See collection
edited by

Oldfield

June 19.

# CIVILIZATION AND BLACK PROGRESS

*Selected Writings of Alexander Crummell on the South*

THE PUBLICATIONS OF THE
SOUTHERN TEXTS SOCIETY

*Michael O'Brien, Chair of the Editorial Board*

*An Evening When Alone:*
*Four Journals of Single Women in the South, 1827–67*
Edited by Michael O'Brien

*Louisa S. McCord: Political and Social Essays*
Edited by Richard C. Lounsbury

*Civilization and Black Progress:*
*Selected Writings of Alexander Crummell on the South*
Edited by J. R. Oldfield

# CIVILIZATION AND BLACK PROGRESS

*Selected Writings of Alexander Crummell on the South*

EDITED BY J. R. OLDFIELD

Published for the Southern Texts Society
by the University Press of Virginia
Charlottesville and London

THE UNIVERSITY PRESS OF VIRGINIA
Copyright © 1995 by Southern Texts Society

*First published 1995*

Library of Congress Cataloging-in-Publication Data
Crummell, Alexander, 1819–1898
    Civilization and Black progress : selected writings of Alexander
Crummel on the South / edited by J. R. Oldfield.
        p.    cm.—(Publications of the Southern Texts Society)
    Includes index.
    ISBN 0-8139-1602-X (cloth)
    1. Afro-Americans—History—1877–1964—Sources. 2. Afro-
Americans—Southern States—History—19th century—Sources.
3. Southern States—Race relations—Sources.    I. Oldfield, J. R.
(John R.)    II. Title.    III. Series.
E185.5.C955    1995
973'.0496073—dc20                                                95-17664
                                                                            CIP

Printed in the United States of America

IN

MEMORIAM

*Sara Dunlap Jackson*

*(1919–91)*

# Contents

# ILLUSTRATIONS

# Acknowledgments

Historical editing, I have discovered, is an arduous task. It can also be very frustrating. Happily in my case help was always near to hand. I owe a special debt of gratitude to John Hammond Moore, Bruce Ragsdale, and Robert Weir, who responded promptly (and cheerfully) to my requests for assistance with biographical notes. John Davies very kindly agreed to cast an expert eye over Crummell's biblical scholarship, while both John McGavin and Anthony Shipps took the trouble to identify some of the less familiar quotations. I would also like to thank the staffs of the British Library, the Hartley Library at the University of Southampton, the Library of Congress, the Moorland-Spingarn Research Center at Howard University, Andover Newton Theological School, and the Domestic and Foreign Missionary Society of the Protestant Episcopal Church in Austin, Texas.

At the University of Southampton, I am fortunate in having colleagues who took a warm interest in this project. In particular, I wish to thank Tony Kushner and Alastair Duke, who not only offered invaluable advice but read portions of the manuscript. I am also grateful to the many students who have taken my third-year course on American race relations. Even if they did not recognize it at the time, their different perspectives have influenced my thinking about Crummell, often in significant ways. Meanwhile, the Cavaliers (a cricket club with a proud history) have provided a welcome diversion from the classroom, the library, and the computer.

On the other side of the Atlantic, Michael O'Brien has been an energetic, resourceful, and supportive editor. The comments of the two independent readers helped to iron out a number of inconsistencies. And I am most grateful to Richard Holway and everyone at the University Press of Virginia for their skill in handling the manuscript. Financial assistance came from the British Academy, whose generosity allowed me to spend a month in Washington, D.C., during the summer of 1992, and the University of Southampton (Advanced Studies Publication Fund).

Finally, I want to thank my wife, Veronica, and our two sons, Thomas and Matthew, who have endured a second stint of Alexander Crummell with great patience and good humor. The book is dedicated to the memory of Sara Dunlap Jackson, a very special Southern lady. Many years ago when I was working in Washington, D.C., Sara took me under her wing, as she did so many young scholars. We became firm friends. She was a brilliant archivist, a wise counselor, and an irresistible dinner companion. The National Archives will never be quite the same without her.

# CIVILIZATION AND
# BLACK PROGRESS

*Selected Writings of Alexander Crummell
on the South*

# Introduction

When W. E. B. Du Bois met Alexander Crummell for the first time in 1895, he bowed before him, "as one bows before the prophets of the world." "I spoke to him politely," Du Bois recalled, "then curiously, then eagerly, as I began to feel the fineness of his character,—his calm courtesy, the sweetness of his strength, and his fair blending of the hope and truth of life."[1] As this language suggests, and he was not given to faint praise, Du Bois discovered in Crummell a spiritual father figure. He also found a source of hope and inspiration, a guide, a mentor, and a soulmate.

Who was this man who made such an impression? Du Bois's *The Souls of Black Folk* (1903) struck a sentimental note. Crummell's life was held up as a mirror which reflected in chilling detail the black experience in the United States, the questioning and searching, the doubts and temptations. The facts spoke for themselves. Buffeted by the inequalities of Jacksonian America and the harsh realities of racial politics on the West Coast of Africa, Crummell's career was a lifelong quest for a place where he might find and fulfill his duty, a pilgrimage which took him from America to England, from England to West Africa, and from West Africa to America. It was a life of great hardship and bitter disappointments. Yet, and this was what instinctively drew Du Bois to Crummell, Crummell had emerged from these experiences strengthened and revitalized and more confident than ever of the "destined superiority of the Negro race." Crummell's suffering, Du Bois believed, had made him a seer.

But Crummell's significance for a generation of black leaders went beyond emotional ties and sympathies. During the late nineteenth century, the debate over race and black culture in the United States took a dramatic and unexpected turn. The death of Frederick Douglass in 1895 coincided with the emergence of a new black leader, Booker T. Washington, with a very different power base and a very different race philosophy. In his now famous address to the Atlanta Cotton Exposition (1895), Washington quite deliberately distanced himself from Douglass's insistence on civil and political equality, preferring instead to emphasize industrial education and his own school at Tuskegee as the key to racial harmony in the South. By the turn of the century, these ideas had gained wide currency. Feted by President Roosevelt, with whom he dined in 1901, Washington came to enjoy immense influence and authority, drawing on the support of a vast network of "friends" and sympathizers, the "Tuskegee Machine," to further his interests.[2]

Washington, however, was not without his critics. One of the first to raise his voice in protest was Alexander Crummell. Initially supportive of Washington's efforts to proffer a hand to Southern whites, Crummell was to become increasingly alarmed at the deteriorating conditions in the South and the exaggerated importance attached to industrial education. Crummell wanted a place for the black intellect as well, a difference of approach and emphasis that he spelled out in his inaugural address to the American Negro Academy in 1897. The academy, a forum for black intellectuals, was Crummell's brainchild. Through it he bequeathed to young men like Du Bois not only a belief in a distinctive black personality but a conviction that blacks were a nascent ethnic group with their own unique destiny.

As Du Bois was quick to appreciate, Crummell provided a link with the past and, more especially, with the nationalist movements of the 1840s and 1850s. But he also spoke to the future. Nobody believed more fervently in the ideas of race and black progress or defended black capabilities more vigorously. These ideas, in turn, underpinned Crummell's commitment to self-help and racial solidarity, a philosophy that at a political level, at least, has obvious parallels with the nationalist movements of the 1960s and speaks to us still. But Crummell was a conservative as well as a nationalist, and here again many of his concerns—law and order, moral discipline, the importance of the nuclear family—have a contemporary significance.

If we are to understand Du Bois and those who followed him, therefore, we must begin by understanding Crummell and those who came before. Richly talented, forthright, and combative, this imposing figure made a vital contribution to the debate over race, intellect, and culture as it affected Southern blacks in the aftermath of slavery.

Alexander Crummell was born free in New York City on March 3, 1819, the first son of Boston Crummell and Charity Hicks.[3] His father was reputedly an African prince and an ex-slave who went on to establish himself as a prominent member of New York's black middle class, first as a grocer and later as an oysterman on Broad Street. His mother, who was freeborn, came from Jericho, Long Island, and, like her husband, was of pure African descent. Crummell's early years were relatively comfortable. Unable to read or write himself, Boston sent all of his five children to the African Free School in Mulberry Street and even employed white tutors to give them private instruction. The family were also members of St. Philip's Church, New York's leading black Episcopal congregation.[4] By virtue of his background and upbringing, therefore, Crummell belonged to an elite group of free blacks who were educated, prosperous, self-confident, and socially ambitious.

Crummell's position was, indeed, a privileged one, but he was no stranger to prejudice or discrimination. In the summer of 1835 he enrolled in Noyes Academy, a biracial boarding school in Canaan, New Hampshire, only to be driven away by an angry antiabolitionist mob.[5] Bitter and humiliated, Crummell went on to Oneida Institute in Whitesboro, New York. It was here that he underwent a conversion experience. By his own admission Crummell entered Oneida "in a state of sinful rebellion—without God and without hope in the world." He emerged from the school "a man of Principle." This was to be the pattern of his life. Writing in 1899, one memorialist would recall that Crummell's "eating and sleeping, recreation and labor, both mental and physical, were all submitted to the most rigid discipline." Like most evangelicals Crummell tried to instill the same sort of discipline in others. "He never hesitated," wrote another acquaintance, "or adopted compromise measures to secure the same end or avoid any bitterness engendered by reproof."[6] It was this domineering manner that made him such an implacable opponent, although there always was a thin line between principle and what was, in fact, pride and a determination to have his own way.

Crummell left Oneida in 1838 determined to become an Episcopal minister and, with the blessing of Bishop Benjamin Treadwell Onderdonk, was admitted to the Diocese of New York. Early in 1839 he took the more controversial step of applying for admission to the General Theological Seminary, also in New York. In theory, there was nothing to prevent blacks from being admitted to this institution, but experience suggested otherwise. In 1836 Bishop Onderdonk had intervened in his capacity as president of the faculty to block the admission of another black candidate, Isaiah De Grasse, fueling speculation that the seminary was for whites only.[7] Crummell's hopes were dashed when on June 27, 1839, he, too, was refused admission to the General Theological Seminary. News of the decision spread quickly through abolitionist circles and in no time at all became a cause célèbre. One of those drawn into the controversy was John Jay (1817–1894), whose vocal criticisms of the action taken by the theological seminary caused Crummell further humiliation. When Onderdonk called upon Crummell, as the subject of these attacks, to make a public apology, Crummell refused, whereupon the bishop removed his name from the list of candidates for holy orders.

Undeterred, Crummell gained admission to the Eastern Diocese and later attended Yale Theological Seminary. He finally left New Haven in June 1841 to take charge of Christ Church, a black Episcopal congregation in Providence, Rhode Island.[8] But within eighteen months he was on the move again, having fallen out with his vestry and his parishioners. From Providence, Crummell moved south to Philadelphia where he organized the small congregation of St. Bartholomew's. It was during this same period, in 1842 or 1843, that he married Sarah Mabbit Elston, a New Yorker who, like her husband, had been educated in the African Free Schools. Beyond these few details we know very little about Sarah. She appears in Crummell's papers as a rather shadowy figure, prone to bouts of illness, who besides bearing her husband six children had to put up with great hardship all her married life.[9]

Marriage was undoubtedly one of the reasons why in 1844 Crummell returned to New York as the minister of St. Matthew's. Crummell's arrival coincided with efforts to breathe new life into the congregation. Larger premises were found at 592 Broadway, and the congregation was reorganized into the Church of the Messiah. But the task was not an easy one. The congregation was invariably short of funds, and if Crummell is to be believed, he and his wife suffered near starvation in New York, losing their first child through lack of nourishment. Crummell's return to New York was disappointing for other reasons, too. Since the early 1840s he had identified himself closely with the suffrage issue, but in 1846 a New York constitutional convention again rejected a call for the removal of the $250 property qualification imposed on black voters in 1821. The result was a serious setback for political abolitionists, and in Crummell's case it signaled a shift to a broadly nationalist position stressing self-help and racial solidarity.[10]

By the fall of 1847, the fortunes of Crummell's New York congregation had reached a point where he finally decided to try his luck at collecting funds in England. The immediate response was favorable. No sooner had Crummell arrived in England than he made contact with members of the evangelical wing of the Church of England, who arranged for his appeal to be launched at a public meeting in London on May 26, 1848.[11] This same group came up with the idea of sending Crummell to Cambridge. More funds were solicited, and arrangements made for his wife and two sons, Alexander and Sidney, to join him in England as soon as possible. On May 23, 1849, following intensive cramming, Crummell was accepted for admission to Queens' College,[12] and in due course he and his family moved into Botolph Lane, within easy walking distance of Queens'. He was then thirty years of age, and though not the first African-American to go to school in England, he was one of the first to be admitted to either Cambridge or Oxford.

Crummell obviously found his studies at Cambridge demanding. Out of 360 candidates who sat the university's previous examination in March 1851, he was one of the 99 classed in the second division, a result that would seem to have justified his decision to enroll for the ordinary Bachelor of Arts degree and not try for honors. To what extent his performance was affected by poor health it is impossible to say. By his own account Crummell was under medical care from the moment he arrived in England, and his fund-raising activities frequently were interrupted by the recurrence of a heart problem that had troubled him since 1839. Then in the winter of 1850, he was laid up for three months with a varicose vein in his left leg, certainly part of the same disorder. Finally, in 1851 he was struck with such a violent agitation of the heart that he was forced to take a rest cure in the little village of Shotley near Ipswich on the Suffolk coast. His doctors, who included Queen Victoria's physician, Sir Benjamin Brodie, diagnosed a functional disorder, "depending on a morbid condition of the sensory nerves." There was evidently no sign of any organic disease, and as was usual in such cases, Crummell was merely advised to rest and to avoid any rigorous activity, even reading and studying.[13]

Crummell sank so low in the fall of 1851 that after great deliberation he decided to resign his position as minister of the Church of the Messiah and find an occupation that was less "exciting and trying than constant preaching and the care of a Congregation." This left him in an awkward position. Teaching was one possibility, but Crummell seemed reluctant to try any "experiments" of this kind. "Out of the pulpit—divorced from pastoral duties—no black clergyman can live in America, that is, as a clergyman," he explained to a meeting in Cheltenham. "There are no schools or colleges which will give him employment." Convinced that his poor health was meant as a sign of some kind, and conscious of the need to provide for the comfort of his family, Crummell concluded that it would be impossible for him to return to the United States. But at this stage he claimed to have no idea where he might go, save that he needed to live in a warm climate.[14]

Almost a year later Crummell applied for a teaching position in Liberia with the Protestant Episcopal church. The decision was a difficult one, for as he explained to John Jay, he was no colonizationist and did not wish to be thought of as one.[15] Liberia, however, had its own attractions. For one thing, it was the only American foothold on the West Coast of Africa. Furthermore, since 1847 it had become an independent republic with its own constitution and laws. Here, in other words, was a fresh field for nationalistic endeavor. Within weeks Crummell was offered a missionary appointment in West Africa, to commence as soon as possible. But first there were his academic studies to complete. Having failed his final university examinations at the first attempt, Crummell was obliged to sit an additional examination in February 1853, which to his relief he passed.[16] "If I had not succeeded at all it wd have given me no surprise, and none to my friends," he confessed. "They know that during the last two years I have been unable to read. . . . I have been a great sufferer—more than I have cared, at times to say."[17]

Crummell spent his last few months in England saying farewell to his many friends and acquaintances and making arrangements for his passage to West Africa. For five and a half years he had moved in what was predominantly a white world, having had very little contact with either black Americans in England or with that country's small indigenous black community. The effect of this experience on Crummell is incalculable. Cambridge, in particular, was an important source of self-esteem. Although it is true that Crummell did not distinguish himself as a student, Cambridge provided him with the rudiments of a liberal education and introduced him to new ideas, new sensations, and a new social world. This was heady stuff and, as Crummell recognized, dangerous, too.[18] England, in short, served to reinforce Crummell's elitism, not to say his snobbery, and filled him with a sense of special distinction that alienated him from the very people he felt it his duty to serve and nourish. Sadly, all this was to become readily apparent as Crummell struggled to come to terms with a new and very different life in West Africa.

Crummell, his wife, and four children arrived in Monrovia, the capital of Liberia, on July 15, 1853.[19] By this date the colonist population of this small, independent republic was about 3,000. Most of these immigrants came from the American South, and over half were ex-slaves. This, in other words, was a frontier community, and the physical isolation of the settlers was reinforced by the psychological and cultural distance that they put between themselves and the native population. Settler society, in turn, was divided within itself, pitting "Negroes," on the one hand, against "mulattoes," on the other, sometimes with disastrous results. "There are no real parties in Liberia," observed one English traveler in 1873. "The real parties consist of mulattoes and negroes. . . . The mulattoes are aristocrats, and call the black men niggers. The negroes, on the other hand, call the mulattoes bastards and mongrels and declare that they are feeble in body and depraved in mind."[20]

Crummell began his missionary career as minister of St. Paul's Church in

Monrovia. It was not long, however, before he found himself at odds with Episcopal authority in the shape of John Payne, the missionary bishop. The problem for Crummell was that whereas he saw Liberia as an experiment in nation building, his superiors in the Episcopal church regarded it principally as a foreign missionary field. The first signs of trouble came in December 1854 when Crummell helped to draft a series of resolutions calling on Episcopal leaders in the United States to place ecclesiastical arrangements in Liberia on "a new and thoroughly National basis at the earliest possible period."[21] Thereafter relations between Crummell and Payne deteriorated rapidly. Not surprisingly, Crummell's involvement in the movement for a national church, which surfaced again in 1855, earned him a reputation as a troublemaker, and it came as some relief to Payne when in March 1857 he suddenly resigned.

Crummell spent the next twelve months in and around Monrovia, but then in the summer of 1858 he accepted an invitation from Payne to take charge of Mount Vaughan High School at Cape Palmas in the south of the republic. At first the experiment proved a great success, but by June 1860 the small school was nearly bankrupt, and toward the end of the year Crummell was persuaded to take leave in the United States. Later, on April 26, 1861, he was summarily dismissed. Crummell had set sail from England in 1853 with the highest expectations, but nearly eight years in Liberia had brought with it only disappointment and frustration. The truth of the matter was that Crummell was ill cast for the role of a missionary. He was too impatient, too unyielding, too much of the disciplinarian. In John Payne, moreover, he had come up against an adversary who not only had no confidence in blacks but seemed intent on standing in the way of their ambitions. Yet at no stage does Crummell appear to have thought of quitting Liberia. For the moment, at least, he remained passionately committed to the idea of a black nationality in West Africa.

Crummell spent the next eighteen months, from April 1861 to October 1862, promoting Liberian emigration in the Northern United States, first in behalf of the American Colonization Society and later as an agent appointed by the Liberian government. By the end of his visit, however, he had become an increasingly isolated figure. Crummell's identification with Liberia had never been well received by black leaders in the United States, and significantly, his closest ties had been forged with white colonizationists like William Coppinger, secretary of the American Colonization Society. After 1861 the task in hand became more difficult still. While Crummell tried to arouse interest in Liberia, the focus of black thought and action in the United States suddenly shifted toward the prospect of an accommodation at home. Nevertheless, nothing that he saw or experienced during these eighteen months caused Crummell to change either his views or his loyalties. He even turned down an offer to take charge of St. Philip's Church in New York in favor of his race work in Liberia.

Crummell returned to Liberia in January 1863 as professor of moral and intellectual philosophy and English language and literature in Liberia College, a nonsectarian institution sponsored by a group of white colonizationists in Massachusetts. But almost at once he found himself in conflict with the mulatto-controlled Board of Trustees over the terms of his appointment and out of sympathy with the college's president, J. J. Roberts, another mulatto. On his return to Liberia, Crummell also became embroiled again in the movement for a national (Episcopal) church. In February 1863 he and five other Liberian clergy finally seized the initiative and established an independent church organization, the Liberian Episcopal church. If these proceedings were designed to frighten church leaders in the United States, they had their desired effect. In October 1865 the General Convention of the Protestant Episcopal church adopted appropriate legislation permitting six clergy resident within the jurisdiction of a foreign missionary bishop to organize themselves into a diocese. Crummell, who was present at the convention in Philadelphia, took the delegates at their word. No sooner had he returned to Monrovia in January 1866 than he tried to persuade his colleagues to abandon their independent organization and to join him in putting the new canon into immediate effect. But nothing came of Crummell's proposals, and amid mutual recriminations the nationalist movement collapsed, leaving Bishop Payne to pick up the pieces.[22]

To add insult to injury, some months later, in July 1866, Crummell was ousted from Liberia College following a long-standing feud with the college authorities. Bitter and disillusioned, he turned instead to politics and threw his energies into the attempt of the Negro party to elect E. J. Roye as president on a platform of national expansion. In 1869 Roye ran against the mulatto incumbent, J. S. Payne, and, in a close-fought contest, won. The Negro party greeted this news with eager anticipation, but when at the end of his two-year term Roye refused to leave office, the country was thrown into turmoil. During the late summer and fall of 1871, Monrovia remained in a fever of excitement. Crummell reported in September that several leading men in the administration feared for their lives. Finally, this mounting racial tension broke out into open hostility. On October 25 Roye was forced from office by a mulatto mob, and in the chaotic events that followed, hundreds of his supporters were either hanged or imprisoned.[23]

These unprecedented events dashed the spirits of the Negro party. Crummell expected nothing from mulatto rule but national ruin. Liberia's moment had passed, he told his American friends. As time went on, Crummell's own position became more and more intolerable. There were death threats, and then on January 16, 1872, he reported that his church had been attacked and his organ "burnt to pieces."[24] Disenchanted with his country, at odds with its leadership, fearful for his life, it is small wonder that Crummell began to think of leaving Liberia. Late in January he tried unsuccessfully to secure a position for himself in Sierra Leone. Crummell was in Freetown again in March, apparently on his way to the United States via England. He arrived in New York in May and almost at once started looking for a suitable position.

Crummell committed himself to Liberia in the hope that in time it would become a Christian state, a sort of black Victorian England. Such ambitions were idealistic to say the least, but they were by no means unusual at a period when philanthropists on both sides of the Atlantic shared a common belief in the absolute superiority of Western, industrial society over tribal life and approached the task of nation building in West Africa with the same brash confidence. (Sixteen years in Liberia failed to convince Crummell that African tribal culture and the rival claims of Muhammadanism were anything but useless.) The irony was that Crummell's nationalistic vision should have been shattered by attitudes that immigrants and white missionaries brought with them from their "superior" civilization. As a black Episcopal minister with a degree from Cambridge University, Crummell had hoped to escape the indignities that he had suffered in the United States and to start afresh somewhere he might find and fulfill his duty. Liberia, however, turned out to be not the "grand theater of the Negro's civilization" but a microcosm of American racial attitudes.

When Crummell returned to the United States in 1872, he was fifty-three years of age and a weak and dispirited man. At a time when he might have expected to look forward to a life of greater ease and relaxation, he found himself in the unenviable position of having to start his career all over again. He settled first in New York and started making arrangements to bring his family home.[25] But then in the spring of 1873, he received an offer to take charge of St. Mary's Chapel in Washington, D.C., with a salary guaranteed, in part, by several of the city's white churches. Well aware that such an offer would provide himself and his family with a measure of financial security, Crummell accepted. St. Mary's soon became a rallying place for District blacks; and in no time at all, plans were afoot to build a larger church in a more centrally located section of the city. This new building, St. Luke's Church, was opened to the public in November 1879. Here Crummell would concentrate his efforts during the next fifteen years.

Despite a shaky start St. Luke's emerged as a vital center of black activity in Washington. Admittedly, there always would be problems, not least of

*Fig. 1.* Alexander Crummell, c.1880. *(Courtesy of the Moorland-Spingarn Research Center, Howard University)*

*Fig. 2.* Crummell's second wife, Jennie, whom he married in 1880. *(Courtesy of the Moorland-Spingarn Research Center, Howard University. Photographer: J. H. Kent)*

which was the debt on the church building, but when Crummell retired in 1894, there were over 300 communicants, and the church supported a boys' club and a flourishing industrial school for girls. In addition, there was a mission in South Washington and another in the north of the city. The success of St. Luke's confirmed Crummell's status within Washington's black community. It also attracted the attention of prominent whites, among them W. W. Corcoran, Senator Samuel Hoar, and President Chester Arthur.[26] As the pieces included in this volume suggest, Crummell was extremely active between 1872 and 1898, and there is little doubt that his position in Washington gave him a visibility that he might otherwise never have achieved.

On December 9, 1894, at the age of seventy-five, Crummell finally took his leave of St. Luke's. As he himself admitted, retirement left him "like a fish out of water; for by temperament I am disposed to active duty; & added to this is the lifelong conviction that to work is to live." He filled the vacuum by undertaking strenuous speaking tours. In 1895, for instance, he was away from Washington for nearly five months, during which time he delivered baccalaureate sermons at commencement exercises at Wilberforce University and at normal colleges in Petersburg, Ohio, and Hayneville, Alabama. It also was on this trip that he revisited Canaan, New Hampshire, the scene of his unhappy experiences at the hands of an antiabolitionist mob nearly sixty years before. Crummell was away from Washington again in the early part of 1896 when he gave the Founder's Day Address at Hampton Institute and spoke before a white congregation at St. Bartholomew's Church in New York.[27]

For the rest of 1896 and the early part of 1897, a good deal of Crummell's time was taken up with a new initiative, the American Negro Academy (ANA), which originated out of his growing unease over Booker T. Washington's leadership. The nucleus of the ANA was a group of young intellectuals active in the Washington area that included John Wesley Cromwell, editor of the *People's Advocate;* the poet Paul Lawrence Dunbar; Walter B. Hayson, a high school teacher; and Kelly Miller, a mathematics professor at Howard University. On December 18, 1896, these men accepted Crummell's outline of a society committed to the promotion of scholarship and the vindication of African-Americans by means of "original articles upon various Literary, Historical and Philosophical topics." Crummell envisaged that membership, limited to forty individuals, would be open only to "graduates or Professors in Colleges; Literary characters, Authors, Artists and distinguished writers." Provision also was made for an annual meeting to be held each year in Washington.[28]

Subsequently, forty-six men were invited to join the ANA, all of them well educated and for the most part professors, lawyers, and ministers.

Twenty-nine of this number took up membership of the society, but only eleven promised to attend an organizing meeting planned for the following March. Among them was W. E. B. Du Bois, then an assistant instructor in sociology at the University of Pennsylvania; Booker T. Washington pleaded a prior engagement. In all, eighteen men were present when the organizing session of the ANA opened on March 5 in Lincoln Memorial Congregational Church with an address by Crummell, the temporary chairman. A constitution was adopted, and officers were elected. Crummell was the unanimous choice for president, but the meeting also made some provision for the future by electing Du Bois vice-president and appointing two other young men, John Wesley Cromwell and Francis J. Grimké, secretary and treasurer, respectively.[29]

Not long after the inaugural meeting of the ANA, Crummell and his second wife, Jennie, left for England to attend Queen Victoria's Diamond Jubilee.[30] The couple arrived in Liverpool on May 20 and went straight to London in readiness for the celebrations on June 23. The whole idea of the visit was a fitting and illuminating tribute from a man who not only had good reason to be grateful to England and to English charity but who loved the country and looked to it as a source of inspiration. Crummell tried to express his emotions on visiting England again in a letter to John Edward Bruce:

> I have been in England on four previous occasions, but just now I am almost over-powered with the impress of greatness, magnificence & power which comes upon me, at every turn! How wonderful is this great city of London in its immense population & vastness of area, its palatial residences & fine equipages, its grand Cathedrals & noble churches, its countless charities & its boundless beneficence, its marvellous sanitation & unparalleled order. And the glory of it all is the unequalled fact that all this earthly magnificence is more or less allied with moral responsibility & the sanctions of religion— both with regard to authority at home & governmental control abroad.[31]

There is perhaps no clearer statement of what impressed Crummell about England or of what influence the country had on his social and political thought.

In all, Crummell and his wife were in England for four months, visiting friends in Lincolnshire and Somerset and going to and from London on various engagements. Late in September they were in Stratford-upon-Avon, having spent a week "perambulating in the Halls, the Chapels, & the gardens of Oxford." The traveling, not to mention English hospitality, took its toll, and by early October, Crummell clearly was exhausted. The couple left England soon after and arrived at Philadelphia on October 20. They had hoped to stop over in New York but decided instead to go straight on to Washington. By this stage Crummell's health was obviously causing his wife grave concern. Nevertheless, he was fit again for the annual meeting of the American Negro Academy in December 1897, which he declared "a notable success."[32]

On March 3, 1898, as he entered his eightieth year, Crummell still was working six or seven hours each day. "But time tells upon me; & at times I have to sit, do nothing, & wait upon the Lord," he told Bruce. "I grow tired of myself constantly! What a mis-thing is a man in the presence of God; laden as he is with sins & guilt & infirmities & transgressions!" In June, Crummell and his wife moved to Red Bank in New Jersey for the summer where they found a "clean, neat, & really attractive cottage; a most pleasant couple—man & wife; bright & cheerful rooms; a clean bed; & a table, appetizing in its appearance, with food & cooking sufficiently stimulating & delightful for an epicure." Except for a little extra "fervidity" of the sun, Crummell was happy to escape Washington, but in July he fell ill with a stomach complaint that affected his heart. By this time it is clear that he was very weak. Late in August he suffered a relapse from which he never recovered. At 10:30 A.M. on September 10, he gently slipped away.[33]

In spite of several appealing qualities, Crummell was never a popular figure. He was too unyielding, too tactless, too sensitive, too much of the disciplinarian. Yet as Du Bois makes clear in *The Souls of Black Folk,* Crummell has a special place in the history of black leadership in America. The inclusion of Du Bois's tribute to Crummell in that work was by no means accidental. If Booker T. Washington represented the brash materialism that Du Bois feared would ultimately impede the development of blacks toward a higher civilization, then Crummell represented the world of ideas, intellect, character, and racial integrity. These divergent ideologies were symptomatic of what Du Bois believed was a fundamental change in the structure of black leadership itself. Du Bois was opposed to Washington because he was identified with a new generation of black leaders, "the farmers and gardeners, the well-paid porters and artisans, the businessmen,—all those with property and money."[34] Crummell, on the other hand, was representative of an old elite, largely comprised of clergymen, that Du Bois believed had traditionally assumed the responsibilities of leadership in the United States.

The eighteen pieces in this collection give substance to Du Bois's claims. They reflect Crummell's maturer thought as he came to terms with the harsh realities of post-Reconstruction America. Crummell may not have known it, but he returned to the United States at a time when the future of African-Americans hung very much in the balance. In 1872 the country was still recovering from the convulsions of a bloody civil war and the emancipation of some four million slaves. Reconstruction had done little to ease the tensions at the root of the sectional conflict, and while the freedmen had been granted civil and political rights, white conservatives already were starting to win back control of Southern state legislatures. The Compromise of 1877 would formally bring Reconstruction to an end and with it the attempt to impose a racial settlement on the South. The next twenty-five years were to prove a critical period in Southern race relations, as a steadily deteriorating situation finally gave way to legal proscription and widespread disfranchisement of black voters.[35]

In Washington, D.C., Crummell found himself face to face with some of the massive dislocations caused by the Civil War. For years the black population of Washington had remained relatively static, rising from just 12,000 to 14,000 between 1830 and 1860, and during this time it had evolved its own hierarchy based on color and social standing. But the war brought with it a huge influx of ex-slaves from the South Atlantic states. Between 1860 and 1867 Washington's black population rose from 14,000 to 38,663, and over the course of the next fifteen years it almost doubled again. Understandably, these demographic changes caused widespread concern among black Washingtonians, resulting in self-conscious distinctions between "newcomers" and "old families" that polarized the city's black community even further.[36]

Crummell, of course, had never been this far south, and he became increasingly preoccupied with the problems he saw around him. One indication of this is the very different emphasis he came to place on the slavery issue. As an evangelical Crummell was keenly interested in God's purposes for black people, and in his early writings he evolved a synthesis of Africa and America that sought to explain slavery in terms of a "restorative agency" that had introduced blacks to the benefits of a superior civilization.[37] But increasingly after 1875 he focused much more on its negative aspects, condemning slavery as a cruel and oppressive institution that was destructive of family life and family values.[38] The native African, he insisted in "A Defence of the Negro Race in America" (1882), was honest, chaste, and frugal, but slavery had corrupted his religious feelings and robbed him of his sense of family order. "The bad, and they were the mass of slaveholders, were full of greed, tyranny, unscrupulousness, and carnality. They herded their slaves together like animals. They were allowed to breed like cattle. The marriage relation was utterly disregarded. All through the rural districts, on numerous plantations, the slaves for generations merely mated and cohabited, as beasts. They were separated at convenience, caprice, or at the call of nature." Crummell made this same point again in "The Black Woman

of the South" (1882), a quasi-sociological piece that anticipated the work of
E. Franklin Frazier.

Crummell also made the crucial connection between the slave experience
and the disposition to regard manual labor as degrading, something that
he had encountered in West Africa. What was needed, he believed, was for
blacks to learn the value of labor as a creative power. "All work is honourable," Crummell argued. "Only throw brains, skill, energy and economy
with your work; and it will lead you on to success, to comfort, and perchance to wealth."[39] Instead, he saw about him an effort to teach young boys
and girls Latin, Greek, science, and art. The result was a "whole regiment
of pretentious and lazy fools" who had no heart for labor and were given
over to profligacy and ruinous pleasure.[40] The remedy, Crummell thought,
was to use higher education only in fit and exceptional circumstances. In
"Common Sense in Common Schooling" (1886), he advised parents to examine their children at twelve or thirteen years of age to determine whether
or not they would benefit from higher education. A child of ordinary ability,
he said, should be taken from school and put to work.

Throughout the 1880s Crummell was struggling with a complex of issues
that he believed were all part of the heritage of slavery; immorality, indisci-
pline, disorder, and the want of a black work ethic. He was under no illusion
as to the enormity of the problem. Neither was he in any doubt that the
solution lay with blacks themselves. In "The Social Principle among a
People" (1875), Crummell spoke of the need for blacks to organize themselves not for "idle logomachy" but for industrial effort, securing trades for
youth, joint-stock companies, and the production of staples and likewise for
the higher purposes of life, mental and moral improvement, and raising the
plane of social and domestic life. "While one remnant of disadvantage abides
in this land, stand by one another!" he exhorted blacks. "While the imputation of inferiority, justly or unjustly, is cast upon you, combine for all the
elements of culture, wealth, and power."

Central to Crummell's philosophy of self-help and racial solidarity was
the need for a class of black leaders. In part, this was a question of common
sense; as Crummell said, who else could be expected to raise blacks to a
higher plane of civilization. But it also was a question of divine will. Running
through Crummell's thought was a profound sense of special racial qualities
that could not be reached by "alien blood." One aspect of this romantic
racialism was his demand for a black ministry in the South; another was
his insistence on the creation of an educated black gentry. To stimulate and
uplift a people was a work of intelligence, and yet, as Crummell explained,
intelligence was not enough on its own. "The intellect is to be used, but
mainly as the vehicle of mind and spiritual aims. And hence, these men must

needs be both scholars and philanthropists; the intellect rightly discerning the conditions, and the gracious and godly heart stimulating to the performance of the noblest duties for a people."[41]

Inspired by wise and responsible leaders, the freedmen of the South were to effect a revolution from within. Once they proved themselves capable of high moral and intellectual achievements, of honesty, self-restraint, and integrity, of thrift, economy, and enterprise, all the "theories of inferiority" would pass away into "endless forgetfulness." Crummell's nationalism, in sum, was a temporary detour or an indirect route to the goal of equal rights and integration into white society. "What is needed," he explained, "is that we should rise to such elevation that the people of this land be forced to forget all the facts and theories of race, when they behold our thorough equality with them, in all the lines of activity and attainment, of culture and moral grandeur."[42] By definition, this meant accepting and assimilating the values of the dominant white society; in short, becoming black Americans. At the same time, however, Crummell was loath for blacks to lose their own special identity. Although he never used the term, what he seems to have had in mind was a pluralistic society in which blacks would enjoy the same civil and political rights as other ethnic groups but in purely social matters would divide along the line of race.

Crummell's separatist ideology was by its very nature nonconfrontational. He expected very little of the federal or state governments and in 1875 dismissed political agitation as the expenditure of forces that would be better directed back into the black community.[43] Yet there were limits even to Crummell's patience, especially when it came to discrimination within the Protestant Episcopal church. The most important question facing the Episcopal church after the Civil War was its relations with the former slave population. For the Baptists and Methodists, the answer was simple; they left the spiritual welfare of the freedmen to separate (black) ecclesiastical organizations already established for that purpose. But Southern Episcopalians were faced with the prospect of trying to accommodate the ex-slave within the existing white organization. The issue came to a head in 1873 when an independent black congregation applied for admission to the Diocese of South Carolina, and it quickly spread to other Southern states. Fearing the upheaval that mixed dioceses might create, white church leaders moved to block black representation and in doing so grew louder in their pleas that the Church South should be allowed to settle the relations between the races according to their view of what was right and best.[44]

During the 1880s this debate took a new turn as a result of the growing popularity of retrogressionist ideology. One of the most effective advocates of retrogressionist beliefs was Joseph Louis Tucker, an Episcopal minister from Jackson, Mississippi. In a paper read before the Church Congress in Richmond in 1882, Tucker told delegates that blacks were dishonest, lewd, and improvident, and that since emancipation there had been a "great deterioration" in their morals and their level of material prosperity. The remedy, he argued, was for Northern Protestants to withdraw their missionaries from the South and to entrust their funds to Southern whites who understood the race and knew how to deal with them. Tucker was speaking in a debate over the merits of blacks being allowed to control their own churches, but his arguments had important social and political overtones. Like many Southerners, Tucker employed retrogressionist ideology to assert the South's right to self-determination.[45]

As the foremost black Episcopal minister of his day, Crummell met Tucker's arguments in a lengthy broadside entitled "A Defence of the Negro Race in America." But as Herbert Gutman has observed, it was Tucker and not his critics who became an "expert on the emancipated Afro-American." The situation deteriorated still further when in 1883 a group of Southern church leaders met in Sewanee, Tennessee, and reached an accommodation in the form of the Sewanee Canon, which proposed to organize blacks into separate missionary districts. But black Episcopalians were not about to be assigned a separate and unequal status within the white hierarchy, and their sense of outrage found expression in the Conference of Church Workers among Colored People, which Crummell called together in September 1883 for the purpose of protesting against the proposed canon at the next meeting of the General Convention of the Episcopal church.[46]

As it happened, the Sewanee Canon was thrown out by the General Convention, but for Crummell and the Conference of Church Workers among Colored People, the struggle did not end in 1883. Undaunted, the Church South continued to assert its right to settle racial questions on its own terms, and by the end of the century the Sewanee Canon was incorporated into diocesan law in several Southern states. White church leaders went some way to recognizing Crummell's work in behalf of his race when in 1895 they made him a member of the Church Commission for Work among the Colored People, the first African-American to sit on that body. Nevertheless, the contest left him tired and dispirited. Writing to a colleague in 1894, he lamented that he could not find anything "to praise in the history of our CH pertaining to our race. . . . She has been a cold & repulsive step-mother to us Col'd Men, for nigh 200 years."[47] There was no sadder commentary on the Episcopal church or on a ministry that had spanned nearly fifty years.

By the late 1880s Crummell was becoming increasingly wary of attempts to impose artificial constraints on black progress in the United States. In "The Race Problem in America" (1887), he argued that beyond the social sphere there should be no compromise; "this country should be agitated and even convulsed till the battle of liberty is won, and every man in the land is guaranteed fully every civil and political right and prerogative."[48] It was these same concerns that led after 1895 to Crummell's growing unease over the lead taken by Booker T. Washington. Washington's endorsement of industrial education, and his generally conciliatory approach toward Southern whites, came at a time when the South was rapidly becoming a segregated society. Racial attitudes in the North, meanwhile, also were hardening under the impact of Social Darwinism and America's imperialistic ambitions in the Pacific. Not least because he was unwilling to speak out against the pace of segregation in the South, Washington was to emerge as the most important black leader of his generation.[49]

The conflict between Crummell and Washington was at bottom a conflict between an idealist and a materialist. But it is important not to exaggerate the differences in their respective positions. Both men thought that blacks could not leap to greatness or superiority, both men believed that blacks had a special contribution to make to American society, and both men were concerned to instill in blacks a high moral and religious tone. Crummell's disagreement with Washington was not over the value of industrial education per se but the "undue or overshadowing exaggeration of it in the case of the Negro."[50] "The American people care for nought save the material outcome of the Negro problem," he explained to Frazier Miller in 1898. "The ideals of the Negro brain, life, character are a triviality! They say to themselves—'we will do the thinking, philosophizing, the scientific work of the nation:—but you Negroes must work. That is your destiny & that will be your gain & advantage.' And there is a lot of Negro leaders who catch at this bait, & are carried away by the delusion." Anticipating W. E. B. Du Bois, Crummell feared that Washington's endorsement of "industrialism" would make "mere animal labor" the peculiar lot of the race and so deprive African-Americans of true leaders and the opportunity of taking the "next step" to a higher civilization.[51]

Crummell expanded on these themes in his inaugural address to the American Negro Academy in March 1897. The special need of the race, he spelled out in an indirect attack on Washington, was civilization (mental culture) and "not mere mechanism; not mere machinery; not mere handicraft; not the mere grasp on material things; not mere temporal ambitions." These were but incidentals. "The greatness of peoples springs from their ability to grasp the grand conceptions of being," he told the meeting. "It is the absorption of a people, of a nation, of a race, in large majestic and abiding things which lifts them up to the skies."[52] Crummell proposed to meet this crisis through a community of true leaders who would nurture scholars and scholarship and through their publications reaffirm the importance of race consciousness and race pride. "We have as yet no wide, stable basis of race-feeling to work upon; it has got to be created," he wrote John Wesley Cromwell in 1897. "Take the average black man in America, & you will find that he thinks that the creation of race was a superfluous act on the part of the Almighty; & that that superfluity is to be corrected in America."[53]

In August 1897 Crummell launched a more direct attack on Washington in the *Independent*.[54] The response was predictably curt. In two articles published in the same paper in January and February 1898, Washington dismissed those who had "gotten the idea that industrial development was opposed to the Negro's higher mental development." "I would not have the standard of mental development lowered one wit, for with the Negro, as with all races, mental strength is the basis of all progress," he protested, "but I would have a larger proportion of this mental strength reach the Negroes' actual needs through the medium of the hand." Washington then went on to explain that industrial education was not intended to make blacks work as they had worked "in the days of slavery" but to teach them "how to make the forces of nature—air, water, horse-power, steam and electric power, work for [them], how to lift labor up out of toil and drudgery into that which is dignified and beautiful." Crummell, however, was unconvinced. Writing to a colleague in July 1898, he reiterated his belief that the education of blacks "must needs be the same as the white man. It must proceed by the same processes. It must begin at the top."[55]

In the same letter Crummell denied that the fad of industrialism was part of a much wider debate going on in the United States between the different proponents of industrial and higher education. "There is no such conflict," he argued.

> Colleges are increasing all over the land. Munificent endowments are constantly poured into the treasures of these Colleges. Many of the colleges are developing into Universities; & ever & anon a new University, full fledged, springs into existence. And you can't name a single college or University in the land wh has grafted mechanical training on its course. All this talk about "Industrialism" is with regard to the Negro, & Negro education; & there is a lot of white men in the land, who pity the Negro, but who have never learned to love him, who take up this miserable fad, & are moving, by one pretext & another, to put this limitation upon our brains & our culture.

Industrialism, Crummell repeated, threatened to make blacks into a race of "black boys, unthinking & uncultivated, to raise cotton, Rice, Tobacco etc.," while whites did all the "thinking, philosophizing & scientific & artistic work of the nation."

Crummell returned to the question of the black intellect in his first annual address to the American Negro Academy in 1898. Subsequently published as a pamphlet, "The Attitude of the American Mind toward the Negro Intellect" was intended to give a lead to black intellectuals as they sought to challenge Washington's supremacy in the late nineteenth century. A key figure in the mounting criticism leveled at Washington was W. E. B. Du Bois, whose own personal debt to Crummell will be obvious. In "The Conservation of Races," delivered before the ANA in 1897, Du Bois reiterated Crummell's belief that, to a large extent, blacks were responsible for their own elevation and consequently needed leaders of character and intelligence, college-bred men who thoroughly comprehended modern civilization.[56] Du Bois's concept of the "talented tenth" owed a great deal to Crummell, and yet he already was beginning to sense the limits of what pure scholarship (and self-contained action) could achieve. In "The Conservation of Races," he set black leaders the task of determining the broad lines of policy and action for blacks on issues like school segregation and discrimination in public accommodations. It was these concerns that would eventually lead to Du Bois's resignation from the ANA in 1903 and his involvement with the National Association for the Advancement of Colored People.

Crummell's approach to the problems confronting blacks in post-Reconstruction America was shaped by his evangelical faith, his firsthand knowledge of mid-Victorian England, and his experiences first as a free black in Jacksonian America and later as a missionary in West Africa. Faced with a people beset by disintegration and doubt, he responded with a nationalistic philosophy of self-help and racial solidarity that rested upon an unshakable faith in black capabilities. Above all, Crummell sought a proper sphere for the black intellect, attacking prejudice and ignorance on both sides of the racial divide. Here was a man to stir the imagination. Where Booker T. Washington spoke only of stint and contraction, Crummell spoke of progress and elevation. To young men like Du Bois, such ideas were as startling in their freshness as they were appealing in their simplicity.

For all that, Crummell held to what was essentially an antebellum view of the problems of race and black destiny. Like Washington, he saw prejudice not as an ineradicable or immutable force in American society but as an artificial construct (a "theory") that could be set aside and rendered obsolete. Race for Crummell was a question only of identity and loyalty; he was unwilling or unable to admit that it might be an obstacle or impediment to mutual understanding. Du Bois, of course, came to see things rather differently, and it is this emphasis which separates the two men and explains the distance between them. Crummell, after all, belonged to an older generation of black leaders. Temperamentally, he identified closely with young intellectuals like Du Bois. Yet at the same time he shared with Washington an enduring faith in the potential of middle-class values (industry, thrift, and character) to break down the barriers of caste and discrimination. Crummell, in other words, was a transitional figure who bridged two very different worlds separated by the bloodshed and upheaval of the Civil War.

A young admirer once described Crummell as "easily the best read among the colored people of his day."[57] Yet we know very little about his reading habits, the books he might have owned, or his method of working. He left no library to speak of and does not appear to have kept a journal or a commonplace book. The only way to approach Crummell's scholarship, therefore, is through his writings. This is not as easy as it might sound, however. Although Crummell quoted extensively, he seldom used notes or, when he did, gave only the briefest of citations. So the first step in putting together this collection was to try and re-create Crummell's mental world by identifying his sources. That done, it is possible to reach some conclusions about his scholarship.

Crummell was first and foremost an Episcopal minister, and it is no surprise to find that his writings are littered with biblical references and allusions.[58] Crummell's theology (and his scholarship) was influenced by American divines like Beriah Greene, president of Oneida Institute, as well as by evangelicals in England, although it is admittedly very difficult to assess the nature and extent of their influence. Certainly, like most evangelicals he warned Christians to cleave to the "whole Bible, and not a portion of it."[59] Indeed, Crummell found most of the inspiration for his understanding of black history in his reading of the Old Testament. Yet it is interesting to note that he seldom quoted from those Old Testament prophets (Amos, for example) who might have supported a call for greater social justice or a reordering of American society.

Crummell's deliberate use of Old Testament texts is perhaps best illustrated in "The Destined Superiority of the Negro Race" (1877), which attempts to draw a parallel between the black experience in slavery and freedom and the history of the Jewish people in exile. Crummell's imagery, his use of words and phrases like "trial," "painful preparation," and "covenant relation," makes explicit this preoccupation with Old Testament history.[60] Blacks were a "chosen people" struggling with accumulated ills for glory and perfection. The same point is made again in "Incidents of Hope for the Negro Race in America" (1895), which, significantly, takes as its text Psalm 107, a celebration of the deliverance of the children of Israel from the "land of bondage."

In the New Testament, on the other hand, Crummell found the source of his faith in moral discipline both as a group ethic and a rule of personal faith. His quotations, as a result, were carefully chosen to emphasize self-denial (1 Corinthians 9:27), obedience (Romans 13:1), and endurance (2 Timothy 2:3). Crummell's references reveal a deep and intimate knowledge of the New Testament, but two books, in particular, figure prominently in the pieces included here. One is St. Paul's rule of Christian life, as set down in his First Epistle to the Corinthians. The other is the Gospel of St. Luke, the most literary of the New Testament writers and Christianity's first historian. Luke had a special place in Crummell's ministry—his church in Washington, D.C., was named for Luke, for instance—not least, one suspects, because of his strong humanitarian appeal.

The Bible clearly played a major part in shaping the overall character of Crummell's scholarship, as it did in shaping his thought. Equally striking is his use of literary references. That Crummell was a voracious reader is self-evident, but without detailed records it is impossible to say what he read or when. Some of his references may have been borrowed secondhand, others acquired firsthand. Whatever their source, his choice of quotations reveals a definite bias toward English as opposed to American writers and a predilection for Romantic poets like William Wordsworth. In the eighteen pieces included here, there are no less than twelve different quotations from Wordsworth, including five from *The Excursion* (1814).[61] In addition, there are quotations from Samuel Taylor Coleridge and several from two pre-Romantics, James Thomson and James Beattie.

Other English writers quoted by Crummell include Shakespeare, Bacon, Milton, Cowper, Pope, Gray, and Tennyson. By contrast, there are only a handful of quotations here from American writers, among them Henry Wadsworth Longfellow and William Ellery Channing. Crummell's "Englishness" is also evident in the range of his historical allusions. Not only did he assume a knowledge of the deeds of eighteenth-century explorers like James Cook and George Anson, but he thought nothing of quoting politicians like George Canning and John Manners, duke of Rutland. This tendency is particularly pronounced in some of the pieces written and published after Crummell's return to the United States in 1872, but it is evident even in his later writings. In "The Race Problem in America," written in 1887, there are references to Sir John Hawkins, John Hampden, Algernon Sydney, the Reform Bill of 1832, and Benjamin Disraeli, earl of Beaconsfield.[62]

The classical allusions in Crummell's writings are also striking. Crummell came to the classics early. He studied Greek and Latin as a schoolboy in New York and later still at Oneida Institute. But it was probably not until he went up to Cambridge University in 1849 that he was taught the classics in any systematic manner. It was here that he was first introduced to Tacitus and

Sophocles, and where he heard men like William Whewell, professor of moral philosophy, lecturing on Plato's *Republic*. Crummell's affection for the classics was genuine and sincere. Speaking in Boston in 1895, he is said to have delighted his young audience with a disquisition on the ancients, "pointing out and reciting the very passages in which they excelled in each division of letters." On the same occasion Crummell spoke of his devotion to Plato: "He greatly preferred the master idealist to his materialist junior Aristotle, holding that no amount of Aristotle's minute observations and myriad diligence could compensate one moment for the poetic vision and splendid generalisations of Plato."[63]

Knowledge of the classics was a sign of social and racial exclusiveness in nineteenth-century America; the (white) man who knew Latin and Greek was a gentleman.[64] Crummell was keenly aware of these prejudices, and he was equally determined to challenge them. Three pieces included in this collection discuss the achievements of the ancients, "Excellence, an End of the Trained Intellect" (1884), "Right-Mindedness" (c. 1886), and "Civilization the Primal Need of the Race" (1897). Plato, like Socrates, is mentioned by name and here, and elsewhere Crummell referred to Tacitus, whose *Germania* and *Historiae* he obviously knew and admired. The only classical authors quoted by Crummell are Horace, Homer, and Pliny the Elder, but his use of Latin phrases and the scattered references to Pegasus, Croesus, Damon and Pythias, and "The Retreat of the Ten Thousand" help to give his scholarship a weight and authority unique among nineteenth-century black intellectuals.

Two other features of Crummell's scholarship are worthy of notice. The first of these is what we might call his race scholarship, a distinctive feature of which was the interest he took in comparative racial or ethnic history. By studying the history of other races, Crummell sought to discover universal qualities necessary for survival and progress—he was particularly fascinated by those groups that had experienced decline or extinction—and to defend race loyalty (and identity) against the threat of amalgamation. Crummell's approach to such matters was broadly historical, drawing on travelers' accounts,[65] for instance, to identify native African qualities, but he also borrowed ideas from Herbert Spencer's *The Principles of Biology* (1864), while his use of terms like *arrested development* suggests a familiarity with Darwinian theories of evolution.[66]

At the same time Crummell developed a profound interest in the history and progress of his own race. In "The Destined Superiority of the Negro Race," for instance, he used biblical images to explain the meaning of the black experience and to set that experience in a wider historical context. Other pieces dutifully record the race's achievements not only in the United

States but in Latin America and the Caribbean as well. His range, like his sources, was impressive, reinforcing a belief in the inherent ties that bound all black people together. History for Crummell, however, was not simply a matter of collecting facts. He gathered information in order to make a point, namely that blacks were assured of a glorious destiny. His was essentially a Whig interpretation of history, emphasizing elevation, progress, and improvement.

These same concerns explain Crummell's evident pride in the achievements of figures like Toussaint L'Ouverture, Henry Christophe, and Phillis Wheatley, all of whom figure prominently in his writings, and those of his immediate contemporaries, such as Henry Highland Garnet, Frederick Douglass, Samuel Ringgold Ward, and J. W. C. Pennington. Over the years his reading led to the discovery and rediscovery of other important black figures. "Incidents of Hope for the Negro Race in America," for instance, includes references to Henry Diaz (d. 1662), Abraham Hannibal, Juan Lateno (c. 1516–c. 1597), and Anthony William Arno (b. 1703). The same piece exhibits the influence of George Washington Williams, whose *History of the Negro Race in America from 1619 to 1880: Negroes as Slaves, as Soldiers, and as Citizens* appeared in two volumes in 1882 and 1883. Later still, in "The Attitude of the American Mind toward the Negro Intellect," Crummell set himself the task of recording the intellectual achievements of a new generation of black leaders, among them Kelly Miller and W. E. B. Du Bois.

Crummell's significance as a chronicler of the black race has not always been fully appreciated by historians. More widely recognized—and this brings us to the other feature of Crummell's scholarship—is the weight he attached to statistics. Crummell was quite deliberate in his use of this kind of evidence. Statistics set measurable standards for black progress in the United States; they were "evidence of incontrovertible fact" and could not be denied (this, presumably, was what Crummell had in mind when he used the word *scientific*).[67] The approach is best exemplified in Crummell's magnificent assault on the retrogressionist beliefs of Joseph Louis Tucker, "A Defence of the Negro Race in America," where census reports, for instance, are used to devastating effect. Other examples can be found in "The Best Methods of Church Work among Colored People" (1887) and "Incidents of Hope for the Negro Race in America."

Crummell's scholarship was all the more remarkable for being allied to a fluent and lucid prose style. It was this, as much as anything, that often caught the eye of his contemporaries. The *Washington Post*, for instance, noted in 1898 that in speaking and writing "his style was chaste, his diction elegant, his command of English beyond criticism."[68] Crummell's facility with the English language is evident from his personal papers. He rarely needed to correct himself and was seldom lost for the right word or phrase. His writings also have a structure and coherence that is often lacking in other black leaders of the period (one thinks of T. Thomas Fortune and Booker T. Washington, for instance). In this, he undoubtedly was helped by the fact that, unlike Fortune, he was not dependent on his writings for his livelihood and had time (and leisure) to develop his ideas before committing them to paper. But Crummell's writings were, in essence, a reflection of the man's background and interests, and here again the most striking parallel is with Du Bois.

Crummell had obvious limitations as a scholar. He paid little attention to either art or music and showed no interest in politics or economic theory. Neither was his scholarship without its faults. He often misquoted (an indication, perhaps, that he quoted from memory) and was not above misrepresenting the views of his opponents.[69] But he never let a challenge pass, and as the pieces here amply demonstrate, he had a firm grasp of what was being said about racial issues in late nineteenth-century America and by whom. Crummell's achievement was an impressive one. During his lifetime he helped to establish a tradition of black scholarship in America, a tradition that was carried on by Du Bois and the other young men that Crummell gathered about him in the American Negro Academy. Here, in other words, was a pioneer, a man of wide learning who recognized that scholarship, and above all a sense of history, had a vital role to play in the defense of black capabilities.

Proud and domineering, Crummell was a frustrating, sometimes irritable, colleague and a fearsome opponent. The key to the man, his thought and his character, is evangelical Protestantism. His dedication to "principle" and his emphasis on discipline and the need for high moral conduct can be traced to a rigid, desentimentalized faith that allowed no room for compromise, either in approach or manner. Crummell's understanding of black history also was firmly rooted in antebellum evangelical theology. He marshaled his facts accordingly, drawing extensively on contemporary scholarship (history, ethnology, sociology) to explain God's purposes for black people, whether they were in Africa or America. The result was a highly distinctive philosophy, stressing elevation, improvement, and "superiority."

Crummell never lost his faith in the ability of blacks to progress and fulfill their own unique destiny. The questions in his mind related to means, not ends; hence his differences with Booker T. Washington. This brings us to the question of intellect. If Crummell believed profoundly in race and progress, he also was convinced that only education, the world of the mind, would liberate and advance black people. Crummell made this clear in

"Right-Mindedness" where he linked the training of the mind to tenacity, endurance, and persistence, qualities that blacks would surely need if they were to make progress in everyday life, not to mention business or the professions. And, as a first step, the lead would have to come from above. Indeed, the idea of an educated black gentry was central to Crummell's nationalistic vision of racial renaissance and reinvigoration.

Crummell's philosophy of education was to have a profound influence on the thought of young intellectuals like Du Bois, Kelly Miller, and John Edward Bruce. This, of course, is Crummell's great fascination and the reason for his enduring significance. But these young men also responded to Crummell's optimism, his pride, and his integrity. If not quite a role model, Crummell offered an important lead to black intellectuals in the late nineteenth century. For so much of his life an outsider, an outcast even, Crummell emerged in his later years as a source of inspiration for those who shared his doubts about Washington's leadership and the philosophy that lay behind it. Perhaps his greatest achievement was the American Negro Academy, a community of scholars dedicated to the ideas of race and intellect. The ANA not only provided a forum for black intellectuals but set the pattern for similar organizations, political as well as cultural.

Crummell's position and authority, both as an Episcopal minister and president of the ANA, placed him at the very center of the debate over race and black intellect in the late nineteenth century. Yet his writings from this period remain relatively inaccessible. Some can be found in Wilson Jeremiah Moses' *Destiny and Race*,[70] others are available only in reprint editions of Crummell's *Africa and America* (1891), and others again are scattered in books and journals. Here, for the first time, Crummell's major later writings have been collected together in a single volume. Most of the essays are directly concerned with Southern blacks; all of them, directly or indirectly, are concerned with their fate. The purposes of the collection are twofold: to help restore Crummell to his rightful place as a major figure in black thought and culture and to promote greater familiarity with Crummell's writings and the depth and range of his scholarship. For here was a man of intelligence and learning, a black patriarch, whose background and experience gave him a unique perspective on black progress in the Gilded Age.

# Editorial Method

In putting together this collection, I have been concerned to include only Crummell's published writings. I have quite deliberately excluded manuscript sermons and addresses, not simply because they are often difficult to date but because they frequently deal with subjects that Crummell treated more extensively elsewhere. (For obvious reasons, Crummell's theological writings and his addresses on Africa lie outside the scope of the present volume.) Some of the pieces were published for the first time in either *The Greatness of Christ* (1882) or *Africa and America* (1891). Others began life as pamphlets or published addresses, sometimes appearing in more than one edition. The provenance and publishing history of all eighteen pieces are given in the Appendix. Where more than óne version of an address is extant, I have chosen the latest edition, on the grounds that this best reflected the author's intentions. Textual variations are listed in the Table of Emendations deposited with the Southern Historical Collection; in most cases the number of such variations is extremely small.

In editing the collection I have tried to be faithful to Crummell's original capitalization, punctuation, and spelling. Crummell seems to have preferred English spelling for words ending in "-or" or "-er," but sometimes "labor" and "labour," to take one example, appear interchangeably in the same text, perhaps reflecting the efforts of printers to standardize his spelling or Crummell's own attempts to adopt American idioms. All names and references appear in their original form, as do Crummell's quotations, even when they are clearly misquotations. On the other hand, I have corrected a number of minor typographical errors ("Lattin," "thesep eople"), just as I have silently added quotation marks wherever they are missing from the original text. Again, these amendments are listed in the Table of Emendations.

As regards annotations, I have done my best to identify people and quotations. Crummell's own annotations are cited in full and identified by the simple form "[AC]." Where these notes are incomplete or vague, I have added a brief note of my own giving a fuller citation. References and other details which appear in the body of the text inside square brackets are Crummell's own interventions and have been retained as per the original. The most difficult task proved to be running down Crummell's quotations. As noted earlier, Crummell often misquoted, and many of his quotations are unattributed. Thanks to the many concordances and dictionaries of quotations now available, tracing Crummell's references proved less daunting than I had at first thought, but a handful of quotations have eluded even my best efforts. Wherever Crummell misquoted, I have given the standard or original version in the note.

One further word of explanation is necessary. After due consideration I thought it appropriate to preface each piece with a short introductory note, explaining the immediate context of the remarks and the date and occasion on which they were delivered. Publication details are given in the Appendix. Throughout I have tried to keep these notes as brief as possible. Crummell's elegant and scholarly writings are quite capable of standing on their own.

# 1.

## The Social Principle among a People and Its Bearing on Their Progress and Development

A special feature of Crummell's ministry in Washington, D.C., was his annual thanksgiving sermon. Typically, these were occasions for celebration and congratulation, but in 1875 Crummell used the opportunity to expand on his distinctive philosophy of self-help and racial solidarity. Drawing on a text originally prepared as an attack on Liberian settler society, he turned his attention to two "heresies" that he believed stood in the way of cooperative efforts among African-Americans: the dogmas that they should forget their color and give up all distinctive efforts in schools, associations, and friendly societies. Crummell's message was clear. Only by building their own powerful and effective nation (a nation within a nation) would blacks succeed in breaking down the barriers of caste and discrimination.

*Thanksgiving Day, 1875*
Isaiah XLI, 6,7

*They helped every one his neighbor, and every one said to his brother, Be of good courage. So the carpenter encouraged the goldsmith, and he that smootheth with the hammer him that smote the anvil, saying, It is ready for the soldering; and he fastened it with nails that it should not be moved.*

More than a month has passed away since we received the proclamation of our Chief Magistrate, appointing the 25th of November a day of public thanksgiving to Almighty God.

And, in accordance with this pious custom, we, in common with millions of our fellow-citizens, have met together this morning, to offer up our tribute of praise and thankfulness to our common Parent in heaven, for all the gifts, favors, blessings, and benefactions, civil, domestic, religious, and educational, which have been bestowed upon us during the year; for the blessings of heaven above; for the precious fruits brought forth by the sun; for the precious things of the earth and the fulness thereof; for the golden harvests of peace, unstained by blood, and unbroken by strife; for the constant stream of health which has flowed through our veins and households, untainted by plague or pestilence; for the babes whom the Lord has laid upon your arms and given to your hearts; for the plentiful supply of food which has been granted us from the fields, and which has laden our boards; for the goodly instruction which trains the mind and corrects the hearts of our children, and prepares them for responsibility, for duty, and eternity; for the civil privileges and the national freedom, in which we are permitted to participate; for the measure of success which God has given His Gospel, and for the hope that is ours that the Cross shall yet conquer everywhere beneath the sun, and that JESUS shall rule and reign through all the world. For these and all other gifts and blessings we render our tribute of praise and gratitude to the Lord, our Maker, Preserver, and Benefactor, through JESUS CHRIST our Lord!

Grateful as is this theme of gratitude, and inviting as it is for thought and further expression, it is not my purpose to pursue it to-day. I feel that we should turn the occasion into an opportunity for improvement and progress.

Especially is this the duty of a people situated as we are in this country; cut loose, blessed be GOD, for evermore, from the dark moorings of servitude and oppression; but not fully arrived at—only drifting towards, the deep, quiet waters of fullest freedom and equality. Few, comparatively, in numbers; limited in resources; the inheritors of prodigious disasters; the heirs of ancestral woes and sorrows; burdened with most manifest duties and destinies; anxious for our children; thoughtful for our race; culpability and guilt of the deepest dye will be ours, if we do not most seriously consider the means and instruments by which we shall be enabled to go forward, and to rise upward. It is peculiarly a duty at this time when there is evidently an ebb-tide of indifference in the country, with regard to our race; and when the anxiety for union neutralizes the interest in the black man.

The agencies to the high ends I have referred to are various; but the text I have chosen suggests a train of thought, in a distinct and peculiar line. It shews us that spirit of unity which the world exhibits, when it would fain accomplish its great, commanding ends.

The prophet shews us here the notable sight, that is, that GOD comes down from heaven to put an end to the devices of the wicked. Whatever discord and strife may have before existed among them, at once it comes to an end. A common danger awaits them; a common peril menaces. At once they join hands; immediately their hearts are united. "They helped every one his neighbor, and every one said to his neighbor, be of good courage."

The lesson is one which we shall do well to learn with diligence; that it comes from the wicked, does not detract from its value. The world acts on many a principle which Christians would do well to lay to heart. Our Saviour tells us that "the children of this world are wiser in their generation than the children of light."[1] So here, this principle of united effort, and of generous concord, is worthy of the imitation of the colored people of this country, if they would fain rise to superiority of both character and achievement. I shall speak, therefore, of the *"Social principle among a people; and its bearing on their progress and development."*

What I mean by the social principle, is the disposition which leads men to associate and join together for specific purposes; the principle which makes families and societies, and which binds men in unity and brotherhood, in races and churches and nations.

For man, you will observe, is a social being. In his mental and moral constitution God has planted certain sympathies and affections, from which spring the desire for companionship. It is with reference to these principles that God declared of the single and solitary Adam, "It is not good for the man to live alone."[2] It was no newly-discovered affinity of the Maker, no after-thought of the Almighty. He had *formed* His creature with a fitness and proclivity for association. He had made him with a nature that demanded society. And from this principle flows, as from a fountain, the loves, friendships, families, and combinations which tie men together, in union and concord. A wider and more imposing result of this principle is the welding of men in races and nationalities. All the fruit and flower of these organisms come from the coalescence of divers faculties and powers, tending to specific ends. For no one man can effect anything important alone. There never was a great building, a magnficent city, a noble temple, a grand cathedral, a stately senate-house which was the work of one single individual. We know of no important event in history, no imposing scheme, no great and notable occurrence which stands as an epoch in the annals of the race, which was accomplished by a single, isolated individual. Whether it is the upbuilding of Imperial Rome; or the retreat of the Ten Thousand;[3] or the discovery of America; or Cook's[4] or Anson's[5] voyages around the globe; or the conquest of India; or the battle of Waterloo; everywhere we find that the great things of history have been accomplished by the combination of men.

Not less is this the case in those more humane and genial endeavors which have been for the moral good of men, and wherein the individuality of eminent leaders has been more conspicuous. We read of the evangelization of Europe, from the confines of Asia to Britain; and, in more modern times, we have the abolition of the Slave Trade and Slavery, the grand efforts for the relief of prisoners, the Temperance Reformation, the Sunday-school system. These were noble schemes, which originated in the fruitful brains and sprung from the generous hearts of single individuals, and which, in their gracious results, have made the names of Howard and Wilberforce, of Clarkson and Robert Raikes,[6] bright and conspicuous. But yet we know that even they of themselves did not achieve the victories which are associated with their names. Thousands, nay, tens of thousands of the good and pious were aroused by their passionate appeals to stirring energy; and only when the masses of the godly were marshalled to earnest warfare, were those evils doomed; and they fell, never to rise again!

The application of this truth to the interests and the destiny of the colored race of America is manifest. We are living in this country, a part of its population, and yet, in divers respects, we are as foreign to its inhabitants as though we were living in the Sandwich Islands. It is this our actual separation from the real life of the nation, which constitutes us "a nation within a nation:" thrown very considerably upon ourselves for many of the largest interests of life, and for nearly all our social and religious advantages. As a consequence on this state of things, all the stimulants of ambition and self-love should lead this people to united effort for personal superiority and the uplifting of the race; but, instead thereof, overshadowed by a more powerful race of people; wanting in the cohesion which comes from racial enthusiasm; lacking in the confidence which is the root of a people's stability; disintegration, doubt, and distrust almost universally prevail, and distract all their business and policies.

Among a people, as in a nation, we find farmers, mechanics, sailors, servants, business men, trades. For life, energy, and progress in a people, it is necessary that all these various departments of activity should be carried on with spirit, skill, and unity. It is the cooperative principle, working in trades, business, and manufacturing, which is the great lever that is lifting up the million masses in great nations, and giving those nations themselves a more masterly superiority than they have ever known, in all their past histories. No people can discard this principle, and achieve greatness. Already I have shown that it cannot be done in the confined sphere of individual, personal effort. The social principle prevails in the uprearing of a nation, as in the establishing of a family. Men must associate and combine energies in order to produce large results. In the same way that a family becomes strong, influential, and wealthy by uniting the energies of parents and children, so a people go on to honor and glory, in the proportion and extent that they combine their powers to definite and productive ends.

*Two* principles are implied in the remarks I have made, that is, the *one* of mutuality, and the *other* of dependence.

By *mutuality* I mean the reciprocal tendencies and desires which interact between large bodies of men, aiming at single and definite ends. I mean the several sentiments of sympathy, cheer, encouragement, and combination, among any special body of people; which are needed and required in distinct departments of labor. Solitude, in any matter, is alien to the human heart. We need, we call for the aid of our fellow-creatures. The beating heart of man waits for the answering heart of his brother.

It is the courageous voice of the venturesome soldier that leads on a whole column to the heart of the fray. It is the cheering song of the hardy sailor as he hangs upon the shrouds, amid the fierceness of the tempest, that lifts up the heart of his timid messmates, and stimulates to boldness and noble daring. On the broad fields of labor, where the scythe, the plough, and the spade work out those wondrous transformations which change the wild face of nature to order and beauty, and in the end, bring forth those mighty cargoes of grain which gladden the hearts and sustain the frames of millions; there the anthems of toil invigorate the brawny arms of labor; while the sun pours down its fiery rays, and the midday heat allures in vain to the shade and to rest. Deep down in the dark caves of earth, where the light of the sun never enters, tens of thousands of men and children delve away in the coal beds, or iron mines, buried in the bowels of the earth; cheered on in their toilsome labor by the joyous voices and the gladdening songs of their companions. What is it, in these several cases, that serves at once to lighten toil, and to stimulate to hardier effort? Several principles indeed concur; but it is evident that what I call mutuality, *i. e.,* sympathy and unison of feeling, act upon the hearts of soldiers, sailors, laborers, and miners, and spur them on to duty and endurance.

So, likewise, we may not pass by the other motive, *i. e.,* the feeling of *dependence.* We need the skill, the energy, the achievement of our fellow-creatures. No man stands up entirely alone, self-sufficient in the entire circle of human needs. Even in a state of barbarism the rude native man feels the need of the right arm of his brother. How much more with those who are civilized and enlightened! If you or I determine upon absolute independency of life and action, rejecting the arm and the aid of all other men, into how many departments of labor should we not at once have to multiply ourselves?

It is the recognition of this principle of association, which has made Great Britain, France, the United States, Holland, and Belgium the greatest nations of the earth. There are more partnerships, combinations, trades-unions, banking-houses, and insurance companies in those countries than in all the rest of the world together. The mere handful of men in these nations, numbering but one hundred millions, sway and dominate all the other nine hundred millions of men on the globe. Or just look at one single instance in our own day: here are England and France—fifty-eight millions of men— who, united, only a few years ago, humbled the vast empire of China, with its three hundred millions of semi-civilized inhabitants.[7]

The principles of growth and mastery in a race, a nation, or people, are the same all over the globe. The same great agencies which are needed to make a people in one quarter of the globe and in one period of time are needed here, at this time, in this American nationality. We children of Africa in this land are no way different from any other people in these respects. Many of the differences of races are slight and incidental, and ofttimes become obliterated by circumstances, position, and religion. I can take you back to a period in the history of England when its rude inhabitants lived in caves and huts, when they fed on bark and roots, when their dress was the skins of animals. When you next look at some eminent Englishman, the personification, perchance, of everything cultivated, graceful, and refined, you may remember that his distant ancestors were wild and bloody savages, and that it has taken ten centuries to change him from the rudeness of his brutalized forefathers into an enlightened and civilized human being.

The great general laws of growth and superiority are unchangeable. The Almighty neither relaxes nor alters them for the convenience of any people. Conformity, then, to this demand for combination of forces is a necessity which we, as a people, cannot resist without loss and ruin. We cannot pay heed to it too soon; for if there has been anything for which the colored people of this country have been and now are noted, it is for disseverance, the segregation of their forces, the lack of the co-operative spirit. Neither in farming operations, nor trades, nor business, nor in mechanical employment, nor marketing, nor in attempts at grocery-keeping, do we find attempts at combination of their forces. No one hears anywhere of a company of fifty men to start a farm, to manufacture bricks, to begin a great trading business, to run a mill, or to ply a set of vessels in the coasting trade. No one sees a spontaneous movement of thirty or forty families to take possession of a tract of land for a specific monetary venture. Nowhere do we see a united movement in any State for general moral and educational improvement, whereby the masses may be delivered from inferiority and degradation.[8] The people, as a body, seem delivered over to the same humble, servile occupations of life in which their fathers trod, because, from a lack of co-operation they are unable to step into the higher callings of business; and hence penury, poverty, inferiority, dependence, and even servility is their one general characteristic throughout the country, along with a dreadful state of mortality.

And the cause of this inferiority of purpose and of action is two-fold, and both the fault, to some extent, of unwise and unphilosophic leaders. For, since, especially emancipation, *two* special heresies have influenced and governed the minds of colored men in this nation: (1) The one is the dogma which I have heard frequently from the lips of leaders, personal and dear, but mistaken, friends, *that the colored people of this country should forget, as soon as possible, that they* ARE *colored people:*—a fact, in the first place, which is an impossibility. Forget it, forsooth, when you enter a saloon and are repulsed on account of your color! Forget it when you enter a car, South or West, and are denied a decent seat! Forget it when you enter the Church of God, and are driven to a hole in the gallery! Forget it when every child of yours would be driven ignominiously from four-fifths of the common schools of the country! Forget it, when thousands of mechanics in the large cities would make a "strike" rather than work at the same bench, in the same yard, with a black carpenter or brick-maker! Forget it, when the boyhood of our race is almost universally deprived of the opportunity of learning trades, through prejudice! Forget it, when, in one single State, twenty thousand men dare not go to the polls on election-day, through the tyranny of caste! Forget it, when one great commonwealth offers a new constitution for adoption, by which a man like *Dumas* the younger,[9] if he were a North Carolinian, could be indicted for marrying the foulest white woman in that State, and merely because she was white![10] Forget that you are colored, in these United States! Turn madman, and go into a lunatic asylum, and then, perchance, you may forget it! But, if you have any sense or sensibility, how is it possible for you, or me, or any other colored man, to live oblivious of a fact of so much significance in a land like this! The only place I know of in this land where you can "forget you are colored" is the grave!

But not only is this dogma folly, it is disintegrating and socially destructive. For shut out, for instance, as I am and you are from the cultivated social life of the superior classes of this country, if I forget that I am a black man, if you ignore the fact of race, and we both, ostrich-like, stick our heads in the sand, or stalk along, high-headed, oblivious of the actual distinctions which *do* exist in American society, what are you or I to do for our social nature? What will become of the measure of social life among ourselves which we now possess? Where are we to find our friends? Where find the circles for society and cheerful intercourse?

Why, my friends, the only way you, and I, and thouands of our people get domestic relations, marry wives and husbands, secure social relations, form good neighborhood and companionship, is by the very remembrance which we are told to scout and forswear.

2. The other dogma is the demand *that colored men should give up all distinctive effort, as colored men, in schools, churches, associations, and friendly societies.* But this, you will observe, is equivalent to a demand to the race to give up all civilization in this land and to submit to barbarism. The cry is: "Give up your special organization." "Mix in with your white fellow-citizens."

Now I waive, for the present, all discussion of abstract questions of rights and prerogatives. I direct my attention to the simple point of practicality; and I beg to say, that this is a thing which cannot be forced. Grieved, wearied and worried as humanity has been with the absurd, factitious arrangements of society in every quarter of the globe, yet men everywhere have had to wait. You can batter down oppression and tyranny with forceful implements; not so social disabilities and the exclusiveness of caste. The Saxon could not force it upon the Norman. Upon this point, if everything is not voluntary, generous, gracious, and spontaneous, the repulsive will is as icy, and as obstinate too, as Mt. Blanc.[11] I wonder that the men who talk in the style I have referred to, forget that nine-tenths of the American people have become so poisoned and stimulated by the noxious influence of caste, that, in the present day, they would resist to the utmost before they would allow the affiliations, however remote, that implied the social or domestic principle.

Nay, more than this: not only would they reject your advances, but, after they had repelled you, they would leave you to reap the fruits of your own folly in breaking up your own distinctive and productive organisms, under the flighty stimulants of imaginative conceit.

And the disaster, undoubtedly, would be deserved; not, indeed, morally, for the inflictions of caste are unjust and cruel; but because of your unwisdom; for it is the office of common sense to see, as well the exact situation, to comprehend the real condition of things as they exist in this nation; as well as to take cognizance of the pernicious and atrocious virulence of caste!

Few things in policy are more calamitous in result than mere conceit. An unbalanced and blind imagination is one of the most destructive, most disastrous of all guides. Such I believe to be the nature of the suggestions which I reprobate. But remember, I do not condemn the men who hold them. Oppression and caste are responsible for many worse things than unwisdom, or blind speculation. How intolerable are the distinctions which hedge up our ardent, ambitious minds, on every side, I thoroughly apprehend! How the excited mind turns passionately to every fancied and plausible mode of escape, I can easily understand! But remember that the pilotage of a whole people, of an entire race, through the quicksands and the breakers of civil and social degradation, up to the plane of manly freedom and equality, while it is, by its very hazards, calculated to heighten the pulse, and to quicken the activity of the brain, is, nevertheless, just that sort of work which calls for the coolest head, and the hardest, most downright reasonableness. When you are pleading for natural rights, when men are endeavoring to throw off the yoke of oppression, you may indeed

> —imitate the action of the tiger,
> Stiffen the sinews, summon up the blood.[12]

But a war against a gross public sentiment, a contest with prejudices and repulsions, is a thing of a different kind, and calls for a warfare of an opposite character. You cannot destroy caste with a ten pounder! You cannot sweep away a prejudice with a park of artillery!

I know, to use the words of another, "how difficut it is to silence imagination enough to make the voice of Reason even distinctly heard in this case; as we are accustomed from our youth up to indulge that forward and delusive faculty ever obtruding beyond its sphere; of some assistance indeed to apprehension, but the author of all error; as we plainly lose ourselves in gross and crude conception of things, taking for granted that we are acquainted with what indeed we are wholly ignorant of";[13] so it seems to me the gravest of all duties to get rid of all delusions upon this subject; and to learn to look at it in the light of hard, serious, long-continued, painful, plodding work. It is *work,* you will observe, not abnormal disturbances, not excitement; but a mighty effort of moral and mental reconstruction, reaching over to a majestic end. And then when that is reached and secured, then all the hindrances of caste will be forever broken down!

Nothing is more idle than to talk of the invincibility of prejudice. The Gospel is sure to work out all the issues and results of brotherhood, everywhere under the sun, and in this land; but, until that day arrives, we are a nation, set apart, in this country. As such, we have got to strive—not to get rid of ourselves; not to agonize over our distinctive peculiarities; but to accept the situation as Providence allows it, and to quit "ourselves as men,"[14] in, if you say so, painful and embarrassing circumstances; determined to shift the groove of circumstance, and to reverse it.

The special duty before us is to strive for footing and for superiority in this land, *on the line of race,* as a temporary but needed expedient, for the ultimate extinction of caste, and all race distinctions. For if *we* do not look after our own interests, as a people, and strive for advantage, no other people will. It is folly for mere idealists to content themselves with the notion that "we are American citizens;" that, "as American citizens, ours is the common heritage and destiny of the nation;" that "special solicitude for the colored people is a superfluity;" that "there is but one tide in this land; and we shall flow with all others on it."

On the contrary, I assert, we are just now a "peculiar people"[15] in this land; looked at, repulsed, kept apart, legislated for, criticised in journals, magazines, and scientific societies, at an insulting and intolerable distance, *as* a peculiar people; with the doubt against us whether or not we can hold on to vital power on this soil; or whether we have capacity to rise to manhood and superiority.

And hence I maintain that there is the greatest need for us all to hold on to the remembrance that *we* are "colored men," and not to forget it!

While one remnant of disadvantage abides in this land, stand by one another! While proscription in any quarter exists, maintain intact all your phalanxes! While antagonism confronts your foremost men, hold on to all the instincts of race for the support of your leaders, and the elevation of your people! While the imputation of inferiority, justly or unjustly, is cast upon you, combine for all the elements of culture, wealth, and power! While any sensitiveness or repulsion discovers itself at your approach or presence, hold on to your own self-respect, keep up, *and be satisfied with,* your own distinctive circles!

And then the "poor, forsaken ones," in the lanes and alleys and cellars of the great cities; in remote villages and hamlets; on old plantations which their fathers' blood has moistened from generation to generation; ignorant, unkempt, dirty, animal-like, repulsive, and half heathen—brutal and degraded; in some States, tens and hundreds of thousands, not slaves, indeed, according to the letter of the law, but the tools and *serfs* of would-be oppressors: stand by THEM until the school-master and preacher reach them as well as us; and the noble Christian civilization of the land transforms their features and their forms, and changes their rude huts into homes of beauty; and lifts them up into such grand superiority, that no one in the land will associate the word "Negro" with inferiority and degradation; but the whole land, yea, the whole world shall look upon them by-and-by, multitudinous in their brooding, clustered masses, "redeemed, regenerated, disenthralled," and exclaim, "Black, but comely!" But, while they are low, degraded, miserable, almost beastly, don't forget that you are colored men, as well as they; "your brothers' keepers."[16]

Do not blink at the charge of inferiority. It is not a race peculiarity; and whatever its measure or extent in this country, it has been forced upon you. Do not deny it, but neutralize and destroy it, not by shrieks, or agonies, or foolish pretence; but by culture, by probity, and industry.

I know the natural resource of some minds, under these painful circumstances, to cry out, "Agitate! agitate!" But *cui bono?* What advantage will agitation bring? Everything has a value, according to its relation to its own natural and specific end. But what is the bearing of agitation to a purpose which is almost entirely subjective in its nature. For, as I take it, the object we must needs have in view, in the face of the disabilities which confront our race in this land, is the attainment of such general superiority that prejudice *must* decline. But agitation has no such force, possesses no such value. Agitation is the expenditure of force: our end and aim is the husbandry of all our vital resources.

Character, my friends, is the grand, effective instrument which we are to use for the destruction of caste: Character, in its broad, wide, deep, and high significance; character, as evidenced in high moral and intellectual attainments; as significant of general probity, honor, honesty, and self-restraint; as inclusive of inward might and power; as comprehending the attainments of culture, refinement, and enlightenment; as comprising the substantial results of thrift, economy, and enterprise; and as involving the forces of combined energies and enlightened cooperation. Make this, *not* the exceptional, but the common, general reality, amid the diverse, widespread populations of the colored people in this country; and then all the theories of inferiority, all the assumptions of your native and invincible degradation will pass, with wonderful rapidity, into endless forgetfulness; and the people of the very *next,* nay, multitudes, in the decline of *this* generation, when they look upon us, will wonder at the degrading facts of a past and wretched history. Only secure high, commanding, and masterly Character; and then all the problems of caste, all the enigmas of prejudice, all unreasonable and all unreasoning repulsion, will be settled forever, though you were ten times blacker than midnight! Then all false ideas concerning your nature and your qualities, all absurd notions relative to your capacity, shall vanish! Then every contemptuous fling shall be hushed, every insulting epithet be forgotten! Then, also, all the remembrances of a servile heritage, of ancestral degradation, shall be obliterated! Then all repulsive feelings, all evil dislikes shall fly away! Then, too, all timid disconcert shall depart from us, and all cramped and hesitant manhood shall die!

Dear brethren and friends, let there be but the clear demonstration of manly power and grand capacity in our race, in general, in this country; let there only be the wide out-flashings of art and genius, from their brains; and caste will slink, at once, oblivious to the shades. But no mere self-assertion, no strong, vociferous claims and clamor, can ever secure recognition and equality, so long as inferiority and degradation, if even cruelly entailed, abide as a heritage and a cancer. And I maintain we must *organize,* to the end that we may attain such character. The whole of our future on this soil depends upon that single fact of magnitude—character. Race, color, and all the incidents thereof have but little to do with the matter; and men talk idly when they say "we must forget that we are colored men." What is needed is not that *we* should forget this fact, but that we should rise to such elevation that the *people of the land* be forced to forget all the facts and theories of race, when they behold our thorough equality with them, in all the lines of activity and attainment, of culture and moral grandeur. The great necessity in this land is that its *white* population should forget, be made to forget, that we are *colored* men! Hence there is a work ahead of us, for the overthrow of caste, which will consume the best part of a century. He, whoever he may be, commits the greatest blunder, who advises you to disband your forces, until that work is brought to its end. It was only *after* the battle of Waterloo that England and her allies broke up their armies, and scattered their huge battalions. Not until we, as a people, have fully vindicated our race; not until we have achieved to the full their rights and prerogatives; not until, by character, we challenge universal respect and consideration in the land, can we sing the song:

> —Come to the sunset tree,
> The day is past and gone,
> The woodman's axe lies free,
> And the reaper's work is done.[17]

Until that time, far distant from to-day, should the cry be everywhere among us: "Combine and marshal, for all the highest achievements in industry, social progress, literature, and religion!"

I hasten to conclude with two brief remarks:

First, then, let me remind and warn you, my friends, that we, as colored men, have no superfluity of powers or faculties in the work which is before us, as a race, in this country. First of all, we all start with maimed and stunted powers. And next, the work before us is so distinct, definite, and, withal, so immense, that it tolerates no erratic wanderings to out-of-the-way and foreign fields.

And yet there are men who tell us that much of our work of the day is objective, that it lies among another people. But I beg to say that we have more than we are equal to in the needs of the six millions of our ignorant and benighted people, yet crippled and paralyzed by the lingering maladies of slavery. If we address ourselves strenuously and unitedly to *their* elevation and improvement we shall have our hands full for more than one generation, without flowing over with zeal and offices to a masterful people, laden with the enlightenment of centuries.

For one, I say very candidly that I do not feel it *my* special calling to wage war with and to extirpate caste. I am no way responsible for its existence. I abominate it as an enormity. *Theirs* is the responsibility who uphold it, and theirs is the obligation to destroy it. My work is special to my own people, and it is constructive. I beg leave to differ from that class of colored men who think that ours is a special mission, to leave our camp and to go over, as it were, among the Philistines, and to destroy their idols.

For my part, I am satisfied that my field of labor is with my own race in these times. I feel I have no exuberance of powers or ability to spend in any other field, or to bestow upon any other people. I say, as said the Shunamite woman, "I DWELL AMONG MY OWN PEOPLE" (2 Kings: IV, 13); not, indeed, as mindless of the brotherhood of the entire species, not as forgetful of the sentiment of fellowship with disciples of every name and blood; but as urged by the feeling of kinship, to bind myself as "with hooks of steel"[18] to the most degraded class in the land, my own "kinsmen according to the flesh."[19] I have the most thorough and radical conviction that the very first duty of colored men, in this our day and generation, is in the large field of effort which requires the regeneration and enlightenment of the colored race in these United States.

And second, from this comes the legitimate inference suggested by the text, *i. e.,* of union and co-operation through all our ranks for effective action and for the noblest ends. Everywhere throughout the Union wide and thorough organization of the people should be made, not for idle political logomachy, but for industrial effort, for securing trades for youth, for joint-stock companies, for manufacturing, for the production of the great staples of the land, and likewise for the higher purposes of life, *i. e.,* for mental and moral improvement, and raising the plane of social and domestic life among us.

In every possible way these needs and duties should be pressed upon their attention, by sermons, by lectures, by organized societies, by state and national conventions; the *latter not* for political objects, but for social, industrial ends and attainments. I see nought in the future but that we shall be scattered like chaff before the wind before the organized labor of the land, the great power of capital, and the tremendous tide of emigration, unless, as a people, we fall back upon the might and mastery which come from the combination of forces and the principle of industrial co-operation. Most of your political agitation is but wind and vanity. *What this race needs in this country is* POWER—*the forces that may be felt.* And that comes from character, and character is the product of religion, intelligence, virtue, family order, superiority, wealth, and the show of industrial forces. THESE ARE FORCES WHICH WE DO NOT POSSESS. *We are the only class which, as a class,* IN THIS COUNTRY, IS WANTING IN THESE GRAND ELEMENTS. The very first effort of the colored people should be to lay hold of them; and then they will take such root in this American soil that only the convulsive upheaving of the judgement-day can throw them out! And therefore I close, as I began, with the admonitory tones of the text. God grant they may be heeded at least by YOU who form this congregation, in your sacred work *here,* and in all your other relations: "They helped every one his neighbor, and every one said to his brother, Be of good courage. So the carpenter encouraged the goldsmith, and he that smootheth with the hammer him that smote the anvil, saying, It is ready for the soldering; and he fastened it with nails, that it SHOULD NOT BE MOVED!"

# 2.

# The Destined Superiority
# of the Negro

Evangelicals were acutely conscious of God's purposes for their lives, and Crummell was not alone in seeing in the history of the black race a sign of future glory and perfection. In this sermon, delivered at St. Mary's Chapel in 1877, Crummell elaborated on these ideas, drawing a parallel between the pain and suffering of blacks and the "servile sojourn of the children of Israel, four hundred years in Egypt." Crummell's imagery, his use of words and phrases like "thraldom" and "painful suffering," is the imagery of evangelical Protestantism, but just as striking is the way in which he elevated potential black stereotypes ("plasticity," "imitation," and "devotion") into universal racial qualities, shared by all successful peoples and nations.

## ISAIAH LXI, 7.

*For your shame ye shall have double, and for confusion they shall rejoice in their portion.*

THE promise contained in the text is a variation from the ordinary rule of the divine government. In that government, as declared in the Holy Scriptures, shame signifies the hopeless confusion and the utter destruction of the wicked. But in this passage we see an extraordinary display of God's forbearance and mercy. Shame, here, is less intense than in other places. In this case it stands, indeed, for trial and punishment, but for punishment and trial which may correct and purify character.

The allusion is supposed to refer to the Jews after their restoration, and the passage is regarded as teaching that, for all their long-continued servitude and suffering, God, in the end, would make them abundant recompense. Great shame and reproach He had given them, through long centuries; but now, when discipline and trial had corrected and purified them, He promises them double honor and reward.

As thus explained, the text opens before us some interesting features of God's dealing with nations; by the light of which we may, perchance, somewhat determine the destiny of the race with which we are connected. My purpose is to attempt, this morning, an investigation of God's disciplinary and retributive economy in races and nations; with the hope of arriving at some clear conclusions concerning the destiny of the Negro race.

1. Some peoples God does not merely correct; He destroys them. He visits them with deep and abiding shame. He brings upon them utter confusion. This is a painful but a certain fact of Providence. The history of the world is, in one view, a history of national destructions. The wrecks of nations lie everywhere upon the shores of time. Real aboriginal life is rarely found. People after people, in rapid succession, have come into constructive being, and as rapidly gone down; lost forever from sight beneath the waves of a relentless destiny. We read in our histories of the great empires of the old world; but when the traveller goes abroad, and looks for Nineveh and Babylon, for Pompeii and Herculaneum, he finds nought but the outstretched graveyards which occupy the sites of departed nations. On the American continent, tribe after tribe have passed from existence; yea, there are Bibles in Indian tongues which no living man is now able to read. Their peoples have all perished!

When I am called upon to account for all this loss of national and tribal life, I say that God destroyed them. And the declaration is made on the strength of a principle attested by numerous facts in sacred and profane history; that when the sins of a people reach a state of hateful maturity, then God sends upon them sudden destruction.

Depravity prepares some races of men for destruction. Every element of good has gone out of them. Even the most primitive virtues seem to have departed. A putrescent virus has entered into and vitiated their whole nature. They stand up columnar ruins! Such a people is doomed. It cannot live. Like the tree "whose root is rottenness,"[1] it stands awaiting the inevitable fall. That fall is its property. No fierce thunder-bolt is needed, no complicated apparatus of ethereal artillery. Let the angry breath of an Archangel but feebly strike it, and, tottering, it sinks into death and oblivion!

Such was the condition of the American Indian at the time of the discovery of America by Columbus. The historical fact abides, that when the white man first reached the shores of this continent he met the tradition of a decaying population.

The New Zealand population of our own day presents a parallel case. By a universal disregard of the social and sanitary conditions which pertain to health and longevity, their physical constitution has fallen into absolute decay; and ere long it also must become extinct.

Indeed, the gross paganism of these two peoples was both moral and physical stagnation; was domestic and family ruin; and has resulted in national suicide! It came to them as the effect, the direct consequence of great penal laws established by the Almighty, in which are wrapped the punishment of sin. Hence, if you reject the idea of direct interference in the affairs of peoples, and take up the idea of law and penalty, or that of cause and effect, it amounts to the same thing. Whether through God's fixed law, or directly, by His personal, direful visitation, the admission is the same. The punishment and the ruin come from the throne of God!

The most striking instances of the working of this principle of ruin are set before us in the word of God. The case of Egypt is a signal one. For centuries this nation was addicted to the vilest sins and the grossest corruption. There was no lack of genius among them, no imbecility of intellect. It was a case of wanton, high-headed moral rebellion. As generations followed each other, they heaped up abominations upon the impurities of their ancestors, until they well nigh reached the heavens! Then the heavens became darkened with direful wrath! The earth quaked and trembled with God's fearful anger; and judgement upon judgement swept, like lava, over that doomed people, assuring them of the awful destruction which always waits upon sin. And the death of the first-born at the Passover, and the catastrophe of the Red Sea, showed that the crisis of their fate had come.[2]

In precisely the same manner God dealt with the wicked people of Assyria, Babylon, Tyre, and Persia. Read the prophecies concerning these nations, and it seems as though you could see an august judge sitting upon the judgement-seat, and, of a sudden, putting on his black cap, and, with solemn gesture and a choked utterance, pronouncing the sentence of death upon the doomed criminals before him!

2. Turn now to the more gracious aspects of God's economy. As there are peoples whom He destroys, so on the other hand there are those whom, while indeed He chastises, yet at the same time He preserves. He gives them shame, but not perpetual shame. He disciplines; but when discipline has worked out its remedial benefits, he recompenses them for their former ignominy, and gives them honor and prosperity.

The merciful aspect of God's economy shines out in human history as clearly as His justice and judgement. The Almighty seizes upon superior nations and, by mingled chastisements and blessings, gradually leads them on to greatness. That this discipline of nations is carried on in the world is evident. Probation, that is, as designed to teach self-restraint, and to carry on improvement, is imposed upon them, as well as upon individuals. It is part of the history of all nations and all races; only some will not take it; seem to have no moral discernment to use it; and they, just like wilful men, are broken to pieces. Some, again, fit themselves to it, and gain all its advantages. What was the servile sojourn of the children of Israel, four hundred years, in Egypt, but a process of painful preparation for a coming national and ecclesiastical responsibility? What, at a later period, the Babylonish captivity,[3] but a corrective ordeal, to eliminate from them every element of idolatry? What was the feudality of Europe, but a system of training for a high and grand civilization?

Now it seems to me that these several experiments were not simply judicial and retributive. For vengeance crushes and annihilates; but chastisement, however severe, saves, and at the same time corrects and restores. We may infer, therefore, that these several providences were a mode of divine schooling, carried on by the Almighty for great ends which He wished to show in human history.

But how? in what way does God carry on His system of restorative discipline? The universal principle which regulates this feature of the Divine system is set forth very clearly in the Eighteenth Psalm: "With the merciful thou wilt shew thyself merciful; with an upright man thou wilt shew thyself upright; with the pure thou wilt shew thyself pure; and with the froward thou wilt shew thyself froward."[4] These words show the principles by which God carries on His government. And they apply as well to organic society as to single persons.

We have already seen that with the froward God showed Himself froward; that is, those who resist Him, God resists, to their utter shame and confusion. Their miseries were not corrective or disciplinary. They were the blows of avenging justice; the thunder-bolts of final and retributive wrath! In their case, moreover, there was a constitutional fitness to destruction, brought upon them by their own immoral perverseness. So, too, on the other hand, we may see qualities which God favors, albeit He does put the peoples manifesting them to trial and endurance. He sees in them cultivated elements of character, which, when brought out and trained, are capable of raising them to superiority. He does not see merit; and it is not because of desert that He bestows His blessings. But when the Almighty sees in a nation or people latent germs of virtues, he seizes upon and schools them by trial and discipline; so that by the processes of divers correctives, these virtues may bud and blossom into beautiful and healthful maturity.

Now, when the Psalmist speaks of the merciful, the upright, and the pure, he does not use these terms in an absolute sense, for in that sense no such persons exist. He speaks of men comparatively pure, upright, and merciful. Some of the nations, as I have already pointed out, were at the lowest grade of moral turpitude. On the other hand, there are and ever have been heathen peoples less gross and barbarous than others: peoples with great hardihood of soul; peoples retaining the high principle of right and justice; peoples with rude but strong virtues, clinging to the simple ideas of truth and honor; peoples who guarded jealously the purity of their wives and the chastity of their daughters; peoples who, even with a false worship, showed reluctance to part with the gleams which came, though but dimly, from the face of the one true God of heaven!

Now the providence of God intervenes for the training and preservation of such peoples. Thus we read in Genesis that, because of man's universal wickedness, "it repented the Lord that he had made man;"[5] but immediately it says that He approved "just Noah, and entered into covenant with him."[6] So, after the deluge, God saw, amid universal degeneracy, the conspicuous piety of one man; for obedience and faith were, without doubt, original though simple elements of Abraham's character. To these germinal roots God brought the discipline of trial; and by them, through this one man, educated up a people who, despite their faults, shed forth the clearest religious light of all antiquity, and to whom were committed the oracles of God.

The ancient Greeks and Romans were rude and sanguinary Pagans; and so, too, the Germans and the Scandinavian tribes. Yet they had great, sterling virtues. The Greeks were a people severely just; the Spartans, especially, rigidly simple and religious. The Romans were unequalled for reverence for law and subjection to legitimate authority. Tacitus, himself a heathen, extols the noble and beneficent traits of German character, and celebrates their hospitality and politeness.[7] The Saxons, even in a state of rudeness, were brave, though fierce; truthful; with strong family virtues, and great love of liberty.

Added to these peculiarities we find the following characteristics common to each and all these people—common, indeed, to all strong races; wanting in the low and degraded. The masterful nations are all, more or less, distinguished for vitality, plasticity, receptivity, imitation, family feeling, veracity, and the sentiment of devotion. These qualities may have been crude and unbalanced. They existed perchance right beside most decided and repulsive vices; but they were deeply imbedded in the constitution of these people; and served as a basis on which could be built up a character fitted to great ends.

Archbishop Trench, in his comment upon the words of the "Parable of the Sower,"—that is, that "they on the good ground are they who, in an honest and good heart, having heard the word, keep it"[8]—says, "that no heart can be said to be absolutely good; but there are conditions of heart in which the truth finds readier entrance than in others."[9] So we maintain that there are conditions of character and of society, to which the divine purposes of grace and civilization are more especially fitted, and adapt themselves. Such, it is evident, is the explanation of the providential spread of early civilization. It passed by the more inane peoples, and fastened itself to the strong and masculine. Such, too, was the spontaneous flow of early Christianity from Jerusalem. It sought, as by a law of affinity, the strong colonies of Asia Minor, and the powerful states along the Mediterranean; and so spread abroad through the then civilized Europe.

Does God then despise the weak? Nay, but the weak and miserable peoples of the earth have misused their prerogatives, and so unfitted themselves to feel after God.

And because they have thus perverted the gifts of God, and brought imbecility upon their being, they perish. The iniquity of the Amorites in Joshua's day was full—as you may see in Leviticus xviii—full of lust and incest and cruelty and other unspeakable abominations; and they were swept from the face of the earth! They perished by the sword; but the sword is not an absolute necessity to the annihilation of any corrupt and ruined people. Their sins, of themselves, eat out their life. With a touch they go. It was because of the deep and utter demoralization of Bois Gilbert that he fell before the feeble lance of Ivanhoe;[10] for, in the world of morals, weakness and death are ofttimes correlative of baseness and infamy.

On the other hand the simplest seeds of goodness are pleasing to the Almighty, and He sends down the sunshine of His favor and the dews of His conserving care into the darkest rubbish, to nourish and vivify such seeds, and to "give them body as it pleaseth Him; and to every seed his own body."[11] And the greatness of the grand nations has always sprung from the seeds of simple virtues which God has graciously preserved in them; which virtues have been cultured by gracious providences or expanded by Divine grace, into true holiness.

3. Let us now apply the train of thought thus presented to the history and condition of the Negro; to ascertain, if possible, whether we can draw therefrom expectation of a future for this race.

At once the question arises: Is this a race doomed to destruction? or is it one possessed of those qualities, and so morally disciplined by trial, as to augur a vital destiny, and high moral uses, in the future?

To the first of these questions I reply that there is not a fact, pertinent to this subject, that does not give a most decisive negative. The Negro race, nowhere on the globe, is a doomed race!

It is now nigh five hundred years since the breath of the civilized world touched, powerfully, for the first time, the mighty masses of the Pagan world in America, Africa, and the isles of the sea. And we see, almost everywhere, that the weak, heathen tribes of the earth have gone down before the civilized European. Nation after nation has departed before his presence, tribe after tribe! In America the catalogue of these disastrous eclipses overruns, not only dozens, but even scores of cases. Gone, never again to take rank among the tribes of men, are the Iroquois and the Mohegans, the Pequods and the Manhattans, the Algonquins and the brave Mohawks, the gentle Caribs, and the once refined Aztecs!

In the Pacific seas, islands are scattered abroad like stars in the heavens; but the sad fact remains that from many of them their population has departed, like the morning mist. In other cases, as in the Sandwich Islands, they have long since begun their

Funeral marches to the grave![12]

Just the reverse with the Negro! Wave after wave of a destructive tempest has swept over his head, without impairing in the least his peculiar vitality. Indeed, the Negro, in certain localities, is a superior man, to-day, to what he was three hundred years ago. With an elasticity rarely paralleled, he has risen superior to the dread inflictions of a prolonged servitude, and stands, to-day, in all the lands of his thraldom, taller, more erect, more intelligent, and more aspiring than any of his ancestors for more than two thousand years of a previous era. And while in other lands, as in cultivated India, the native has been subjected to a foreign yoke, the negro races of Africa still retain, for the most part, their original birthright. Their soil has not passed into the possession of a foreign people.[13] Many of the native kingdoms stand this day, upon the same basis of power which they held long centuries ago. The adventurous traveler, as he passes farther and farther into the interior, sends us reports of populous cities, superior people, and vast kingdoms; given to enterprise, and engaged in manufactures, agriculture, and commerce.

Even this falls short of the full reality. For civilization, at numerous places, as well in the interior as on the coast, has displaced ancestral heathenism; and the standard of the Cross, uplifted on the banks of its great rivers, at large and important cities, and in the great seats of commercial activity, shows that the Heralds of the Cross have begun the conquest of the continent for their glorious King. Vital power, then, is a property of the Negro family.

But has this race any of those other qualities, and such a number of them, as warrants the expectation of superiority? Are plasticity, receptivity, and assimilation among his constitutional elements of character?

So far as the first of these is concerned there can be no doubt. The flexibility of the negro character is not only universally admitted; it is often formulated into a slur. The race is possessed of a nature more easily moulded than any other class of men. Unlike the stolid Indian, the Negro yields to circumstances, and flows with the current of events. Hence the most terrible afflictions have failed to crush him. His facile nature wards them off, or else, through the inspiration of hope, neutralises their influence. Hence, likewise, the pliancy with which, and without losing his distinctiveness, he runs into the character of other people; and thus bends adverse circumstances to his own convenience; thus, also, in a measurable degree, linking the fortunes of his superiors to his own fate and destiny.

These peculiarities imply another prime quality, anticipating future superiority; I mean imitation. This is also universally conceded, with, however, a contemptuous fling, as though it were an evidence of inferiority. But Burke tells us that "imitation is the second passion belonging to society; and this passion," he says, "arises from much the same cause as sympathy." This forms our manners, our opinions, our lives. It is one of the strongest links of society.[14] Indeed, all civilization is carried down from generation to generation, or handed over from the superior to the inferior, by the means of this principle. A people devoid of imitation are incapable of improvement, and must go down; for stagnation of necessity brings with it decay and ruin.

On the other hand, the Negro, with a mobile and plastic nature, with a strong receptive faculty, seizes upon and makes over to himself, by imitation, the better qualities of others. First of all, observe that, by a strong assimilative tendency, he reduplicates himself, by attaining both the likeness of and an affinity to the race with which he dwells; and then, while retaining his characteristic peculiarities, he glides more or less into the traits of his neighbors. Among Frenchmen, he becomes, somewhat, the lively Frenchman; among Americans, the keen, enterprising American; among Spaniards, the stately, solemn Spaniard; among Englishmen, the solid, phlegmatic Englishman.

This peculiarity of the Negro is often sneered at. It is decried as the simulation of a well-known and grotesque animal.[15] But traducers of the Negro forget that "the entire Grecian civilization is stratified with the elements of imitation; and that Roman culture is but a copy of a foreign and alien civilization." These great nations laid the whole world under contribution to gain superiority. They seized upon all the spoils of time.[16] They became cosmopolitan thieves. They stole from every quarter. They pounced, with eagle eye, upon excellence wherever discovered, and seized upon it with rapacity. In the Negro character resides, though crudely, precisely the same eclectic quality which characterized those two great, classic nations; and he is thus found in the very best company. The ridicule which visits him goes back directly to them. The advantage, however, is his own. Give him time and opportunity, and in all imitative art he will rival them both.

This quality of imitation has been the grand preservative of the Negro in all the lands of his thraldom. Its bearing upon his future distinction in Art is not germain to this discussion; but one can clearly see that this quality of imitation, allied to the receptivity of the race, gives promise of great fitness for Christian training, and for the higher processes of civilization.

But observe, again, that the imitative disposition of the negro race leads to aspiration. Its tendency runs to the higher and nobler qualities presented to observation. Placed in juxtaposition with both the Indian and the Caucasian, as in Brazil and in this land, the race turns away from the downward, unprogressive Indian, and reaches forth for all the acquisitions of the Caucasian or the Spaniard. And hence wherever the Negro family has been in a servile position, however severe may have been their condition, without one single exception their native capacity has always

> —glinted forth
> Amid the storm;[17]

preserving the captive exiles of Africa from utter annihilation; stimulating them to enterprise and aspiration; and, in every case, producing men who have shown respectable talent as mechanics and artisans; as soldiers, in armies; as citizens of great commonwealths; not unfrequently as artists; not seldom as scholars; frequently as ministers of the Gospel; and at times as scientific men, and men of letters.

I referred, at the beginning, and as one of the conditions of a Divine and merciful preservation of a people—for future uses, to the probation of discipline and trial, for the cultivation of definite moral qualities. Is there any such large fact in the history of this race? What else, I ask, can be the significance of the African slave-trade? What is the meaning of our deep thraldom since 1620? Terrible as it has been, it has not been the deadly hurricane portending death. During its long periods, although great cruelty and wide-spread death have been large features in the history of the Negro, nevertheless they have been overshadowed by the merciful facts of great natural increase, much intellectual progress, the gravitation of an unexampled and world-wide philanthropy to the race, singular religious susceptibility and progress, and generous, wholesale emancipations, inclusive of millions of men, women, and children.

This history, then, does not signify retribution; does not forecast extinction. It is most plainly disciplinary and preparative. It is the education which comes from trial and endurance; for with it has been allied, more or less, the grand moral training of the religious tendencies of the race.

Here, then, are the several conditions, the characteristic marks which, in all history, have served to indicate the permanency and the progress of races. In all other cases they have been taken as forecasting greatness. Is there any reason for rejecting their teachings, and refusing their encouragements and inspirations, when discovered in the Negro?

I feel fortified, moreover, in the principles I have to-day set forth, by the opinions of great, scrutinizing thinkers. In his treatise on Emancipation, written in 1880, Dr. Channing says: "The Negro is one of the best races of the human family. He is among the mildest and gentlest of men. He is singularly susceptible of improvement."[18]

Alexander Kinmont, in his "Lectures on Man," declares that "the sweet graces of the Christian religion appear almost too tropical and tender plants to grow in the soil of the Caucasian mind; they require a character of human nature of which you can see the rude lineaments in the Ethiopian, to be implanted in, and grow naturally and beautifully withal."[19] Adamson, the traveller who visited Senegal, in 1754, said: "The Negroes are sociable, humane, obliging, and hospitable; and they have generally preserved an estimable simplicity of domestic manners. They are distinguished by their tenderness for their parents, and great respect for the aged—a patriarchal virtue which, in our day, is too little known."[20] Dr. Raleigh, also, at a recent meeting in London, said: "There is in these people a hitherto undiscovered mine of love, the development of which will be for the amazing welfare of the world. . . . Greece gave us beauty; Rome gave us power; the Anglo-Saxon race unites and mingles these; but in the African people there is the great, gushing wealth of love which will develop wonders for the world."[21]

1. We have seen, to-day, the great truth, that when God does not destroy a people, but, on the contrary, trains and disciplines it, it is an indication that He intends to make something of them, and to do something for them. It signifies that He is graciously interested in such a people. In a sense, not equal, indeed, to the case of the Jews, but parallel, in a lower degree, such a people are a "chosen people"[22] of the Lord. There is, so to speak, a *covenant* relation which God has established between Himself and them; dim and partial, at first, in its manifestations; but which is sure to come to the sight of men and angels, clear, distinct, and luminous. You may take it as a sure and undoubted fact that God presides, with sovereign care, over such a people; and will surely preserve, educate, and build them up.

2. The discussion of this morning teaches us that the Negro race, of which we are a part, and which, as yet, in great simplicity and with vast difficulties, is struggling for place and position in this land, discovers, most exactly, in its history, the principle I have stated. And we have in this fact the assurance that the Almighty is interested in all the great problems of civilization and of grace carrying on among us. All this is God's work. He has brought this race through a wilderness of disasters; and at last put them in the large, open place of liberty; but not, you may be assured, for eventual decline and final ruin. You need not entertain the shadow of a doubt that the work which God has begun and is now carrying on, is for the elevation and success of the Negro. This is the significance and the worth of all effort and all achievement, of every signal providence, in this cause; or, otherwise, all the labors of men and all the mightiness of God is vanity! Nothing, believe me, on earth; nothing brought from perdition, can keep back this destined advance of the Negro race. No conspiracies of men nor of devils! The slave trade could not crush them out. Slavery, dread, direful, and malignant, could only stay it for a time. But now it is coming, coming, I grant, through dark and trying events, but surely coming. The Negro—black, curly-headed, despised, repulsed, sneered at—is, nevertheless, a vital being, and irrepressible. Everywhere on earth has been given him, by the Almighty, assurance, self-assertion, and influence. The rise of two Negro States[23] within a century, feeble though they be, has a bearing upon this subject. The numerous emancipations, which now leave not more than a chain or two to be unfastened, have likewise, a deep, moral significance. Thus, too, the rise in the world of illustrious Negroes, as Touissant L'Ouverture, Henry Christophe, Benjamin Banneker, Eustace the Philanthropist, Stephen Allan Benson, and Bishop Crowther.[24]

With all these providential indications in our favor, let us bless God and take courage. Casting aside everything trifling and frivolous, let us lay hold of every element of power, in the brain; in literature, art, and science; in industrial pursuits; in the soil; in cooperative association; in mechanical ingenuity; and above all, in the religion of our God; and so march on in the pathway of progress to that superiority and eminence which is our rightful heritage, and which is evidently the promise of our God!

# 3.

# The Assassination of
# President Garfield

On July 2, 1881, President James Garfield was shot and mortally wounded by Charles Guiteau, a disappointed office seeker. Like many other Americans, Crummell looked upon this incident as a brutal yet fitting judgment on the political excesses of the Gilded Age. A lifelong conservative, he distrusted and feared what he called "wild and lawless Democracy" and subscribed to a political faith that stressed duties, not rights. As this sermon makes clear, Crummell was equally anxious that blacks should be "ranked alongside conservative men" in the United States, and to this end he sought to instill in them self-restraint and the traditional virtues of thrift, honesty, and family order. "The Assassination of President Garfield" was preached at St. Luke's on July 10, 1881, as Garfield lay on his deathbed.

### St. John, XI: 49, 50

*And one of them named Caiaphas, being the High Priest that same year, said unto them, Ye know nothing at all, nor consider that it is expedient that one man should die for the people, and that the whole nation perish not.*

ALL through the week,[1] my brethren, we, in common with the people of this land, have been passing through an ordeal of suspense, of agony, of almost despair, rarely parallelled in the history of this or any other country. Pain and suffering are the common lot of all men; but it is seldom that a whole nation is called to the intense, long-lingering anxiety which has been the lot of the many millions who make up this great nation. Day by day, nay, hour by hour, this entire republic has been on the rack, fearful of a report which would have brought anguish and bereavement to unnumbered hearts and households. For the entire people of this land have felt that the dreadful deed which brought our Chief Magistrate well nigh the shades of death was personal to themselves. When President Garfield was shot by a wild and reckless assassin, every citizen was shot at. His wounds were our wounds. His agonies were our agonies. It was not only that he, as President and Chief, stood officially before the people and the world the representative of the nation, and hence that to attack him was like an assault upon the flag of the country—an assault upon its every citizen; but, added to this, is the further fact, seen in various ways before this sad occurrence, that the genuine and intense personality of this man had "bowed the heart" of its whole population, "as the heart of one man."[2] Hence it is that a whole people have stood breathless, anxious, and appalled at his bedside; and strong men, when they heard of this calamity, fainted, and the tender hearts of women and children gave way to uncontrollable emotions, and the aged, in known instances, shocked at the awfulness of this assault, lay down and died!

Such interest, such sympathy, such fellowship in suffering with a suffering man has never before been witnessed. We know somewhat how great has been his anguish. But is it too great an exaggeration to say that thousands of people in this land, have suffered well nigh as much in *his* suffering as he himself has suffered? Is there any man here who can estimate the intense mental anguish, the harassing care of multitudes, as they have stood, day by day, trembling, almost despairing, for the life of this eminent man? Many years ago I read a poem, "The Death-Bed," by Thomas Hood. It is a most graphic representation of the aching anxiousness of the soul at the dreaded death of a sufferer; but never have I so felt them in my heart as, day by day, with an anxiousness beyond expression, I have sought the bulletins from the "White House."

> We watched her breathing through the night,
> Her breathing soft and low,
> As in her breast the wave of life
> Kept heaving to and fro.
>
> So silently we seemed to speak,
> So slowly moved about,
> As we had lent her half our powers
> To eke her living out.

> Our very hopes belied our fears,
>     Our fears our hopes belied—
> We thought her dying when she slept,
>     And sleeping when she died.[3]

It is a terrible event, my brethren! The fruit of the distempered brain and
the wild will of a reckless and bloody-minded man! But the Divine will runs
right beside it, with beneficent intent, and corrective and saving ends. Just
so it is in all the dark and dreadful occurrences of life. The Almighty maintains His omnipresent power amid dread disaster, as well as in benignant
event.

Neither man nor devil can shut God out of the currents of history. And
we see that He moves, that He *will* move, in all the shady, murky occurrences
of life, ever

> —from seeming evil
> Still educing good.[4]

It is this counteracting and governing will of Deity, seen everywhere, in
the dark as well as in the bright histories of men, which we call *Providence*.
We see it in this occurrence. There is a providence in this dreadful tragedy.
President Garfield is not allowed, you may be sure, to suffer in vain. There
are great moral uses discoverable in his sore trial. Albeit not intended by the
Evil One, our great sufferer is manifestly a sacrifice for national good. And
the flippant words of Caiaphas, which were, after all, an unconscious prophecy, set forth the great principle of expiation which runs through all the
relations of life; but which reaches its highest point in the sufferings of the
Crucified. Although it be one of its lower senses, we may see it exemplified
in our suffering Chief Magistrate.

1. See, first of all, the sudden check this event has given to the gross
secularization of the American mind. The race for wealth in this country, the
eager, outstretched ambitions for mere earthly good, outstrip the rivalries of
all other nations. They are so absorbing and so immense that they allow only
the most slender intrusion of things sacred and divine. They make men
earthly in all the purposes of life, and create that intense thirst for mere
temporal gratification which is the special temptation of the young, and
proves so widely the ruin of the old. The mind of the men of this land,
beyond the general mind of other civilized nations, alien, for the most part,
from art, unaddicted, save in the schools, to science and philosophy, runs
with an eager, almost insane, craving after mere earthly good.

And yet, in an instant, as it were, this whole nation's secularity was
brought to a stop. By one single flash of the telegraph, millions of men sickened of trade, and barter, and money-making. At a single whisper of national

calamity, handicraft and farming, labor and service, are given up. The busy wheel of the factory ceases its whirl, and the song of the anvil is hushed. Wall street turns with disgust from its trade in stock, and mechanism puts aside the hammer and the plane.

In *this one* aspect undoubtedly that is a good which serves to arrest the blind rush after mere material ends. No one can measure the benediction, almost sacred in its nature, which lifts up a people, above earth and sense, into the domain of sentiment and feeling. It is a glorious incident in the life of any nation, when of itself it pushes out of sight the gross and carnal, and advances spontaneously and in one mighty phalanx into the sphere of sensibility.

And next observe that with this sudden collapse of the temporal, uprises, as by a divine impulse, the grand outburst of a whole nation's intense and tearful sensibility. Not only women with their tender sympathies, and children with their warm and ardent feelings, but millions of men, with throbbing hearts, rushed, as it were, to this man's bedside, offering sympathy, devotedness, and gifts; nay, almost ready to tender their life-blood, to save the life of their loved and honored chief. See how this nation, for well nigh a week, has been given up to tears and indignation; alternate hope and fear; to prayer and supplications; and now, at the last, note the generous outpouring of riches, that the wife and children of this Chief Magistrate may not, in any event whatever, be left unprovided for and destitute!

My brethren, there is nothing fortuitous in these stirring occurrences. God's hand is manifestly visible, bright and beneficent, amid its darkest shades. Satan, indeed, and his dark-scarred instrument, "thought evil" in this bloody deed; but "God meant it unto good;"[5] even the sudden wresting of a nation from gross, material purposes, and the uplifting them to the highest, noblest aims of life. And this I call a blessing. It is, indeed, almost a salvation, this sudden rising tidal wave of affection and sympathy in this nation's heart. Whether its gross materialism could have been disturbed in any ordinary way, is doubtful. Whether its dull lethargy could have been galvanized even into temporary life, by common occurrence, is a question. It seems as though some terrible thrill was needed; as though nothing but the threatened life of a grand victim could sweep away the film from the eyes of this nation, and enable it, of a sudden, to *see*.

I feel, as much as any man, the horror of this murderous act. But when I observe this grand demonstration of a nation's moral nature; when I see the *spiritual* bursting forth from the caverns of a people's cold, calculating secularity; I behold a providence that cannot be mistaken, and learn, besides, that it is sometimes expedient "that one man should die, that a whole nation perish not"!

2. But neither the keenness of our feelings nor the depth of our sensibilit-

ies should cause us to pass by great lessons which spring immediately from this sad event. People talk of it as a casualty. Some look at it as a mystery. But remember "that affliction cometh not forth of the dust, neither doth trouble spring out of the ground."[6] There is nothing of chance or hap-hazard in this calamity. It requires no extraordinary insight to discover in it the principle of sequence. For, unless I make the greatest of mistakes, cause and effect are as plainly evident in this tragic occurrence as in any of the other incidents which go to make the history of the times.

Let me set before you some of the lessons which it seems to me that this nation is called upon, just now, to learn.

And (1) this attempted assassination brings vividly before us the intoxicating and demoralizing effects of our political system. It is a system calculated most directly to carry men beyond themselves, to taint the brains of thousands with incipient insanity, and to hurry them on to wild and irresponsible actions. We talk, in common parlance, of the wildness of money speculations and of the madness of unlawful lottery schemes. But these ventures are actual soberness compared with the intense and extravagant incitements which come out of our political agitations. We have, in our country, settled organisms and established modes in politics, which, in their operations, seem designed as certainly they do to produce widespread and convulsive upheavals. Why, the very caucusses of parties, and they are multitudinous, are flames. Our vast political assemblages, what are they but burning blasts? Our national conventions, but tempests? Our tumultuous and swarming canvasses, but paroxysms? Our grand elections, what but tremendous tornadoes? And then, when success has attended these almost frenzied partisan efforts, what can we call the uprising and the passionate pressure of the mighty army of anxious, greedy, determined office-seekers—what but blasting hurricanes?

There can be no doubt, as it strikes me, that this homicidal attack has sprung directly from this exciting system. This assassin's career goes to show that he possessed that temperament and that sort of brains, fitted, most precisely, to the counter-cries and the intemperate incitements of our recent political and partisan upheavals. His very letters, words, and utterances show that his mind for a long time had become stimulated to frenzy by agitations and strifes, of which you all know, but which may not be dwelt upon nor too plainly spoken of in this sacred place. The anxiousness for office was indeed an element in his conduct; and that is another feature of this deadly political inebriation. But the main characteristic of the assassin's motive and act, was partisan spleen and political dudgeon, chafed and inflamed to murderous purpose.

The clear-minded citizen of every name has seen somewhat, in the last ten days, the bane of this whole system. By blood, perchance—which God forbid—by death, a sudden revelation has been made of the organic but destructive system of fire, storm, and tempest which characterizes our national politics. This discovery, sad and humiliating as it may be, is somewhat compensatory for the prodigious evil which fathers it. And if this great lesson is thoroughly learned at this time, then, in the divine providence, it will be clearly seen how, at times, it is "expedient that one man should die, and that the whole nation perish not." For perish it will if reason, restraint, unselfishness, and sober duty are not made stronger and more conspicuous elements in our political strife.

2. Turn to another lesson suggested by this dark occurrence. We may see, just now, the ignoble fact that our people hold government and governmental rule as too cheap a thing in estimation. I have the impression that, outside of the thinking, cultured classes, the average American thinks that the governmental system of the land is simply his tool, the republic as only a thing for personal convenience. Allied to this notion is the other feeling, that neither nation, nor any officer thereof, must trench too much upon personal desire or individual purpose.

What is the common sentiment abroad in the land with regard to the Republic, as a nation? Do not men declare that it is a man-made thing? Do they not vociferate that civil government is merely human? That it is "of and by the people," with the narrow limitations of the assertion which they make? Nay, are there not large masses of people in the land who would resent as an insult and an outrage, the *denial* that any government, that is organic in its nature, was made "by the people"? And is it not owing to this that we look in vain on this soil for that filial, that reverential sentiment toward government which characterized even the higher pagan nations of antiquity?

It is this cheap idea of government, an idea as false as it is puerile, which has served to demoralize the American mind, and which has produced such wide unrestraint, not only in the civil, but in all the other relations of life. For if there is one special peculiarity of our national character, it is dislike of rule and authority. It comes out in civil affairs, in churches, in colleges, in common schools, and in families.

The notion of government most widely prevalent among us is that it is mostly a subjective thing. People feel that they must be left to govern themselves. External authority is a grievance and an irritation. And hence it arises that not only men and women, but children, in our day, and at a very early age, chafe under rule, reject authority, and spurn control.

One of the most alarming things in the life of the nation is the perversion that we discover in all the lines of life—the perversion of liberty into license. And when a people reach such a state that they lose sight of the magnitude of the very idea of government, and begin to eschew the principle of rule and authority, then they are rapidly verging toward anarchy, toward speedy and certain ruin.

One grand corrective to this error lies in the region of thought and principle. "People who have been entrapped by false opinions must be liberated by convincing truths." Hence, in these days, when the idea of obedience to constituted authority seems fading away, it is the duty of ministers of the Gospel to press upon the attention of the people the truth, that government is, *per se,* in itself, in idea, a grand and majestic thing. The fact must be set forth with prominence, that the nation is a creation and manifestation of God. For, my brethren, all civil power is from God Himself. When St. Paul, in one place, declares, "there is no power but of God,"[7] he asserts the magnitude of the very principle of government, and that in *all* relations. And when, in another, he commands, "Honor the king,"[8] he inculcates the duty of subjection to and reverence for constituted magisterial authority.

One of the deep undercurrents of American thought, in responsible circles, has been with regard to the drift of society to lawless freedom. Everywhere it has given thinking men the greatest concern and anxiety. It comes up, in this month of July, on the very eve of Independence Day, with a force and significance never felt before since 1776. It cannot be put down now until some true, solid basis is found, not only in opinion, but in practice and in law, for the security of that reverence and subjection to authority which is so much needed in civil, domestic, and, indeed, in all the other relations of life. And, in this respect, grieved and heart-sore as we all are at our President's sufferings, we may be brought to see "how expedient it is that one man should die for the people, and that the whole nation perish not."

3. Immediately connected with the point just considered is the common irreverence among us for rulers and persons in authority. Even (so-called) great men think that they show their superiority when they stand before multitudes and proclaim the dogma, that "civil officers are only the people's servants." And, certainly, if the notion of government just attacked, be true, then *this* notion concerning civil officers is certainly its legitimate inference. For, if government be the cheap thing men claim that it is, then its official representatives are cheap things too.

But, my friends, the notion is thoroughly false. The statement that officers are servants is only a half-truth; and half-truths are most generally whole lies. The President is indeed to serve the people. His office is, without doubt, an office of service; and this is no new discovery of this country, because it is a republic. Kings and emperors, in the oldest dynasties of the old world have, from time immemorial, acknowledged this obligation. One of the oldest royal houses of Europe has kept, as its perpetual family motto, the words, *"Ich dien,"* I serve.[9] Even pagan rulers have been awfully impressed with the idea that "they acted in trust." But the notion that, because authority is a trust, and then, because it *is* a trust, that rulers are only the people's servants, shows blindness to the grander factor in the constitution of authority, viz., that "the powers that be are ordained of God,"[10] and that "they are the ministers of God attending continually upon this very thing,"[11] i. e., the exercise of civil authority.

Yes, there are two factors in all civil government, and in the exercise of all civil authority; and it is one of the gravest of all mistakes that it was not laid down thus, in the infancy of the nation, in the great charter of our freedom, the "Declaration of Independence." When Thomas Jefferson declared that "governments derive their just powers from the consent of the governed,"[12] and left his dogma crudely, at that point, he shut out a limitation which the pride and self-assertion of degenerate humanity is always too reluctant to yield, and too tardy to supply.

The theory of the Declaration is incomplete and misleading. Governments, my brethren, derive their just authority, *first* of all, from the will of God; and then *next,* from the consent of the governed. It is because of the exclusion of this prime factor in this axiom that the governments of the earth are all more or less sick and diseased. It is owing very considerably to national blindness to this truth that *we* have had so many sore evils in this land, and now, at last, a great, national disaster. The people of this country, in vast self-importance, have been accustomed to look down upon the chief magistracy of the land as a convenient instrumentality for personal ends. The office has been too much regarded as the facile agent of grand politicians, for party objects and partisan ambitions. But in this matter they have not been the only sinners. It has been the wont of the people, as well, to regard both the office and its functions as "good for use." This, in too many cases, has been one-half the meaning of the term "availability," applied to presidential candidates. The grand authority of a ruler, the reverence due to the Chief Magistrate, have been too generally forgotten. People in other lands do not look thus upon their kings and emperors and great chieftains. "Ah!" is the rebuke I hear coming up from the pews; "This is a Republic. Ours is a democratic country." "Well, what of that?" is my reply. Your President is as much a ruler, he is as truly a potentate as the Emperor of Russia or the Queen of Great Britain. He is your ruler and grand magistrate, and mine. And he sits in his chair of authority by the will of God, declared in governmental arrangements, as distinctly and positively as though he had been born to the office.

Alas! instead of thus regarding the dignities of the presidency as representing the *divine* sovereignty in human government; instead of honoring the President as incarnating the dread sovereignty of the nation; the habit has prevailed of regarding him as the biggest servant in the land. And intense canvasses have been carried on, the main stimulant to which has been the disposal, as through an elected instrument or machine, of thousands of offices. And then when an election has been carried, we have seen how cheap a thing people regarded their chief ruler, in the fact that the meanest men, greedy of office, could demand an audience at the "White House," and get it, too, with a facility which would be scouted by a manufacturer at Lowell, or a merchant in Boston. Nay, and worse than this—the cases have been numerous of men, when their applications have been rejected, who have turned, with "proud and haughty wrath," from the Chief Magistrate, taken his refusal as a personal insult, and assailed him with revenge and unforgiving malice.

Almighty God, in all the histories, has spoken "in divers manners"[13] to various peoples. He has spoken by angels, by oracles and prophets, by dreams and revelations, and so made known His will to nations and to men. And He still speaks to them. He speaks to them at times by providences. Just now he has spoken to *this* nation, through the pistol-shot of an assassin. The miserable wretch, we know, is an execration to the Almighty, but He overrules his bloody deed to immediate good. In the flash of a murderer's pistol the whole nation sees suddenly and in glaring light the sin of its cheap estimate of the presidential office. And I venture to predict that, from this time, the office of Chief Magistrate will be withdrawn from the pressure of office-seekers; the White House will get the dignity, the reserve, the sanctity of national sovereignty; and the person of the chief ruler will henceforth be accessible only to persons of character, reputation, and personal responsibility.

And thus again, my friends, while our anguished hearts go out with tenderest sensibility and solicitude to our still endangered President, we learn "how expedient it is that one man should die for the people, and that the whole nation perish not!"

What I have spoken this day is nothing new. I make no pretence whatever to originality in the views I have expressed. The main truths I have brought before you have been not infrequently suggested by eminent persons; and I have been, and for a long time, so thoroughly convinced of their truth that they rush with unusual force upon my mind, at this juncture, and demand utterance. That great political prophet, Alexander Hamilton, predicted not a few of the evils I have pointed out, although he did not live to see them.[14] In more recent times they have been seen and pointed out by a small body of men, called "Civil Service Reformers."[15] And no body of men in the land has been more laughed at and ridiculed than they. Their publications have been numerous, and, I may add, in many cases, as fruitless as numerous. But the lightning, the lightning of disaster, has done more for them than all their books and speeches and essays. It has shivered our civil service system, as now ordered, to pieces; and scattered the multitudinous swarms of office-seekers from the portals of the presidential mansion.

2. I have brought this subject before *this* congregation in particular, because, although we colored men are not yet allowed either a large participation in politics, or governmental rule, or offical patronage, I am, nevertheless, anxious that *my* people should be ranked among the conservative men in this land, and stand among the firmest upholders of law and authority. The sudden rise to freedom, the newness of our participation in political prerogatives, above all the oscillation from extreme servitude to the right of suffrage—all naturally tend to land us in the extreme of wild and thoughtless democratic opinion, and expose us to the danger of mistaking license for liberty. Thank God, these dangers have been but little realized as yet. And may they never show themselves amid the black population of this country! As in the past, so in the future may it ever be, that the blood of this race may furnish no nursing-plot for treasons, seditions, and assassinations!

A people numbering more than six millions, with a rapidly-increasing birth-rate, growing on every side in knowledge and material power, must, from the very nature of things, become, ere long, a most formidable phalanx in the multitudinous population of the country. I pray Almighty God that *this* race may ever be found strong and determined for good, stable government, their influence weighty in the state for authority and order, the constant foes of revolutions, communism, and revolt;

> Zealous, yet modest, innocent, though free,
> Serene amidst alarms, inflexible in faith.[16]

3. My words, this morning, have had respect, almost entirely, to the vicarious position of our Chief Magistrate. I have dwelt all along upon the fact that this chief ruler has been called to suffering, perhaps to death, so that the nation may not die! I have preferred this line of thought, albeit the tender, sympathizing aspects of the case were far more inviting to every Christian heart. I know full well that

> —Tears to human suffering are due.[17]

And our deepest sympathies have thrilled at this awful tragedy, our hearts been faint and sickened many an hour, many a moment since its occurrence; and our prayer and cries constantly ascend to heaven for the recovery of the great sufferer. The other aspect of the case, however, seems to me no less tender and interesting. Certainly, if any man in this nation must needs be a victim, for mysterious, but definite national good, no nobler offering can be laid upon the altar of a nation's sacrifice than this man. If great good is to spring from this dreadful visitation, no more exalted victim could have been chosen than he. His personal virtues have been long conspicuous. His clear, unconcealed, yet unostentatious piety is everywhere known and acknowledged. The fine, unequalled qualities—a rare thing in our national history—which he has brought to the seat of national authority have excited both unusual surprise and unusual admiration. Statesmanlike in national politics, strong in intellectual capacity, pure in life and reputation, his character and abilities would give moral fitness to his sacrifice, if it should please God that he should succumb to the assassin's bullet!

# 4.

## *The Dignity of Labour; and Its Value to a New People*

During the 1880s Crummell became increasingly concerned about the "condition of labor" and, in particular, the disposition to regard manual work as degrading. What was needed, he argued in this address, was for blacks to learn the value of labor as a creative power and to seize hold of servant life, wherever necessary, as a first step in their temporal prosperity. The gradualism implicit in these statements is noteworthy, and so, too, is Crummell's analysis of the impact of slavery on the development of a black work ethic. "The Dignity of Labor" was delivered to the Working Men's Club of Philadelphia in 1881.

THERE are two ways of knowing things in this world. The *one* is to know them in a crude, blind, uninformed and mechanical manner, *i. e.,* by the senses merely, and the bodily powers; somewhat as an animal knows a thing. This kind of knowing is altogether outward, and pertains mainly to our physical nature. But the *other* mode of knowing is the apprehension of principles and essences; the seeing into the very life of things; and the seizing upon the highest uses and advantages which they may offer.

Now, in just these two ways we can understand the fact and the principles of labour. The beasts of burden that toil in the fields and carry heavy loads, *they* understand what labour is. Void of reason though they be, they have nevertheless understanding. When trained, they know their places before carts and vehicles; know the times of service; know the routines of work;

know how to fit themselves to severest tasks; come to know painstaking and endurance in their tasks and toil. But they don't know the full value of their labour; they don't know the skill whereby they might participate in the rich gains which their sweat and toil yield to their owners.

But the skill and cunning of men have enabled them to fall upon devices, whereby they have been able to reduce vast numbers of their fellow men to well nigh the same state and condition of the beasts of the field, and to lead them, almost blindly, to the same dull, laborious and animal-like endurance of mere bodily toil. Multitudes of men, in every land, know labour, in precisely the way domestic animals do. They know the mere physical toil, and all the accessories to it; know the severest tasks; know the iron routines of service; know the soulless submission and the slavish drudgery; but alas they have never come to know the dignity of labour; never been permitted to share its golden values, and its lofty requitals. And in this we may see the difference between enlightened labour, on the one hand; and unskilled and unenlightened labour on the other. Skilled labour knows its own value and contends for it. It knows *two* things: it knows (*a*) what labour *is,* in its excellence and glory; *not* as mere service and dredging, but as a creative power amid the divers materials of earth, clay, minerals, wood and stone; and (*b*) it knows too the values of all labour; *i. e.,* the noble worth and real merit which belong to the plastic and formative use of the trained hand and the cunning intellect of man. Unskilled and ignorant labour is wanting in both these respects. For 1st, it does not know in its best sense what labour is. For, divorced from the nobler results of toil, it can not see; it is *unconscious* of the dignity of labour; and digs and delves mechanically from necessity, or, compulsion, or from mere animal impulse. Untrained and unenlightened, the hand is awkward, and the eye is blind.

There is no mingling of the active brain with strained exertion. No reaching over of the mind to the grand results which flow, in golden streams, from the sweated pours of labour.

And 2d, the deficiency of untaught labour shows itself in its unconsciousness of values. The rude untutored labourer does not know himself; does not know his powers; does not know the value of his powers; does not know the worth of his pains and toil and sufferings in labour; does not know the weight of every sweat-drop that bursts from his pores, and rolls, like beads, from his moistened brow. The wild Indian in the West hunts, day by day, for a few skins of animals. He sells them to a Trader for a simple gewgaw, or a jug of rum; but the Trader brings them East, and sells them for a sum which would have been a fortune to the whole tribe of simple Indians.

What makes the difference? The red man ran, day after day, amid exposure, without food, without shelter; with constant strain and effort of limb;

but did not know the value of his labour, and parted with the fruit of his toil—for nothing! The Trader turns it into solid gold, and in a few years is a wealthy Capitalist. Ignorant labour is service and drudgery, and yields but bare subsistence. It takes but the slightest cognizance of the higher faculties of men, and pertains almost entirely to the animal of our nature. But skilled and enlightened labour, starts from the centre. Its spring is the intellect. It runs continually in the orbit of human thought and skill. And it yields all the productive realities which serve body, mind and spirit; and which tend to the development of a high humanity.

Now, if I do not make a very great mistake, the former is the characteristic of the black labour in this country for two and one half centuries. It has been labour with the following most evident peculiarities:—It has been rude, untutored, unenlightened. It has been to a large extent, unmingled with brains and intelligence. It has been plodding, mechanical, and very largely merely animal. It has been unskilled. It has been labour alienated, from dignity and manhood. It has been labour divorced from the grand ends, and the large and golden values, which are the legitimate product of human toil! Just here the question arises,—"are these characteristics to be perpetuated in our line and blood,—in all our future?" Is the labour of the black man in the time to come, to be a menial, boorish serfdom, spent only for food, and a dilapidated hut; unassociated with intelligence; without the adornment of competency, of superiority, and of art. Or, on the other hand, is it to be a joyous, remunerative and a fruitful system of toil, allied to everything manly and elevating, and yielding the grand products of comfort, improvement, intelligence, and domestic refinement. Doubtless there are sanguine minds here who, carried away by the seeming show of things, are ready on the instant to cry out to me—"Yes, the future of our labour is to be glorious! The past is dead and can never be revived! Slavery is doomed, and all its fruits are withered, and blasted forever!"

But my friends I can't speak so confidently as some of you upon this question. I am indeed hopeful; but I have my apprehensions. When I look at the present condition of the black race in this country, I see serious and formidable obstacles which array themselves in their way, preventing, so largely, the securing of land, and the acquisition of wealth; I am sorely troubled with misgivings, least the opposing forces may so far prevail as to keep their labour, for a long period to come, inferior, servile and unremunerative.

Two special dangers threaten the race with respect to labour. *One* of these is the danger of a labour system, semi-servile in its nature, and feudalistic in its working; binding the labourer to service, but allowing him the slenderest interest in the soil, and when possible, shutting him off from the ownership of land.

The actual state of things, all through the south, justifies my fears. There is evidently a very wide conviction in the southern mind that the special function of the black man is to be a humble tiller of the soil; the mere functionary of the old landed proprietor. In making this statement I intend nothing offensive. I am speaking of the legitimate tendencies of human nature. Emancipation, you will remember was a terrible dislocation, it broke up everything suddenly and disastrously. It was like the upheaval of the great deep, by an earthquake. It tore up the foundations of systems which had had the rooting of two centuries and more. It left chaos on every side. The whites of the south felt it, and still feel it. All dislocations are injurious, and leave wounds and sorrows behind. They injure material interests, and they grievously confuse the brain. Herein lies the peril for the future. The old landed proprietor, bewildered as by an earthquake, mindful only of the past, unable to settle in the grooves of the future, holds on to the soil; holds on to his old notions as to the fit tillers of the soil; holds on to his old convictions of the natural place and destiny of the black race, as *the* tillers of the soil.

Hence arises the disposition, as by an instinct, to hold on to the soil, and to keep the black race from possessing it. "The Negro has no right to be a proprietor. He was born for service and for toil. If he does not know his place as a hewer of wood and a drawer of water, he must be taught it."

Now these convictions are the most natural conceivable. They are not the exclusive characteristic of southern gentlemen. Men of power and property act so everywhere. You will find the same sentiment among land owners in England; among planters in the West Indies; among manufacturers in New England; among proprietors in the East Indies; will you believe it? Yea, among black emigrants in Liberia surrounded by crude and ignorant pagans. Everywhere on earth men like to hold on to power; like to use their inferiors as tools and instruments; plume and pride themselves as superior beings; look with contempt upon the labouring classes, and strive by every possible means to use them to their own advantage.

Indeed, it is generally the selfish instinct of Capital to regard the labouring man as fit for use; regardless of his comfort, his rights, and his well being, as a man, a citizen and an immortal being.

> "For why? Because the good old rule
> Sufficeth them, the simple plan,
> That they should take who have the power
> And they should keep who can."[1]

But not only have these opinions and this past system been injurious to the whites, but they have seriously affected *us,* as a people. They have injured us in two diverse and opposite ways. For, first they have served to settle in the minds of large numbers of our race the idea that servitude *is* the normal condition of the black man. Two centuries of service in this land has thoroughly driven this idea into the souls of thousands of our people; so that you can find numbers of black men and black women who really think that they themselves are inferior because they are black; that the race was born for inferiority; and that they reach the highest state of honour when they become servants of white men. These convictions have injured our race nearly as much in an *opposite* direction. They have bred the notion in another larger class, that labour is degrading; that superior people ought not to work; that as soon as one gets up a little in the world, soiled or horny hands, are vulgar and debasing; that those who can get a little learning, should give up hardy toil and aim after something higher!

Let me lay down here a few principles which may help us, as a people, to settle upon a solid basis this most important subject for the future. And, in this attempt, I wish to speak intelligently and with an eye to practicality.

First of all then, let me urge the primary importance of recognizing the duty and dignity of labour. Very many things have served to disturb such recognition. All the usages of society, all the habitudes of life, all the instructions of superiors, have tended to fasten upon us the idea of the degradation of labour. We have been brought up under a most artificial system, wherein on the one hand, all the glory and the beauty of life have been associated with ease, luxury and mastery; and where all the toil, the drudgery, the ignorance and the suffering, have been allied to the Negro and to servitude. What sort of a school was this, in which to learn the dignity of labour? Nay, rather was it not the very condition in which to convince the whole race that labour was the grandest curse of humanity? We cannot unlearn this conviction too speedily. For the very first step in a people's temporal prosperity is the material one of self-dependence, of personal support, through toil. Not until a people are able, by their own activities and skill, to raise themselves above want, and to meet the daily needs of home and family, can they take the next great step to the higher cultivation which comes by letters, refinement and religion; and which lifts them up to civility and power. The kernel of this higher cultivation is labour. Go back in the history of mankind, trace the progress of human culture from its earliest buddings, to its fullest blossomings and fruitage; in either Egyptian, or Eastern, or Grecian, or Roman civilization; and the same identical facts, and allied to them, the same identical principles show themselves in all human history.

1st, for the facts: The *facts* are these, namely, that regular, systematic and plodding toil, in all the diversified fields of human action, anticipated and lay at the base of all national greatness, in all the great empires. Everywhere we come to the sight of labour, in the fields, in the rivers, in the aqueducts, on the roads, in the navies, in the architecture, in the domiciles, in the temples, of these great peoples.

And 2d, the principle which is interfused in all these human endeavours is this,—viz., that toil and material greatness, sustain the abiding relation of cause and effect. Underlying all this grandeur and this glory of nations lies the solid fact, of all the multitudinous activities of men, in all the divers trades and occupations of life. It was a magnificent result, to which every hardy worker was a contributor. All the splendour of Athens or of Rome; in temples or senate houses, or bridges, or columns, or aqueducts, or baths; in vast empire, or extended commerce; was a gift bestowed by the brawny arms, and the vigorous frames of hardy, humble labourers.

None of these things come without labour. It is the grand creator of all things superior in the world. Without its presence, barrenness, rudeness, sterility prevail. But when labour comes upon the scene, then the wilderness with its gigantic trees and its forests of stubble, vanish from sight; then the rocks fall to dust, and the hills are unseated from their beds; then the valleys are filled up, and wasteful rivers are turned from their courses; then the useless herbage of the soil is swept away, and fields of corn and wheat wave their golden tassels, and invite the scythe and sickle of the reaper; then the wild confused face of nature departs; and is changed by rule and genius, into regulated surfaces, and the seats of orderly towns and villages; then the fitful, wasteful labour of barbarism is changed into the systematic toil of the mechanic and the artizan; then the rude and barbarous life of the savage becomes subverted; and the stimulated desires and the cultivated wants of society, bring in civilization; then the rude bark and the dangerous canoe are rejected; and noble vessels strike out into the ocean for trade and commerce; then grand cities spring up into existence, and art and science and generous culture, and noble universities elevate society, and bring nobleness to the breed of men.

All these my friends are the direct and legitimate results of labour. The very first step from savage life to grand civility, is the throwing off the disorganized, irregular toil of the uncivilized man; and turning sharply, into the ways of systematic, orderly, regulated labour.

You thus see friends that the very first thing is labour. It is not, observe, a sleight-of-hand, or cunning artifice; or skillful ingenuity whereby gain, or advantage, or sustenance can come to you or me. It is labour whereby we are to get daily bread, and all the other accessories of sustenance and living. And this labour is a personal demand and requirement, as a means reaching over to an end. Don't listen for a moment to the too popular but lying adage—"The world owes every man a living." Wherever a debt is contracted there is always an antecedent equivalent which goes before the indebtedness.

If—*if* I say, if the world owes you a living, labour goes before and anticipates the indebtedness. Labour, I say then, again—Labour is the first thing.

Turn now to another limitation. It is labour I am speaking of, not *drudgery.* Man has got tired of drudgery. He is not tired of labour. Everywhere he is willing to work; but he is dissatisfied with 'mere animal toil, and the bare subsistence which the lowly workers of life, all over the globe, have for cen- turies, been getting. The demand for freedom in Russia; the grand emanci- pations in the West Indies and America; the turbulence of the working classes in every European state and kingdom; the labour upheavals in our own country, all serve to show that the days of human drudgery are coming to an end. The labour world is craving for more rest; more time to read and think; more time for comfort and enjoyment; more time for home and fam- ily, and the reading room and the church. Its battle now in our day is against DRUDGERY; not always a wise battle; but, nevertheless, a battle, and a pro- test against mere bodily toil divorced from the best desires and the nobler aspirations of the living soul. It is not a demand for indolence. Man is, by his constitution, a toiler. Every limb, every faculty, within and without calls for labour. All the necessities, requirements, appetencies, aspirations, desires, instincts, of both body and soul, not only fit him for, but *make* him a labourer.

So here, I repeat myself, viz.—that the very first thing is labour. This is the root, this is the foundation of all natural superiority in the world. It is the fountain of all excellency, power and mastery. It is the kernel of all human greatness. Nothing of might and majesty ever spring up in this world, which did not owe its origin and completion to labour.

Labour then is the most honorable, the most glorious thing in human society, and he who knows it not; he who refuses participation in it, is a nobody; I care not if he owns millions. Every man in the world is bound to be productive, in some definite way, by *labour;* or else he is a dead man or a dog!

We see too, from this, what a vulgar, what an insensible, what a brainless thing it is, in anybody, to despise work; and to look down upon labourers. Let me repeat just here the strong and pointed language of Carlyle:—"Two men I honour, and no third. First the toil-worn craftsman that, with earth- made implements, laboriously conquers the earth and makes her man's! Ven- erable to me is the hard hand, crooked, coarse; wherein notwithstanding, has cunning virtue indefeasibly royal, as of the sceptre of this planet. Vener- able too is the rigid face, all weather-tanned, besoiled with its rude intelli- gence; for it is the face of a man living manlike. Oh but the more venerable for thy rudeness and even because we must pity, as well as love thee! Hardly entreated brother! For *us* was thy back bent, for *us* were thy straight limbs and fingers so deformed; thou wert our conscript, on whom the lot fell; and fighting our battles wert so marred! For in thee too lay a God-created form, but it was not to be unfolded; encrusted must it stand with the thick adhesions and defacements of labour; and thy body, like thy soul, was not to know freedom. Yet toil on, toil on; thou art in thy duty, be it out of it, who may; thou toilest for the altogether indispensable, for daily bread.

A *second* man I honour, and still more highly: Him who is seen toiling for the spiritually indispensable; *not* daily bread, but the Bread of life. Is he not too in his duty; endeavouring towards harmony, revealing this by act or by word, through all his outward endeavours, be they high or low? Highest of all, when his outward and his inward endeavours are *one,* when we can name him Artist,—not earthly craftsman only, but inspired thinker; that with heaven-made implement conquers heaven for us! If the poor and humble toil for him in return, that he have light, have guidance, freedom, immortality. These two, in all their degree, I honour; all else is chaff and dust, which let the wind blow whither it listeth.

Unspeakably touching is it however, when I find both dignities united; and he that must toil outwardly for the lowest of man's wants, is also toiling inwardly, for the highest. Sublimer in this world, I know nothing than a peasant Saint, could such anywhere be met with. Such a one will take you back to Nazareth itself! Thou wilt see the splendour of heaven spring forth from the humblest depths of earth, like a light shining in great darkness!"[2]

You see in these words of Carlyle how he extols, first of all, the toiler in the fields, the bread-winner by agricultural labour; and rightly so. For farming, *i. e.,* the tilling of earth was the first of all human work. And well it would be for us, as a people, if *we* cherished large solicitudes for the labours of the fields. It is at once one of the simplest, purest, health-giving, independent, and lucrative of all employments. In every land, the farming people, the yeomanry of a nation, produce the staunchest, bravest, most hardy and virtuous part of the population. No nobler sons, no chaster more excellent women can be found in our land, than those who come from the rural districts.

Just this has been, for 200 years, the main employment of our race in this land; and it is a cause of deep regret to me that, since emancipation, hundreds and thousands of our people, partly through abuse and fraud, and partly from an injudicious choice, have deserted the labour of the land, to seek the temporary and uncertain employments of cities. How desirable it is that our brethren should seek once more the independence of country life and country toil! Would that scores and hundreds crowding the lanes and alleys and tenement houses of the cities, would return to the tillage of the soil! I say to young men—"Seek country homes. Get small farmsteads. Cultivate small fruits. Raise chickens. Strive to possess land!" Observe the wisdom of the new immigrant. He sees, on his arrival, the glare and glitter of New York. But he does not think that the metropolis is heaven, and that he can live nowhere else! No, he pushes his way into the country; clears the forest, and becomes a farmer; and in a few years amasses a comfortable future. And so I say to ambitious colored young men—Get out of the cities; leave the hotels; go to mother earth for sustenance, independence and wealth.

But I know that all men can't be farmers; and all men don't *want* to be farmers. Choose then *other* employments. Diversify your labours. When you *can,* engage in trade and barter and merchandise. It is difficult I know thus to break through the barriers of caste, to the height of such occupations; but try; and try; and try again; until you carve your way, to the higher avenues to wealth and superiority. Seek trades for your children. The difficulties in your way are formidable. Don't be satisfied with the exclusion of your sons and daughters from the workshops of mechanics. Strive; push; argue; protest; remonstrate; demand; until importunity, shame and justice give you triumph; and multitudes of your sons ply the plane, the hammer, the saw and all the other implements of mechanism in every quarter of the land. Until then use all the occupations of service, which houses, hotels and restaurants offer, without hesitation, and with alacrity.

1. Since labour of any kind and all kinds, is in itself, such a prime and valuable thing, I beg to caution my brethren against that vulgar sentiment one meets in colored society, I mean the contempt of servant life. I call it a vulgar sentiment; for first, *all* labour is honourable; and next, the service of others is one of the grandest vocations to which *any* man can be called. All the great heroes, all the noble martyrs, in human history, served their generation, and died. The grandest illustration of this noble duty is the Lord Jesus Christ. He came to serve. He did serve! He suffered in serving; and in the service of man he died!

And the calling and the duties of servants will be perpetual. *Some* people, and at all times, will have to be servants; and I know no reason why *coloured* people should not be, as well as any other. In the United States I am aware there is a disposition to avoid servant life. Free-born white Americans think it beneath them to serve in the houses of the rich. And the same feeling is gradually spreading among our people.

But believe me it is an ignorant and contemptible feeling. For observe, we *all,* whether rich or poor, have to serve. First of all, our parents, are our servants, before we are born; immediately *at* our birth; many weary weeks and months and years, *after* we enter upon life. Then elder brothers and sisters are our servants. Then schoolmasters. Then hired persons. Then Policemen. Then Ministers, and Judges, and Governors, and Magistrates! See, how, all through life, men are the servants of others.

Hence, I say the vocation of a servant is one which is established by the

Almighty; which pervades life; and is therefore a divine institution. But notice again, that the vocation of domestic servant has its generous and gracious advantages. It has its disadvantages I know; for it serves to soften; it produces luxurious tastes; it begets a liking for things rich and expensive; it indisposes for hard and severe toil; it is adapted to make people fastidious. But my sober conviction is that if people have well regulated minds, the advantages of servant life exceed the disadvantages. For first, it trains people to regular, systematic and orderly modes of living. In this consists the superiority of the rich that they must have order and system. This gives a training to those who serve them; and which they are likely to carry into their own homes, when *they* commence life.

2. Service cultivates neatness. This is another demand of the rich; and it aids domestics in renouncing untidiness and slovenliness.

3. It teaches people economy; for the wealthy and affluent are a deal more economical than the poor; and this is a great lesson to learn.

4. It teaches people obedience and humility. There can be no true servant-life without these two grand qualities; for they *are* grand qualities. No man, no matter who he be, can do the work of life well, unless he learns to obey and be humble. I say, *no man;* and I mean the Chief Magistrate of the nation, as well as the humblest servant boy here to-night. Humility and obedience are Christian graces; and it is our duty to learn them. But observe, I am not inculcating servility. A man who is a servant is bound to remember that he is a man, just as much as his master; and he ought not to allow that master to trench upon his manhood. But, within that limit, servant life is a grand educator of obedience and humility.

5. It gives us the opportunity of securing the purest English, and learning the very best manners. More than one foreign tourist in this country has remarked that the colored people of America were among the most polite people he met with. Many have spoken of the correct English we speak. Contact with affluent classes give us these advantages both of manners and speech.

6. The advantages of money making are worthy of consideration here; for if wages *are* moderate, the expenses of servants are light; and if they are prudent they can, in a few years, with the presents good servants are sure to get,—purchase a small homestead for themselves; and—

7. And lastly servants have the grand privilege of doing good, and of blessing the life of others. I am not speaking of hirelings; I am speaking of servants who do their duty, with diligence, from principle, and with affection. What a noble privilege is it not, with such feelings, to serve both the old and the young—aged people, little children, babes and the sick. And hence I say— *if* you have the gifts of service, the willing mind, the gentle hand, the soft

voice, the tender heart, follow the calling of a servant; and show yourselves friends to your employers, in your honorable calling! The humble spheres of labour then must still be recognized. The humbler spheres of labour still abide; and we, as a people, are to participate in them, just the same as all other people, in the several nationalities.

But while indeed recognizing the full legitimacy of service, I must here present the due meets and bounds of this recognition. I am willing that *some* colored people who *desire it,* should be servants; but I protest against making this the condition of the whole people; for it is not every man who wants to be a servant. I maintain that we must have the same division of labor among *us* that the English, the French, and the German and the Irish have. If the colored people of this country only are to be servants, then you make the colored people a CASTE in this country; and consign, not only them in one generation, to servile employment, but their children, and their children's children, perpetually. In India, Brahmins and Soodras and Casters, are fixed and separated, in definite spheres; and tied down to distinctive employments *forever.* What the father was, so the son must be, and the grandson after him. The blood of a family can never be turned to duties different from their ancestors. The particular caste must run in one simple groove forever! Now I say that no class of men have the right to cramp the intellect of any set of men by such arbitrary distinctions. If men, in the humbler spheres of life, are gifted with a genius superior to their parents, no artifical arrangements of society should be allowed to consign them to lowly occupations. All men have the natural right to rise to any position to which talent and energy may fit them. The coloured people of this country must assert this natural right. If they have fitness for the loftier spheres of activity; then perish every barrier which would

"Cloud young genius brightening into day."

What right has society, in this country, to say that no black man shall be an engineer, an architect, a manufacturer, an artist, or a Senator? If God has given him the capacity for any such craft or position; whence comes the authority to keep him in a servant's place and condition, merely on account of race? I say therefore that while indeed willing to serve in humble duties, we must resist the attempt to make us a caste of servants in the land. And the only way to effect this is by careful and systematic endeavors to secure a proper division of labour among us. By concert, by general understanding, by wise forecast, by systematic action we must strive to introduce among the rising generation, every sort of trade and business which other men engage in.

Can you tell me a single craft or calling in which white men are occupied, to which black men are utterly unfitted? Is there anything *they* do, which we can't do?

I have been referring this evening more especially to physical toil. I have said nothing concerning professional life, and the intellectual labours allied thereto; and simply for the reason that I fear there is too often extravagance among young men, in this regard. Work, I fear, is getting to be ungenteel in some classes among us; and so it comes to pass that many a good Barber, Caterer or Mechanic, is turned into a booby Doctor, or, a briefless Lawyer.

How much better if they had spent the time lost on law books in endeavoring to build up a business, or in farming; in successful catering, or the occupation of a trade. Clever physicians we have. Keen and successful lawyers honour our race at the Bar. May their numbers be multiplied. We need a large school of such clever and efficient men. But you and I know instances not a few, where young men would have done a deal better by abiding in the callings of their parents; working with their hands; and throwing as much talent and respectability as possible in the old family craft, humble though it be.

If I could catch the ears of scores of such young men, whose vain ambition tires me, I would say—"Young men don't despise the humble positions of your parents. *All* the crafts of men are honourable. Dignify the toil of your family by your fine personal qualities. Raise their occupations, by genius and talent, to honour and competency. All work is honourable. Only throw brains, skill, energy and economy into your work; and it will lead you on to success, to comfort, and perchance to wealth. Don't be too anxious for soft places. 'Endure hardness as a true man.'"[3]

May I join to this another suggestion: that is, that no man, no class of men, leap into superiority. Society never, anywhere, leaps into progress, greatness or power. The black race in this land cannot leap into might and majesty. It is to reach the higher planes in just the same way all other peoples have, in all the past of human history. The same conditions apply to us as to them. And these conditions are, first, humble labour; then, a gradual uprise; and then dogged and persistent effort, unfailing hope, living and undying aspiration, and pluck and audacious ambition, which brooks no limitations in the spheres of enterprise! In this process take the first step of the ladder! Never mind how lowly the duty may be. God has ordained that duty in the arrangements of society! Take it! Off with your coat. Bare your arms. Make a manly grasp of duty; do that duty, well and thoroughly, as a man; so that men of earth, and angels above you may see that it is work finished and complete!

And then, when that work is thoroughly done and the way is opened;— and *you* must keep your eyes open to see the time and opportunity,—step out of that work, upon the next round of the ladder; content there to abide:—but watchful for a higher vocation and a nobler field:—always alert to open your way, by manly resolution to a loftier vocation. And so go on, from one round of the ladder to another, and another;—if God so wills and helps. And there is no danger about your progress and success; if you are patient, industrious, vigilant and aspiring.

"My Father worketh hitherto and I work."[4]

This is one of the most marvelous sayings which fell from the lips of the "Son of man!" I have studied it, year by year, through long periods of my life; but never yet been able to get the plummet line whereby to fathom and to sound its mighty depths of meaning. But a few things lie upon its surface.

The first of these is that while the primary significance of these words pertains to God's vast spiritual economy, it includes, likewise, the broad physical and material universe and the prodigious fabrics which He has produced therein. And second, it implies that work is one of the inherent necessities of all intelligent beings. To work is a law of existence with God, with Angels, and with men: and then, third, as we see that all the productions of the Divine hand, through all the realms of nature.

"Up from the creeping plant to sovereign man,"[5]

—all show, in all things evidence of law, system, organization, so we may learn that the work of man is the noblest and most majestic which is characterized by intelligence, and which manifests skill. In the work then of life let us eschew the ephemeral; let us rise up as a people to the apprehension of the organic laws which pertain to all human endeavour; and so grasp the permanent and abiding forces of nature and society:—and through them press on to power, to majesty, to wealth, and to social and political prerogatives which, ere long, will be the common inheritance of both our manhood and our intelligence!

# 5.

## A Defence of the Negro Race in America from the Assaults and Charges of Rev. J. L. Tucker, D.D., of Jackson, Mississippi

Following the end of Reconstruction, Episcopal leaders in the South began to call for greater autonomy in dealing with the former slave population. In 1882 this debate took a new turn when Joseph L. Tucker, an Episcopal minister from Jackson, Mississippi, told delegates to the Congress of Episcopal Churches in Richmond, Virginia, that since emancipation there had been a "great deterioration" in the moral, spiritual, and material condition of the freedmen. Tucker's retrogressionist beliefs, and the underlying assumption that black Episcopalians were unfit to control their own churches, were the immediate context of this address, published in 1882, which is remarkable not only for its bitter irony but its scholarly and "scientific" method.

THIS is peculiarly the age of criticism, and neither the sensitiveness nor the weakness of peoples can exempt them from its penetrating search or its pointed strictures. Criticism, however, in order to perform its functions aright, must submit to certain laws of responsibility, and be held by certain rules of restraint. It must deal with facts, and not with fancies and conjectures. It must not indulge what Butler calls the "forward and delusive faculty" of the imagination, "ever intruding beyond its sphere."[1] It must avoid coloring its facts with the hues of its own self-consciousness or feelings. It must be rigidly just in its inferential processes. Nothing can be more ludicrous than to make a wide generalization from the narrow circle of a provincialism, and nothing more unjust.

It is because Dr. Tucker's paper "ON THE RELATIONS OF THE CHURCH TO THE COLORED RACE"[2] is defective in these several points that I have undertaken, at the suggestion of reverend brethren of my own race and Church, a refutation of it. We are all fully aware of the weaknesses, and, to a large extent, of the degradation of our race in this country; for the race has been a VICTIM race. Our children have been victimized, our men have been victimized, and alas! worse than all, our women have been victimized—generation after generation, two hundred years and more, down to the present! We make no pretense that our people, by miraculous impulse, have of a sudden risen entirely above the malarial poison of servitude. We know better than this, and we mourn their shortcomings. But we know, also, that a marvelous change has taken place in all the sections of their life—social, civil, educational, ecclesiastical—since the day of freedom; and we regard it a most grievous misdemeanor in Dr. Tucker that he has blindly ignored that change.

I have read Dr. Tucker's pamphlet with very much care and attention, and I cannot resist the conclusion that it is one of the most unjust and injurious statements that I have ever met with. First of all, on the hypothesis that his representation of the moral condition of the Negro is correct—but which I deny—his pamphlet, instead of being a lamentation over wrong and injustice, is an INDICTMENT, alike gross and undeserving, of a deeply-wronged people. Unless I greatly misunderstand Dr. Tucker, and his endorsers also, he attributes gross moral depravity, general lewdness, dishonesty, and hypocrisy as *Negro* peculiarities, and as such constitutional to him. But I beg to say that these charges are unjust. These traits of character, so far as they maintain at the South, are *American* characteristics—the legitimate outcome of the pernicious system of bondage which has crushed this race for more than two hundred years. For, first, when Dr. Tucker and his endorsers declare that the Negro, *as such*, is void of the family feeling; that moral purity is an unknown virtue; that dishonesty is almost an instinct; that both economy and acquisitiveness are exotics in his nature, they testify that of which they do not know.

## THE NATIVE CHARACTER OF THE NEGRO.

I have lived nigh twenty years in West Africa. I have come in contact with peoples of not less than forty tribes, and I aver, from personal knowledge and acquaintance, that the picture drawn by Dr. Tucker is a caricature. I am speaking of the *native* Negro. (*a*) All along the West Coast of Africa the family tie and the marriage bond are as strong as among any other *primitive* people. The very words in which Cicero and Tacitus describe the homes and families of the Germanic tribes can as truly be ascribed to the people of the

West Coast of Africa. (*b*) Their maidenly virtue, the instinct to chastity, is a marvel. I have no hesitation in the generalization that, in West Africa, every female is a virgin to the day of her marriage. The harlot class is unknown in all their tribes. I venture the assertion that any one walking through Pall Mall, London, or Broadway, New York, for a week, would see more indecency in look and act than he could discover in an African town in a dozen years. During my residence there I only *once* saw an indecent act. Of course polygamy—and polygamy is the exceptional fact—brings, in Africa, all its common disastrous fruits: intrigue, unfaithfulness, adultery. But these are *human*, not Negro, results, cropping out from an unnatural system. (*c*) And then, when you come to the question of honesty, the state of society in Africa settles that point. Heathen though these people are, their system is a most orderly one—filled everywhere with industrious activities; the intercourse of people regulated by rigid law. The whole continent is a beehive. The markets are held regularly at important points. Caravans, laden with products, are constantly crossing the entire continent; and large, nay at times immense, multitudes are gathered together for sale and barter at their markets. Such a state of society is incompatible with universal theft and robbery.

I know somewhat the reputation of the "Yankee;" and the nature of the *Jew* has made his name a synonym. But if either Jew or Yankee possesses more of the acquisitive feeling than the native African, then I have failed in my knowledge of human nature.

Of course the *wants* of the African are inferior to those of the Yankee or the Jew; but that the masterful instinct of greed stimulates the entire continent is witnessed by the strong trading tendencies of almost every tribe; by the universal demand for foreign goods; by the search for outlets for native products; and by the immense trade which is poured out of every river into the hold of foreign vessels.[3]

### THE DEBASED AMERICAN NEGRO.

But perchance Dr. Tucker will insist that the portrait he gives of the SOUTHERN Negro is a true one. He is void of family feeling; he is lewd; he is a liar and self-deceiver; he is dishonest and improvident. Grant, for the moment, that this representation of the American Negro is correct. I have shown that these characteristics are not *native* to the race. Whence then this divergence of character from the original type? Why is the black man *in America* so different in morality from his pagan brother in Africa?

Look at Dr. Tucker's picture of the moral degradation of this people. I do not wish to do him the least injustice. Nevertheless I think I may repeat St. Paul's summary of the moral condition of the Pagan Romans, of his day, as the equivalent of Dr. Tucker's characterization of the *American* Negro. I leave it to the reader to strike out the few epithets in Rom. 1, 29; or 1 Tim. 1, 9 and 10, which may seem inapplicable to this case,[4] for Dr. T. charges the race, as a class, with hypocrisy, lying, stealing, adultery, &c.

Now this is one of the most appalling representations that has ever been put upon paper. (*a*) Here is a nation of people, for a population that runs up its numbers to six or seven millions, is not merely a people—it is a NATION. Here then is a nation, resident for more than seven generations amid the vast populations of this Christian country; and yet, as Dr. Tucker avers, so low and degraded in moral character, that he, himself, is forced even now, after twenty years of freedom, to declare that they are a demoralized people on the downward track to ruin.

(*b*) Yet notice that this Negro nation has been for two centuries under the absolute control and moulding of the Christian Church and people of the South. They have not been separate in locality, as the Israelites in Goshen were, from the Egyptians.[5] They have been living, in all their generations, on the farms and in the houses and families of their masters. So thoroughly intermingled have they been with the life and society of their superiors that they have lost entirely their native tongues, and have taken English as their vernacular. Moreover, they presented the resistance of no *organic* religion to the faith of their masters. They had a heterogeneous paganism when they came from Africa—so inchoate and diversified that it soon fell before the new circumstances in which they were placed.

(*c*) Hence, it is evident (1) that the paganism of the African was no formidable obstacle to the Christian Church; (2) that the Christian Church had the opportunity of easy conquest; and (3) joining to the numerical inferiority of the Negro population the vast resources of the Southern Christian, in all the elements of power and available resources, we can see at once the high vantage ground of the Christian Church.

(*d*) But what now is the fact presented by Dr. Tucker? It is this, viz.: That after two and a half centuries, the black race in the South is still in a state of semi-barbarism, slightly veneered by a Christian profession. Their religion (I use his own words) is "an outward form of Christianity with an inward substance of full license given to all desires and passions." (Page 18.)[6]

Let us take Dr. Tucker at his word; and what, I ask—what is the inference to be drawn from this state of things? I state the conclusion with the greatest sorrow; but it seems irresistible, *i. e.*, that the Christian Church in the South, with the grandest opportunity for service for Christ, and with the very best facilities, has been a failure! It has had one of the widest missionary fields! It has had this field of service open before it two hundred years, and it has hardly attempted to enter it! It has been full of missionary zeal for the peoples of Greece and Asia, for India, and even the West African Negro, but it has lacked the missionary heart for the millions of Negroes on its own plantations and in its own households!

## THE SOUTHERN BLACK MAN THE PRODUCT OF THE SOUTHERN "SCHOOLMASTER"—SLAVERY.

I do not deny that there is wide-spread demoralization among the Southern black population. How could it be otherwise? Their whole history for two hundred years has been a history of moral degradation deeper and more damning than their heathen status in Africa. I am speaking of aggregates. I grant the incidental advantages to scores and hundreds which have sprung from contact with Christian people. I am speaking of the moral condition of the MASSES, who have been under the yoke; and I unhesitatingly affirm that they would have been more blessed and far superior, as pagans, in Africa than slaves on the plantations of the South.

Bishop Howe,[7] of South Carolina, calls slavery "a schoolmaster to the black man."[8] Bishop Gregg declares that "it brought its benefits and blessings."[9] I am filled with amazement that men of sense and reason can thus travesty plain, common English, and talk such senseless stuff! "Schoolmaster!" And pray what sort of a schoolmaster has slavery proven? Why, the slave system has had the black man under training two hundred years, and yet never in all this period has it developed *one* Negro community of strength or greatness! Never raised up anywhere an intelligent, thrifty, productive peasantry! Never built up a single Negro institution of any value to mankind! Never produced a single scientific or learned black man! Its only fruit has been darkness, degradation, semi-barbarism, immorality, agonies, and death! GARNET, DOUGLASS, WARD, and PENNINGTON[10] were men of the largest mould. But each had to run away from the South to get the development of their colossal natures amid Northern institutions!

And so, too, *since* emancipation. All the black men of conspicuous genius or character South have had to get out of the old slave region and come North for the training and development of their intellect. The little Colony of Sierra Leone, with a population of 90,000, has been in existence one hundred years. Will their Reverences show me anywhere in America any such results as that Colony exhibits in letters, civilization, commercial enterprise, manhood, and religion, which have come from two hundred years' tenure of slavery on American soil? Will they declare that their "SCHOOLMASTER" has bred such men, started such enterprises, and developed such missionary ventures as the handful of Negroes in that little English colony? "Schoolmaster" indeed! Is it not an abuse of the English language and of common sense to print such verbiage? Look for a few moments at the moral status and training of the black race under slavery, and see if anything else but demoralization could be the fruit thereof?

1st. They were left, as to religion, to themselves. Their ministers were almost universally ignorant and unlettered men. As the ambition and cleverness of the race, under slavery, could find no other channel than the ministry, the piety of ministers was but an incident; and so men anxious for rule and authority, but withal ofttimes unscrupulous and godless as well as ignorant, became their preachers. Not all such indeed; but alas! in large proportions! Good but illiterate men numbers of the field preachers were. But large numbers of them were unscrupulous and lecherous scoundrels! This was a large characteristic of "plantation religion;" cropping out even to the present, in the extravagances and wildness of many of their religious practices!

2. Their religion, both of preachers and people, was a religion without the Bible—a crude medley of scraps of Scripture, fervid imaginations, dreams, and superstitions. So thorough was the legal interdict of letters and teaching, that the race, as a whole, knew nothing of the Scriptures nor of the Catechisms of the churches. I state it as a strong conviction, the result of wide inquiry, that at the close of the civil war not five hundred blacks among four and a half millions of my race could be found, in the entire South, who knew the "ASSEMBLY'S CATECHISM;"[11] not five hundred who knew, in its entirety, the CATECHISM of the Episcopal Church. The Ten Commandments were as foreign from their minds and memories as the Vedas of India or the moral precepts of Confucius. Ignorance of the MORAL LAW was the main characteristic of "PLANTATION RELIGION!"

3. Sad as are these facts in the history of the race, one further item is horrifying; and that is that the prime functions of the race, under slavery were 1st, LUST, and 2d, UNREQUITED LABOR. This the most serious feature of the whole slave system; and upon it a volume might be written. But I confine myself to the statement of a few simple glaring facts.

In speaking of the licentious and demoralizing nature of slavery, I am speaking of its *general* influences. I have no time to waste upon exceptional features. There are black men who tell me that *all* slave-holders were tyrants and Legrees;[12] but such men I know to be fanatics. There are white men who tell me that slave-holders in general were fathers to their slaves; but such men are manifestly fools. Slave-holders, like all other sorts of men were divided into two classes—the good and the bad: the *good*, like Baronial lords, like Patriarchs of old, like the grand aristocrats of civilized society, were kind, generous, humane, and fatherly; they were NOBLEMEN; and there was a large class of such men. The *bad*, and they were the mass of slaveholders, were full of greed, tyranny, unscrupulousness, and carnality. They herded their slaves together like animals. They were allowed to breed like cattle. The marriage relation was utterly disregarded. All through the rural districts, on numerous plantations, the slaves for generations merely mated and cohabited, as beasts. They were separated at convenience, caprice, or at the call of interest. When separated each took up with other men or women as lust or inclination prompted. Masters and ministers of the gospel taught their slaves, not only that there was no sin in such alliances, but that it was their duty to make new alliances and exercise the animal function of breeding. And hence the cases are numerous where men, sold from one plantation to another, have had six and eight living wives; and women, as many living husbands. Nay more than this, I have the testimony where one man less than fifty years old was the father of over sixty children; of another man who was kept on a plantation with full license as a mere breeder of human beings! And from this disastrous system, so wide has been the separation of families and the rending of the ties of relationship, that now after twenty years of freedom, one cannot take up a copy of the eighty or ninety COLORED NEWSPAPERS printed in the United States without finding at times a score of inquiries of husbands for wives and of wives for husbands; of children for parents and of parents for children. Ever and anon I meet with a woman who had a dozen children sold from her; and in her old age, with living children, is childless, not knowing where they are! And one case came to my knowledge where a woman married her own son, sold from her in his early boyhood; and only discovered the relationship months after the marriage!

Of this gross carnality of the slave system, trained into the blood for generations, until they became mere animals, we see symptoms cropping out ever and anon, in the atrocious acts which are reported in Southern newspapers. The slave system is indeed dead, but its deadly fruit still survives. But it should be remembered that these gross sins are common as well among the whites of the South as among its black population. It filled *them* full of lust as well as their victims.[13]

One would have supposed that with these appalling facts staring him in the face, Dr. Tucker would have taken up the wail of lamentation—

> "We have offended. Oh, my countrymen!
> We have offended very grievously,
> And been most tyrannous. From East to West
> A groan of accusation pierces Heaven!
> The wretched plead against us; multitudes,
> Countless and vehement, the sons of God,
> Our brethren! Like a cloud that travels on
> Steam'd up from Cairo's swamps of pestilence.
> Even so, my countrymen! have we gone forth

And borne to injur'd tribes slavery and pangs;
AND, DEADLIER FAR, OUR VICES, whose deep taint
With slow perdition murders the whole man,
His body and his soul."

COLERIDGE[14]

Alas, nothing of the kind is visible in all this pamphlet! It is an INDICT-MENT, from beginning to end, of the victimized and wronged people! Bishops, presbyters, and laymen all unite in a dark picturing of an entire race, almost oblivious of any wrong-doing on their part! Some of these men are painstaking in the endeavor to show that the difficulty lies in the INHERENT NATURE OF THE NEGRO! Poor miserable obtuse creature, he has been to SCHOOL two hundred years! He has had Bishop Howe's "SCHOOLMASTER," and all his teachings; but he still remains an ignorant, stupid, semi-barbarous animal! It is the Negro! the Negro!

And Dr. Tucker, instead of a wail of lamentation at the neglect and outrage which has brought this race to degradation, not only ignores all the conspicuous facts of Negro progress *since* emancipation, but actually enters a gross and exaggerated charge of deterioration against the entire race. Nay, worse than this; when confronted by brother clergymen, who deny his charges, he goes to work to gather in from every quarter every possible charge of infamy against them! It is evidently a disguised attempt to prove EMANCIPATION A FAILURE!

## THE NEGRO RACE SOUTH, PROGRESSIVE IN NUMBERS, IN PROPERTY, IN EDUCATION, IN RELIGION.

This indictment of the black race is a false one. I care not how generous may be the professions of Dr. Tucker, his statement before the Episcopal Congress at Richmond was an outrage, and his charges untrue and slanderous. I set before me, at this point, especially, the following summary of his charges. He says (p. 21); "*The great facts stare us in the face—that the race is increasing largely in numbers; that since the war but few of them have come up above the moral level of the race; that the average level in material prosperity is but little higher than it was before the war; that in morality there has been a great deterioration since the removal of the restraints of slavery; that there is now no upward movement whatever in morals, and if there is any change it is downward.*"

I address myself to the proof that these charges are false.

## PROOF FROM VITAL STATISTICS.

1st. The admission in this paragraph, viz: that "*the race is increasing largely in numbers,*" is a refutation of the charge of general deterioration. Nothing is more established than the fact that a people given up to concubinage and license lose vitality and decline in numbers. Through unbridled lust and the commonality of their women whole islands in the Pacific seas have long since taken up

"funeral marches to the grave;"[15]

and their populations have become utterly extinct. And so everywhere on earth the integrity and the advance of a people's population have been conditioned on the growth and the permanency of the family feeling. The last census of the nation (1882) bears out these fundamental principles. The increase of the black population from 4,880,009, in 1870, to 6,577,497, in 1882, is in itself a complete refutation of Dr. Tucker's assertion. Its full force can only be seen in connection with another fact, viz: that in the face of the enormous immigration from Europe, added to the natural increase of the American white population, the rate of increase is 34.8 for the black race to 29.2 for the white.

Observe that the rate of increase of the *slave* population in the decades, viz., from 1850 to 1860, was 23.38, from 1860 to 1870, was 9.9.

But now we have the fact that as soon as slavery declines, up springs this population to the enormous rate of 34.8.[16] Will Dr. Tucker tell me that no moral facts underlie this growth of a people? That numerical increase is merely the manifestation of animality? Such an assertion is both false and unphilosophical. The vitality of a people is a sure indication of several high qualities. Mere human animals can live and increase nowhere. They are doomed everywhere to destruction. "No country," says Mr. BURKE—I substitute "people"—"No people in which population flourishes and is in progressive improvement can be under a very mischievous government."[17] Freedom then is a better government than slavery.

No, the growth of population evinces the presence of moral qualities. It is a manifestation of industrial forces. It witnesses the existence of the family instinct. It points out forecast, the use of material agencies, and the play of divers intelligent qualities which are absolutely necessary to the persistency of life and the attainment of some of the higher planes of being.

But, *second*, the educational progress of the race, refutes Dr. Tucker's charge of deterioration. Previous to emancipation the black race, so far as the intellect is concerned, was a dead race! Look at this people at the present. There is, I know, vast illiteracy among the southern blacks. But there are two sides to all questions; and there is a view of this question which is full of cheer and encouragement.

Remember, then, that previous to emancipation there were not more than 30,000 people of color in the Union who could read and write. At the *North* those trained in the schools were chiefly confined to the large cities.

In the rural disticts tens of thousands were cruelly neglected. At the *South*, education was a thing universally interdicted by law; secured only by stealth; and then confined to only a small fraction of the race. Take these facts into consideration, and then consider the grand fact that this day there are 738,164 of this race in annual attendance at school.[18] Consider that a large number of these have advanced to a knowledge of grammar, geography, and history! Consider that no small portion of these are persons who have stretched forth to philosophic acquaintance and some of the acquisitions of science and literature! Consider that over 15,000 of them are employed as teachers! Consider that in this immense army of scholars there is a grand regiment of undergraduates in fifteen colleges; then another, smaller, but not less important, phalanx fitting themselves for the legal and medical professions; and then a larger host of sober, thoughtful, self-sacrificing men, who are looking forward to the pains, trials, and endurance of a thankless but glorious service as ministers of the Gospel of Jesus Christ.

Consider these large and magnificent facts, and you get somewhat an idea of the wonderful contrast between the bright and hopeful present and the dark and disastrous night of our past intellectual history!

Join to this the other significant fact that this large reading population has created a demand for a new thing in the history of the race—NEWSPAPER LITERATURE. And thus have sprung into existence over EIGHTY newspapers edited by men of the Negro race. All this, be it noticed, in a downward-going race!

## STATISTICS OF EDUCATION, FURNISHED BY BUREAU OF EDUCATION, WASHINGTON, D.C.

ENROLMENT OF COLORED YOUTHS, as far as reported by State school officers, for the year 1880, 784,709.

Per cent. of the colored youth of school age enrolled, about 48.

COLORED SCHOOL TEACHERS IN U. S. A.

| | |
|---|---|
| Males | 10,520 |
| Females | 5,314 |
| Total | 15,834 |

NORMAL SCHOOLS for colored youth, 44; teachers in these, 227; pupils in them, 7,408.

HIGH SCHOOLS or ACADEMIC, for them, 36; teachers in them, 120; pupils, 5,327.

UNIVERSITIES and COLLEGES for the race, 15; teachers in them, 119; students, 1,717.

SCHOOLS OF THEOLOGY for them, 22; teachers in them, 65; pupils reported, 880.

SCHOOLS OF LAW, 3; teachers in these schools, 10; pupils in the same, 33.

SCHOOLS OF MEDICINE, 2, with 17 teachers and 87 pupils.

## THE RELIGIOUS ADVANCEMENT OF THE FREEDMAN.

Upon this topic Dr. Tucker gives us simply dogmatism and assertion. He never—to use his own language in reply to his critics—*"undertakes to furnish proof"*[19] of his assertions. A man evidently of deep convictions, he is content to use frequent and most positive affirmations. "No one knows better than himself" the grave statements he makes! He "knows" what he asserts "to be absolutely true!" "The consensus of all authorities(?) establish them beyond the power of any man to overthrow them."[20] This is Dr. Tucker's usual style.

All this, let me remind Dr. Tucker, is but OPINION, unsupported, as are the statements of himself and his endorsers, by a single item of documentary or official testimony. And "opinion," says no less an authority than JOHN LOCKE, is "the admitting or receiving any proposition for true upon arguments or proof that are found to persuade us to receive it as true without certain knowledge that it is so."[21] Or, in other words, opinion is altogether a *subjective* thing. But FACTS, Dr. Tucker will observe, are *objective, i. e.*, outside of the range of imagination, conjecture, and likewise of dogmatism.

I shall not follow Dr. Tucker in his peculiar mode of setting forth his case. I yield to him a monopoly of self-assertion and positiveness. Nevertheless, I shall present a few facts upon this subject which, if I do not greatly err, will lessen the weight of Dr. Tucker's cartloads of intensity and exaggeration.

I present here statistics of the religious status of the black race in the Southern States. These statements are very imperfect. Items of considerable importance, such as baptisms, marriages, contributions, &c., are omitted, from the impossibility of securing details. I have not included the facts relating to Congregationalists, Episcopalians, Campbellites, and Lutherans. I have only taken the work of those denominations which embrace the MASSES of the black population.

### Church Statistics of Black Population

| DENOMINATION. | MINISTERS. | MEMBERSHIP. |
| --- | --- | --- |
| Baptists | probably 3,000 | 700,000 |
| Methodist Episcopal Church (Colored Membership) | not known | 300,000 |
| African Methodist Episcopal | 1,832 | 390,000 |
| Zion African Methodist Episcopal | 2,000 | 300,000 |
| Colored Methodist Episcopal | 638 | 125,000 |

| Colored Methodist Episcopal Union ............... | 101 | 2,550 |
| Presbyterians ........................................... | 75 | 15,000 |
| | 7,646 | 1,832,552 |

Here, then, we have an aggregate of nigh TWO MILLIONS of professed disciples amid the black population of the South. Putting aside all the other items relating to their religious life and conduct, I shall confine myself to this single point of *membership*. What is to be said concerning it? We will, for Dr. Tucker's sake, make large concessions, *(a)* on account of the *ignorance* of these people; *(b)* for the taint of *immorality*, the heritage of slavery, which, doubtless, largely leavens their profession; and *(c)* because their religion is certainly greatly alloyed with phrensy and hysteria, and tinged with the dyes of superstition.

But, after all, is it not, in the main, genuine and true? Is it not, simple and childish though it be, *in its essence*, CHRISTIANITY? Does it not lead to prayers, and faith, and Sabbath keeping, and holy meetings, and sacramental observances? Does it not produce fruits of righteousness? Does it not beget astonishing self-sacrifice for the glory of Jesus, and the lavish outpouring of moneys for the extension of Christ's kingdom and the building of churches?

Surely this is the testimony of scores and hundreds—Presbyterians, Congregationalists, above all, Methodists and Baptists, the very men who have done the most for them, lived most with them, and who know them better than any others.

Dr. Tucker, however, has deliberately declared of this immense multitude of Christians (1) "that they have a form of Christianity without its substance, and that they have no comprehension of what that substance ought to be!"[22] (2) "That the great mass of them are hypocrites, and do not know it." (3) "That their religion is an outward form of Christianity, with an inner substance of full license given to all desires and passions." (4) "That almost a whole race of them is going down into perdition before our eyes!"[23]

We have a dreadful picture in the 1st Epistle of the Corinthians of the demoralization of an Apostolic Church; and yet the holy Apostle St. Paul did not dare to speak of that church in the sweeping and destructive way that Dr. Tucker speaks of millions of disciples of our Lord Jesus Christ in the Southern Negro churches. And I cannot but ask, if it is not a horrible thing that a minister of the Gospel of our Lord Jesus Christ should thus assume the prerogative of Deity, and thus sit in judgement upon the character and piety of multitudes of people whom he has never seen, and of whom he knows nothing!

> "Snatch from His hand the balance and the rod,
> Rejudge His justice, be the God of God!"[24]

## INDUSTRIAL FACTS.

Fourth. I turn from the religious advance of my people to their monetary and industrial condition. And here, too, as in the other cases referred to, there is every cause for thanksgiving. We are indeed a poor people—most likely *the* poorest, as a class, in the whole nation. The fact of poverty is unavoidable, for our history has had one conspicuous peculiarity, viz.: that while enriching others, both law and slavery prevented us from enriching ourselves. At the period of emancipation both these hindrances were removed, and for the first time in two hundred years my people saw open before them the pathway to wealth. The change in their monetary condition has been rapid. They have not, indeed, succeeded as yet in amassing wealth; for, first, no people can extemporize a state of opulence suddenly; nor, second, has it been possible to break down straightway all the unhappy influences and hindrances of slavery. CASTE, the eldest child of slavery, still exists. But, notwithstanding all the difficulties in the way, the black race in this country has begun the race of wealth; has succeeded in entering some of the golden avenues of prosperity and affluence.

Twenty years ago it was a slave race. Over four millions of men and women did not own the bodies in which were enshrined the immortal spirits which resided therein.

Out of those immortal spirits slavery had crushed every noble impulse and all the springs of action. And see now at once the marvelous change. The instinct of greed, dead for centuries under the palsying influences of slavery, has been resurrected by the genius of civil freedom.

To-day this same people are the possessors of a wide domain of lands. Immense tracts of land have been brought by them into cultivation, and by this cultivation they have become producers of the most valuable staples.

I am indebted to the Editor of the "PEOPLE'S ADVOCATE"[25] for the following facts: "In the State of Georgia the Negro owns 680,000 acres of land, cut up into farms; and pays taxes on $9,000,000 worth of property. In the Cotton States he owns 2,680,000 acres." And he adds to this the significant remark: "Think of it, that in the Cotton States, including a fraction of over two-thirds of the race, the Negro, in seventeen years, has accumulated territory equal in extent to the size of the STATE OF CONNECTICUT."

Let me suggest here another estimate of this landed property of the Negro, acquired *since* emancipation. Taking the old slave States in the general, there has been a large acquisition of land in each and all of them. In the State of Georgia, as we have just seen, it was 680,000 acres. Let us put the figure as low as 400,000 for each State—for the purchase of farm lands has been everywhere a passion with the freedman—this 400,000 acres multiplied into 14, *i. e.* the number of the chief Southern States, shows an aggregate of 5,600,000 acres of land, the acquisition of the black race in less than twenty years.

But Dr. Tucker will observe a further fact of magnitude in this connection: It is the increased PRODUCTION which has been developed on the part of the freedmen since emancipation. I present but *one* staple, and for the reason that it is almost exclusively the result of FREE NEGRO LABOR.

I will take the five years immediately preceding the late civil war and compare them with the five years preceding the last year's census-taking; and the contrast in the number of cotton-bales produced will show the industry and thrift of the black race as a consequent on the gift of freedom:

| YEARS | BALES | YEARS | BALES |
|---|---|---|---|
| 1857 | 2,939,519 | 1878 | 4,811,265 |
| 1858 | 3,113,962 | 1879 | 5,073,531 |
| 1859 | 3,851,481 | 1880 | 5,757,397 |
| 1860 | 4,669,770 | 1881 | 6,589,329 |
| 1861 | 3,656,006 | 1882 | 5,435,845 |
| Total | 18,230,738 | The five years' work of *freedom* | 27,667,367 |
| | | The five years' work of *slavery* | 18,230,738 |
| | | Balance in favor of freedom | 9,436,659 |

Now this item of production is a positive disproof of Dr. Tucker's statement, "that the average level in material propserity is but little higher than it was before the war." Here is the fact that the Freedman has produced one-third more in *five* years than he did in the same time when a slave!

Another view of this matter is still more striking. The excess of yield in cotton in seven years [*i. e,* from 1875 to 1882] over the seven years [*i. e,* from 1854 to 1861] is 17,091,000 bales, being AN AVERAGE ANNUAL IN-CREASE OF 1,000,000 BALES. If Dr. Tucker will glance at the great increase of the cotton, tobacco, and sugar crops South, as shown in Agricultural Reports from 1865 to 1882, and reflect that NEGROES have been the producers of these crops, he will understand their indignation at his outrageous charges of "laziness and vagabondage;"[26] and perhaps he will listen to their demand that he shall take back the unjust and injurious imputations which, without knowledge and discrimination, he makes against a whole race of people.

This impulse to thrift on the part of the Freedmen was no tardy and reluctant disposition. It was the *immediate* offspring of freedom, and the result was—

First. The founding of the FREEDMAN'S BANK in the city of Washington.

The following facts are worthy of notice:

(*a*) This bank was opened in 1865 and closed in 1874.

(*b*) No less than 61,000 Freedmen were the depositors in this bank.

(*c*) The depositors were men and women in *every* Southern State from Maryland to Louisiana.

(*d*) The sum total of moneys deposited amounted to over $56,000,000. All which evidences character, industry, moral energy, and the capability of self-support.

The destruction of this Bank, through the rascality of white men, was a great calamity; but it did not quench the ambition of the race. Since then other notable demonstrations of manly power have been shown by the freedmen.

Second. The uprising of thousands in the South-west and their emigration with great loss of property, health, and life to the West, was not the act of degenerate beings, but of high-souled and aspiring men—albeit they were poor and ignorant.[27] They were cheated wholesale out of their wages by the very men—Dr. Tucker's neighbors—who, he tells us, "know the Negroes and love them" with the "tender remembrances of childhood!"[28] These men, owners of wide, uncultivated tracts of land, refused to sell these Freedmen the smallest patches, in order to keep them perpetual serfs of the soil. So, in deep indignation, they shook the dust of the South from their feet and carried their families into free Kansas, to secure freeholds, liberty, and education for their children.

Third. "The last census shows us that the colored people are assessed for over $91,000,000 worth of taxable property. Does this look like an incurably thriftless race?"[29]

I have referred above to the large landed estate of the black man; and I may add here that it is the result of his own sweatful toil. He has earned his own property. Unlike the Indian, he has had no one to prop him up. He was turned loose suddenly, without any capital, to undertake the duty of self-support. The nation acted as though it owed him no duty and no debt. It gave him his freedom to save its own life; and then left him to struggle for life, if not to die! Justice demanded that, after centuries of slavery, he should have been made the ward of the nation—at least until he learned the ways and provinces of freedom. He was turned out to die.

But neither failure nor death was to be the destiny of the Negro. It never has been in any of the lands of his emancipation. Everywhere, when freedom has come to him, he has discovered all the proclivities to enterprise and personal sustentation. It has been conspicuously so in this nation. The Freedmen of this country, on coming out of bondage, began at once all the laborious activities which their needs demanded, and which were required for the securing a foothold in this land.

Of course this industrial enterprise was not universal. It never is universal in any people. Large numbers could not understand the situation; could not see the grand vistas of opportunity and success which freedom opened before them. My own estimate of their progress since emancipation is this, viz: (1) That about one-third have fallen to a lower level than they were previous to emancipation, viz: the aged, the decrepid, the imbruted, and the slaves of the meanest, lowest, whites. (2) That *another* third stand a little *above* their condition when freedom was given them. And, (3) lastly, that the *last* third have risen to a state of superiority which already rivals the energy and progress of the American people in general. To start *one-third* of any people earnestly on the road of glorious progress is a grand result. For in all revolutions of society there is sure to be a great loss of man. For it is with men as it is with seeds—some spring up into life, and some seem to have no productive vitality at all. Says Bishop Butler: "For of the numerous seeds of vegetables and bodies of animals which are adapted and put in the way to improve to such a point or state of natural maturity and perfection, we do not see that one in a million actually does. For the greater part of them decay before they are improved to it, and appear to be absolutely destroyed."[30] So, too, some men—large classes of men—are sure to fall behind in the race of life. But, as the immense loss of seeds does not contradict the fact of the prodigious wheat harvests of the West which supply the world with food, so the actual loss or decline of a third of the Freedmen does not contravene the fact of the real progress of the race. For this same relative loss is discovered in all peoples. It is seen in the white population of this land, notwithstanding all their advantages. Look into the alms and poor houses; into the jails of the country; into the indigent quarters of the large cities; examine the statistics of crime and poverty, and you will see that fully one-third of the white population is constantly going down. Indeed society everywhere advances only by the force and energy of minorities. It is the *few* who lift up and bear the burdens and give character to the many. But, nevertheless, it is advance; and the human race in civilized countries is ever going upward.

Just here I rest my case; and I submit that I have disproved Dr. Tucker's gross indictment of my race. I have shown, by the evidence of incontrovertible fact, by figures and statistics which cannot be denied—

1st. That their numerical increase has been prodigious;

2d. That their acquisition of property has been enormous;

3d. That they show almost a reduplicated capacity for production, the direct result of freedom;

4th. That their rise in education and religion has been almost like the resurrection of a people from death to life!

### DR. TUCKER'S REMEDIAL SYSTEM.

I close this paper with a brief reference to Dr. Tucker's plans for the elevation of the Negro.

They are as follows:

1st. That the Northern people shall furnish supplies of money for work among the Negroes;

2d. That Southern Missionaries shall use and disburse these moneys in church work among the black race;

3d. That Northern Missionaries shall be excluded from this work.

4th. That black men shall not be entrusted with the training and education of their brethren.

As Dr. Tucker is evidently serious in these suggestions, I presume that I must take them up in as serious a manner as he presents them.

Now, I beg to say that nothing can be more non-natural than the plans thus proposed. People, however philanthropic, are rarely prepared to go it blind in the disbursements of moneys. Christian people especially give as "stewards" of their Divine Master. They want to know, first of all, the quality of fitness in their almoners; and, next, that they will use their moneys aright. But here is a proposition which reverses all the settled principles of almsgiving. For—

1st. It cleverly lays the burden of obligation in this matter upon the Northern people. Dr. Tucker says, "You freed the slaves and left them on our hands." . . . . "Blood and trouble have come of it so far, and for this you of the North are largely to blame."[31] But the question arises, Has freedom made the alleged heathenism of the Southern blacks any denser than slavery did? Has emancipation plunged the Southern blacks into ignorance and benightedness? And, if not, whence arises the special obligation of the North to perform this duty of evangelization! And then—

2d. Why should *Southern* men be the chosen missionaries to the black race? Whence arises *their* special fitness for this work? From experience? From high achievement or from large success? Why, Dr. Tucker admits the failure of the South. The Negro has been moulded and fashioned by Southern Christians two centuries and more; and Dr. Tucker avers—I am using his own language—"the Negro is retrograding in morality," (p. 2). "I say deliberately, with a full realization of what the words mean, that the great mass of the Negroes in the South professing religion have a form of Christianity without its substance; and, further, that they have no comprehension of what that substance ought to be," (p. 3). And this after two hundred years of Southern training!

Then, next, Dr. Tucker, self-contradictory as usual, exhorts—"Work through the Church South;" that is, be it noticed, through this inept and fruitless Church South, which has brought the Negro to a state of ignorance of "what the substance of Christianity ought to be!" But let us follow our author: "Work through the Church South . . . and then you will enlist those who *thoroughly know what they are about;* know how to reach the colored people; who love them with the remembrances of childhood and youth and manhood, as strangers can never learn or grow to care for them" (p. 27).

Did ever any one hear such assumption! The Church South "thoroughly knows what they are about!" But for two hundred years they have had an awkward way of showing it! "*They* know how to reach the colored people!" But, alas, in two hundred years they have failed to reach them; and now Dr. Tucker himself is calling for a new departure; exhorts an attempt *de novo* in order to reach and christianize them! This is logic with a vengeance! But lastly comes the claim—"WE SOUTHERN PEOPLE KNOW THE NEGRO BETTER THAN YOU DO!"[32] This is the old claim which the American people have heard *ad nauseam*. Alas, for all their knowledge they never knew them well enough to treat them as men! They never knew them well enough to give them freedom! They never knew them well enough, *after* freedom came, to stimulate culture, manhood, and superiority among them.

Precisely this same claim was made by the slaveholders in the British West Indies. They were constantly telling the English people, "we know the Negro better than you do." And yet emancipation had to be *forced* upon both West Indian and American slaveholders! With all their knowledge of the Negro, and their exuberant love of him, they both resisted to the utmost the unfettering of their bondmen!

How was it *after* emancipation? The great work of elevating and educating the Freedmen had to be undertaken by philanthropists *outside* of the former domains of slavery; by the friends of the black man in England; by Northern men in the United States. I don't know of one single instance in the history of Negro bondage where slaveholders, as *a class*, have ever voluntarily emancipated the Negro, or, when raised to freedom, have ever voluntarily put themselves to pains to elevate him to manhood, intelligence, and superiority.

I challenge Dr. Tucker to point out one such instance.

3d. The main reason Dr. Tucker gives for the rejection of Northern Missionaries is that the "Northern man don't know the Negro." When they (*i. e.,* the Northern Christians) propose to help the Negroes, the Southern (white)

Christians "draw back," he says, "with a feeling of despair, mingled with anger, that God's servants should in wilful ignorance build up the kingdom of evil."[33] Passing strange language this! Here these Northern people, from divers denominations of Christians, have been sending forth missionaries to every quarter of the heathen world—Presbyterians, Baptists, Congregationalists, Methodists, Episcopalians. Everywhere they have gone their work has been so graciously attended by the gifts of God the Holy Ghost, they have shown such wonderful knowledge of human nature, and plied such marvelous skill and practicality that English Civilians, great Governors-General, French and German tourists, yea, even infidel travelers, have spoken of these Northern American missionaries as equal, and in many cases superior, to all other modern Missionaries. And yet Dr. Tucker gravely tells us, "Send no Northern Missionaries down here!"[34] And why, forsooth, this mandate? Because, without doubt, something besides the grace of God, and high literary culture, and a knowledge of human nature is needed. And pray *what* is this special quality needed? Why, to use the grotesque language of a humorous acquaintance, "these Northern men—wise, learned, experienced in God's work, full of the Holy Ghost—lack a knowledge of the special science of NEGROOLOGY." *That*, Dr. Tucker would have us believe, is the exclusive possession of Southern slaveholders!

But how comes it to pass that Northern people *"rarely know a Negro when they see him?"* As Dr. Tucker seems oblivious of some facts in American history, let me briefly set before him *two* classes of facts:

*The first class:*

(*a*) Let me say that Northern people from Massachusetts, Rhode Island, Connecticut, New York, &c., went to Africa in slave ships, stole and bought native Negroes from the predatory chiefs, and brought them in cargoes to the Northern States. And *this fact*, first of all, shows some "acquaintance" of a very sorry nature "with Negroes" on the part of Northern people.

(*b*) These captured Negroes were bought by Northern people by thousands; worked on their farms and in their houses; and ofttimes were put upon the auction block, and sold as goods and chattels. And *this* fact implies, secondly, a further acquaintance with Negroes.

(*c*) And, lastly, that these Northern people were NOT Negro-worshippers is evidenced by the fact that these Negroes were kept in ignorance by their owners; whipped at the whipping-post; families were separated; treated as brutes; *once*, under the suspicion of insurrection, were hung up in the streets of New York as dogs![35] And then, *after* emancipation, for nigh fifty years they were cruelly treated; excluded from cars, coaches, and steamboats; frequently mobbed; and late as 1863, in an awful riot, their houses were sacked, their women whipped in the streets, and their men hung up at the lamp-posts![36] Does not all this look as though "Northern people knew Negroes when they saw them?"

I turn to the *second class of facts:*

(*a*) During the whole period of Northern slavery there was always a class of Northern men, philanthropists, who revolted at human bondage.

(*b*) This class of men—Quakers, Episcopalians, and others —were never afraid of slaveholders, and would never allow themselves to be bullied by them.

(*c*) At a very early period, even in Colonial times, they asserted themselves, and demanded the abolition of slavery.

(*d*) Hence arose the "ABOLITION SOCIETIES" of the Middle States, who both established schools for Negro children and demanded the abolition of slavery. It was these men—the Jays, Clarksons, Kings, and Kents,[37] of New York; the Boudinots, Shotwells, the Benezets,[38] of New Jersey; the Rushs and Franklins,[39] of Pennsylvania—who ameliorated the condition of Northern Negroes, and, in some cases, destroyed their slavery. They looked upon these people as *men*, and secured their citizenship. They regarded them as *intelligent beings*; and so, at last, through their efforts, schools, and the colleges of the North—Dartmouth, Harvard, Yale, Brown, Columbia, Princeton, and Pennsylvania—have been opened to Negroes. Nay, beyond this, they counted them as *brethren* in Christ; and so they have been received in their churches; and in many cases they have been cordially welcomed to their pulpits.

And now I trust these facts will serve to convince Dr. Tucker that Northern people "know a Negro when they see him!" And I beg to add, if he has any doubt of these historical facts, he can easily verify them by any "COMMON SCHOOL HISTORY of the United States of America."

Dr. Tucker may also learn from this that Northern people have had some experience in the endeavor to civilize and elevate the black race; and so, when they come South on such a mission, they will come, not as novices, but as adepts. In every State North they can point to schools and churches, to intelligent and thrifty communities, nay, in some cases, to wealthy and learned colored men, the result of the endeavors of their fathers to elevate a wronged and injured people, and to redress a dark and shameful past. When the South has done as much for the Negro as the North, then it will be unjust as well as absurd to say that "Southern Missionaries barely know a Negro when they see him!"

For my own part, I differ *toto cœlo* from Dr. Tucker. I rejoice in the aid of all sorts of Christians in this great work. I am glad to have the assistance not only of Northern, but also, and especially, of Southern white missionaries. When, with their other knowledge of the Negro, they come to a recognition of him as a MAN, then they will make the very best missionaries to the Negro. This was the case of old with the Abolitionists. None were so true to the Negro cause as the Grimkes, the Birneys, the Brisbanes,[40] and others.

But I must say, with all candor, that the deliverance of the black race South into the hands exclusively, of Southern whites, has its dangers. I would not, for the life of me, say one word in least derogatory of Southern white men. They are just the same—no better, no worse—than other men. They are in no way responsible for the acts nor the sentiments of their forefathers. Nay, their fathers themselves were the heirs, NOT the creators, of the heritage of human bondage. But Southern men are but men; and Southern or any other men, who are the descendants of a long line of slaveholders, or of a feudality, or of a nobility, or of an aristocracy, are the heirs of a spirit of dominancy; and carry in their blood all the proclivities to undue mastership and control. Placed in juxtaposition with a degraded and illiterate race, they will naturally, albeit unconsciously, be tempted to a system of feudality or peonage, unless the most careful safeguards are guaranteed that race. There is no such guarantee in placing the Negro entirely in the hands of his former masters. It would be to look for too much from poor human nature to expect of the Southern white man such large disinterestedness as Dr. Tucker demands. He has too many personal interests involved in this problem for him to rise to the height of such lofty virtue; and therefore the temptation should not be set before him.

Nor is this mere speculation. The South has shown its hand. Ever since emancipation the Legislatures of the South have resorted to every possible expedient to neutralize the force of the "AMENDMENTS" which gave freedom to the black man. They, the aristocracy of the South, have left no stone unturned to narrow the limits of the black man's new-born liberty and his rights. Hence it is evidently unsafe to put the Freedman's future entirely in the hands of his former master.

No, the Southern black man needs teachers of diversified characteristics. He needs the Southern Missionary, for he is to the "manner born," and understands certain phases of life, society, and character which no other man knows. But he needs, too—and *so does the Southern white man need*—the Northern element. No civilization on this continent will be worth a cent which lacks a large infusion of the large common-sense, the strong practicality, the fine intelligence, the lofty culture, the freedom-loving spirit, and the restless aspiration of the people of the North.

Hence, it seems to me, that there must be an element of aberration in Dr. Tucker's constitution when he deliberately ejaculates "Send no more Northern Missionaries down here!" Here, when the whole civilized world is instinct with curiosity at the manifestation of the peculiar civilization of the North; and delegates are coming hither from England and China, from France and Japan, from Germany and Madagascar, to study it, and carry away with them its very best elements as contributions to the higher civilization of the future; Dr. Tucker peremptorily demands that the Negro is to be entirely shut out from it.

Dr. Tucker is mistaken. He has not the ability to erect another Chinese wall to keep out this (to him) objectionable element. What has been so graciously and fruitfully begun by Northern teachers, preachers, and philanthropists will be continued, until the Negro in the South is re-fashioned, enlightened, and lifted up to the very highest planes of civilization, grace, and manhood.

4th. Equally mistaken is Dr. Tucker in another most important point. He seems to think that the work of educating the Negro race is to be entrusted chiefly to white men. "The Negroes," he says, "are not well enough educated, not yet on a high enough level, to make good use of any help you may extend to them. The Southern white people, who know all about the race, and how to deal with them, are the only ones who can work judiciously to lay sure foundations."[41]

I cannot dwell upon this topic. I only wish to say three or four things:

1st. That hundreds of well-furnished and efficient colored teachers (about 16,000 at present) are now in the field doing noble service as teachers.

2d. That hundreds more can be obtained for the same service at any time.

3d. That hundreds more *besides* these are preparing in schools, academies, and colleges for a life service as teachers among their race; and there is no likelihood of a lack of supply of colored teachers in the farthest future.

4th. That an INDIGENOUS AGENCY in the evangelization of a people is a UNIVERSAL PRINCIPLE. Negroes are no exception to this principle; and the man or the organization which attempts the training of the black race by ignoring this principle may surely expect these two inevitable results:

(*a*) They will doubtless get a certain following of people; but their gatherings, save in the rarest exceptional cases, will be nothing more nor less than useless "snobberies," to be perpetually petted or paid for their allegiance, and everlastingly deficient in strength and manliness. And,

(*b*) They will find the *masses* about them will resist all their inducements, and, under the *racial impulse*, will go off to any standard lifted up by a man of their own blood.

True leaders of a race are men of that race; and any attempt to carry on missions opposed to this principle is sure to meet disastrous failure!

The Negro race is a living, not a dead race—alive in the several respects of industry, acquisitiveness, education, and religious aspiration. Not entirely divorced as yet from the sore diseases of the Egypt from which they have only recently been delivered, they are, nevertheless, making mighty efforts for cure and healing by both the appliances of education and the Blood of the Lamb. It is a race instinct in every section with HOPE and aspiration. All the springs of action are moving in it. Its leaders, everywhere, conscious, indeed, of deep, radical defects within, and most formidable hindrances without, have, notwithstanding, but few misgivings as to the future. They have very great confidence, first of all, in certain vital qualities inherent in the race! They trust those universal and unfailing tendencies of TRUTH, JUSTICE, and EQUITY, which have ever attended their history on this continent! They look with no uncertainty to the large and loving BROTHERHOOD of countless Christians, of every name, in this land, whose hearts are alive with pity for the past sorrows of the Negro; whose prayers go up as clouds of incense for his restoration; and whose purses pour forth annually tens of thousands for his well-being and salvation! And they repose in quiet confidence upon the marvelous mercy and loving-kindness of a divine DELIVERER and SAVIOUR, who has wrought out a most gracious and saving providence for them!

These succors and assistances cannot fail! They will surely serve to realize the qualities and justify the character implied in the epithet of Homer, when he speaks of

"ÆTHIOPIA'S BLAMELESS RACE."[42]

# 6.

---

## *The Black Woman of the South:*
## *Her Neglects and Her Needs*

Crummell was one of the few black leaders of the nineteenth century who addressed himself to the condition of black women. His reasons for doing so were quite straightforward; the reform of women's morals was to be the basis of a revolution in the status of the black family. It was these assumptions that prompted Crummell to write "The Black Woman of the South." Significantly, Crummell attributed the sad moral condition of the freedwomen to the heritage of slavery, which he discussed here in some detail. The remedy, he argued, was continued missionary effort and the setting up of an industrial school for black girls in every Southern state. "The Black Woman of the South" was delivered before the Freedman's Aid Society of the Methodist Episcopal Church at Ocean Grove, New Jersey, on August 13, 1883, and is reported to have sold over 500,000 copies.[1]

IT is an age clamorous everywhere for the dignities, the grand prerogatives, and the glory of woman. There is not a country in Europe where she has not risen somewhat above the degradation of centuries, and pleaded successfully for a new position and a higher vocation. As the result of this new reformation we see her, in our day, seated in the lecture-rooms of ancient universities, rivaling her brothers in the fields of literature, the grand creators of ethereal art, the participants in noble civil franchises, the moving spirit in grand reformations, and the guide, agent, or assistant in all the noblest movements for the civilization and regeneration of man.

In these several lines of progress the American woman has run on in advance of her sisters in every other quarter of the globe. The advantage she has received, the rights and prerogatives she has secured for herself, are unequaled by any other class of women in the world. It will not be thought amiss, then, that I come here to-day to present to your consideration the one grand exception to this general superiority of women, viz., "THE BLACK WOMAN OF THE SOUTH."

In speaking to-day of the "black woman," I must needs make a very clear distinction. The African race in this country is divided into two classes, that is—the *colored people* and the *negro population*. In the census returns of 1860 this whole population was set down at 4,500,000. Of these, the *colored* numbered 500,000; the *black* or *negro* population at 4,000,000. But notice these other broad lines of demarkation between them. The colored people, while indeed but *one-eighth* of the number of the blacks, counted more men and women who could read and write than the whole 4,000,000 of their brethren in bondage. A like disparity showed itself in regard to their *material* condition. The 500,000 colored people were absolutely richer in lands and houses than the many millions of their degraded kinsmen.

The causes of these differences are easily discovered. The colored population received, in numerous cases, the kindness and generosity of their white kindred—white fathers and relatives. Forbidden by law to marry the negro woman, very many slave-holders took her as the wife, despite the law; and when children were begotten every possible recognition was given those children, and they were often cared for, educated, and made possessors of property. Sometimes they were sent to Northern schools, sometimes to France or England. Not unfrequently whole families, nay, at times, whole colonies, were settled in Western or Northern towns and largely endowed with property. The colored population, moreover, was, as compared with the negro, the *urban* population. They were brought in large numbers to the cities, and thus partook of the civilization and refinement of the whites. They were generally the domestic servants of their masters, and thus, brought in contact with their superiors, they gained a sort of education which never came to the field hands, living in rude huts on the plantations. All this, however casual it may seem, was a merciful providence, by which some gleams of light and knowledge came, indirectly, to the race in this land.

The rural or plantation population of the South was made up almost entirely of people of pure negro blood. And this brings out also the other disastrous fact, namely, that this large black population has been living from the time of their introduction into America, a period of more than two hundred years, in a state of unlettered rudeness. The Negro all this time has been an intellectual starvling. This has been more especially the condition of the black woman of the South. Now and then a black man has risen above the debased condition of his people. Various causes would contribute to the advantage of the *men:* the relation of servants to superior masters; attendance at courts with them; their presence at political meetings; listening to table-talk behind their chairs; traveling as valets; the privilege of books and reading in great houses, and with indulgent masters—all these served to lift up a black *man* here and there to something like superiority. But no such fortune fell to the lot of the plantation woman. The black woman of the South was left perpetually in a state of hereditary darkness and rudeness. Since the day of Phillis Wheatly[2] no Negress in this land (that is, in the South) has been raised above the level of her sex. The lot of the black *man* on the plantation has been sad and desolate enough; but the fate of the black woman has been awful! Her entire existence from the day she first landed, a naked victim of the slave-trade, has been degradation in its extremest forms.

In her girlhood all the delicate tenderness of her sex has been rudely outraged. In the field, in the rude cabin, in the press-room, in the factory, she was thrown into the companionship of coarse and ignorant men. No chance was given her for delicate reserve or tender modesty. From her childhood she was the doomed victim of the grossest passions. All the virtues of her sex were utterly ignored. If the instinct of chastity asserted itself, then she had to fight like a tigress for the ownership and possession of her own person; and, ofttimes, had to suffer pains and lacerations for her virtuous self-assertion. When she reached maturity all the tender instincts of her womanhood were ruthlessly violated. At the age of marriage—always prematurely anticipated under slavery—she was mated, as the stock of the plantation were mated, *not* to be the companion of a loved and chosen husband, but to be the breeder of human cattle, for the field or the auction block. With that mate she went out, morning after morning to toil, as a common field-hand. As it was *his,* so likewise was it her lot to wield the heavy hoe, or to follow the plow, or to gather in the crops. She was a "hewer of wood and a drawer of water."[3] She was a common field-hand. She had to keep her place in the gang from morn till eve, under the burden of a heavy task, or under the stimulus or the fear of a cruel lash. She was a picker of cotton. She labored at the sugar mill and in the tobacco factory. When, through weariness or sickness, she has fallen behind her alloted task then came, as punishment, the fearful stripes upon her shrinking, lacerated flesh.

Her home life was of the most degrading nature. She lived in the rudest huts, and partook of the coarsest food, and dressed in the scantiest garb, and slept, in multitudinous cabins, upon the hardest boards!

Thus she continued a beast of burden down to the period of those maternal anxieties which, in ordinary civilized life, give repose, quiet, and care to expectant mothers. But, under the slave system, few such relaxations were allowed. And so it came to pass that little children were ushered into this world under conditions which many cattle raisers would not suffer for their flocks or herds. Thus she became the mother of children. But even then there was for her no suretyship of motherhood, or training, or control. Her own offspring were *not* her own. She and husband and children were all the property of others. All these sacred ties were constantly snapped and cruelly sundered. *This* year she had one husband; and next year, through some auction sale, she might be separated from him and mated to another. There was no sanctity of family, no binding tie of marriage, none of the fine felicities and the endearing affections of home. None of these things were the lot of Southern black women. Instead thereof a gross barbarism which tended to blunt the tender sensibilities, to obliterate feminine delicacy and womanly shame, came down as her heritage from generation to generation; and it seems a miracle of providence and grace that, notwithstanding these terrible circumstances, so much struggling virtue lingered amid these rude cabins, that so much womanly worth and sweetness abided in their bosoms, as slaveholders themselves have borne witness to.

But some of you will ask: "Why bring up these sad memories of the past? Why distress us with these dead and departed cruelties?" Alas, my friends, these are not dead things. Remember that

"The evil that men do lives after them."[4]

The evil of gross and monstrous abominations, the evil of great organic institutions crop out long after the departure of the institutions themselves. If you go to Europe you will find not only the roots, but likewise many of the deadly fruits of the old Feudal system still surviving in several of its old states and kingdoms. So, too, with slavery. The eighteen years of freedom have not obliterated all its deadly marks from either the souls or bodies of the black woman. The conditions of life, indeed, have been modified since emancipation; but it still maintains that the black woman is the Pariah woman of this land! We have, indeed, degraded women, immigrants, from foreign lands. In their own countries some of them were so low in the social scale that they were yoked with the cattle to plow the fields. They were rude, unlettered, coarse, and benighted. But when they reach *this* land there comes an end to their degraded condition.

"They touch our country and their shackles fall."[5]

As soon as they become grafted into the stock of American life they partake at once of all its large gifts and its noble resources.

Not so with the black woman of the South. Freed, legally she has been;

but the act of emancipation had no talismanic influence to reach to and alter and transform her degrading social life.

When that proclamation was issued she might have heard the whispered words in every hut, "Open Sesame;" but, so far as her humble domicile and her degraded person was concerned, there was no invisible but gracious Genii who, on the instant, could transmute the rudeness of her hut into instant elegance, and change the crude surroundings of her home into neatness, taste, and beauty.

The truth is, "Emancipation Day" found her a prostrate and degraded being; and, although it has brought numerous advantages to her sons, it has produced but the simplest changes in her social and domestic condition. She is still the crude, rude, ignorant mother. Remote from cities, the dweller still in the old plantation hut, neighboring to the sulky, disaffected master class, who still think her freedom was a personal robbery of themselves, none of the "fair humanities"[6] have visited her humble home. The light of knowledge has not fallen upon her eyes. The fine domesticities which give the charm to family life, and which, by the refinement and delicacy of womanhood, preserve the civilization of nations, have not come to *her*. She has still the rude, coarse labor of men. With her rude husband she still shares the hard service of a field-hand. Her house, which shelters, perhaps, some six or eight children, embraces but two rooms. Her furniture is of the rudest kind. The clothing of the household is scant and of the coarsest material, has ofttimes the garniture of rags; and for herself and offspring is marked, not seldom, by the absence of both hats and shoes. She has rarely been taught to sew, and the field labor of slavery times has kept her ignorant of the habitudes of neatness, and the requirements of order. Indeed, coarse food, coarse clothes, coarse living, coarse manners, coarse companions, coarse surroundings, coarse neighbors, both white and black, yea, every thing coarse, down to the coarse, ignorant, senseless religion, which excites her sensibilities and starts her passions, go to make up the life of the masses of black women in the hamlets and villages of the rural South.

This is the state of black womanhood. Take the girlhood of this same region, and it presents the same aspect, save that in large districts the white man has not forgotten the olden times of slavery, and, with, indeed, the deepest sentimental abhorrence of "amalgamation," still thinks that the black girl is to be perpetually the victim of his lust! In the larger towns and in cities, our girls, in common schools and academies, are receiving superior culture. Of the fifteen thousand colored school teachers in the South, more than half are colored young women, educated since emancipation. But even these girls, as well as their more ignorant sisters in rude huts, are followed and tempted and insulted by the ruffianly element of Southern society, who think that black *men* have no rights which white men should regard, and black *women* no virtue which white men should respect!

And now look at the *vastness* of this degradation. If I had been speaking of the population of a city, or a town, or even a village, the tale would be a sad and melancholy one. But I have brought before you the condition of millions of women. According to the census of 1880 there were, in the Southern States, 3,327,678 females of all ages of the African race. Of these there were 674,365 girls between twelve and twenty, 1,522,696 between twenty and eighty. "These figures," remarks an observing friend of mine, "are startling!" And when you think that the masses of these women live in the rural districts; that they grow up in rudeness and ignorance; that their former masters are using few means to break up their hereditary degradation, you can easily take in the pitiful condition of this population, and forecast the inevitable future to multitudes of females, unless a mighty special effort is made for the improvement of the black womanhood of the South.

I know the practical nature of the American mind, I know how the question of values intrudes itself into even the domain of philanthropy; and, hence, I shall not be astonished if the query suggests itself, whether special interest in the black woman will bring any special advantage to the American nation.

Let me dwell for a few moments upon this phase of the subject. Possibly the view I am about suggesting has never before been presented to the American mind. But, Negro as I am, I shall make no apology for venturing the claim that the Negress is one of the most interesting of all the classes of women on the globe. I am speaking of her, not as a perverted and degraded creature, but in her natural state, with her native instincts and peculiarities.

Let me repeat just here the words of a wise, observing, tender-hearted philanthropist, whose name and worth and words have attained celebrity. It is fully forty years ago since the celebrated Dr. Channing said: "We are holding in bondage one of the best races of the human family. The Negro is among the mildest, gentlest of men. He is singularly susceptible of improvement from abroad. . . . His nature is affectionate, easily touched, and hence he is more open to religious improvement than the white man. . . . The African carries with him much more than *we* the genius of a meek, long-suffering, loving virtue."[7]

I should feel ashamed to allow these words to fall from my lips if it were not necessary to the lustration of the character of my black sisters of the South. I do not stand here to-day to plead for the black *man*. He is a man; and if he is weak he must go to the wall. He is a man; he must fight his own way, and if he is strong in mind and body, he can take care of himself. But for the mothers, sisters, and daughters of my race I have a right to speak.

And when I think of their sad condition down South, think, too, that since the day of emancipation hardly any one has lifted up a voice in their behalf, I feel it a duty and a privilege to set forth their praises and to extol their excellencies. For, humble and benighted as she is, the black woman of the South is one of the queens of womanhood. If there is any other woman on this earth who in native aboriginal qualities is her superior, I know not where she is to be found; for, I do say, that in tenderness of feeling, in genuine native modesty, in large disinterestedness, in sweetness of disposition and deep humility, in unselfish devotedness, and in warm, motherly assiduities, the Negro woman is unsurpassed by any other woman on this earth.

The testimony to this effect is almost universal—our enemies themselves being witnesses. You know how widely and how continuously, for generations, the Negro has been traduced, ridiculed, derided. Some of you may remember the journals and the hostile criticisms of Coleridge and Trollope and Burton,[8] West Indian and African travelers. Very many of you may remember the philosophical disquisitions of the ethnological school of 1847, the contemptuous dissertations of Hunt and Gliddon.[9] But it is worthy of notice in all these cases that the sneer, the contempt, the bitter gibe, have been invariably leveled against the black *man*—never against the black woman! On the contrary, *she* has almost everywhere been extolled and eulogized. The black man was called a stupid, thick-lipped, flat-nosed, long-heeled, empty-headed animal; the link between the baboon and the human being, only fit to be a slave! But everywhere, even in the domains of slavery, how tenderly has the Negress been spoken of! She has been the nurse of childhood. To her all the cares and heart-griefs of youth have been intrusted. Thousands and tens of thousands in the West Indies and in our Southern States have risen up and told the tale of her tenderness, of her gentleness, patience, and affection. No other woman in the world has ever had such tributes to a high moral nature, sweet, gentle love, and unchanged devotedness. And by the memory of my own mother and dearest sisters I can declare it to be true!

Hear the tribute of Michelet: "The Negress, of all others, is the most loving, the most generating; and this, not only because of her youthful blood, but we must also admit, for the richness of her heart. She is loving among the loving, good among the good (ask the travelers whom she has so often saved). Goodness is creative, it is fruitfulness, it is the very benediction of a holy act. The fact that woman is so fruitful I attribute to her treasures of tenderness, to that ocean of goodness which permeates her heart. . . . Africa is a woman. Her races are feminine. . . . In many of the black tribes of Central Africa the women rule, and they are as intelligent as they are amiable and kind."[10]

The reference in Michelet to the generosity of the African women to travelers brings to mind the incident in Mungo Park's travels, where the African women fed, nourished, and saved him. The men had driven him away. They would not even allow him to feed with the cattle; and so, faint, weary, and despairing, he went to a remote hut and lay down on the earth to die. One woman, touched with compassion, came to him, brought him food and milk, and at once he revived. Then he tells us of the solace and the assiduities of these gentle creatures for his comfort. I give you his own words: "The rites of hospitality thus performed toward a stranger in distress, my worthy benefactress, pointing to the mat, and telling me that I might sleep there without apprehension, called to the female part of her family which had stood gazing on me all the while in fixed astonishment, to resume the task of spinning cotton, in which they continued to employ themselves a great part of the night. They lightened their labors by songs, one of which was composed extempore, for I was myself the subject of it. It was sung by one of the young women, the rest joining in a sort of chime. The air was sweet and plaintive, and the words, literally translated, were these: 'The winds roared and the rains fell; the poor white man, faint and weary, came and sat under our tree. He has no mother to bring him milk, no wife to grind his corn. Let us pity the white man, no mother has he,'"[11] etc., etc.

Perhaps I may be pardoned the intrusion, just here, of my own personal experience. During a residence of nigh twenty years in West Africa, I saw the beauty and felt the charm of the native female character. I saw the native woman in her *heathen* state, and was delighted to see, in numerous tribes, that extraordinary sweetness, gentleness, docility, modesty, and especially those maternal solicitudes which make every African boy both gallant and defender of his mother.

I saw her in her *civilized* state, in Sierra Leone; saw precisely the same characteristics, but heightened, dignified, refined, and sanctified by the training of the schools, the refinements of civilization, and the graces of Christian sentiment and feeling. Of all the memories of foreign travel there are none more delightful than those of the families and the female friends of Freetown.

A French traveler speaks with great admiration of the black ladies of Hayti. "In the towns," he says, "I met all the charms of civilized life. The graces of the ladies of Port-au-Prince will never be effaced from my recollections."[12]

It was, without doubt, the instant discernment of these fine and tender qualities which prompted the touching Sonnet of Wordsworth, written in 1802, on the occasion of the cruel exile of Negroes from France by the French Government:

"Driven from the soil of France, a female came
  From Calais with us, brilliant in array,
  A Negro woman like a lady gay,
Yet downcast as a woman fearing blame;
  Meek, destitute, as seemed, of hope or aim,
  She sat, from notice turning not away,
But on all proffered intercourse did lay
  A weight of languid speech—or at the same
Was silent, motionless in eye and face.
  Meanwhile those eyes retained their tropic fire,
  Which burning independent of the mind,
  Joined with the luster of her rich attire
To mock the outcast—O ye heavens be kind!
And feel thou earth for this afflicted race!"[13]

But I must remember that I am to speak not only of the neglects of the black woman, but also of her needs. And the consideration of her needs suggests the remedy which should be used for the uplifting of this woman from a state of brutality and degradation.

I have two or three plans to offer which, I feel assured, if faithfully used, will introduce widespread and ameliorating influences amid this large population.

(*a*) The *first* of these is specially adapted to the adult female population of the South, and is designed for immediate effect. I ask for the equipment and the mission of "sisterhoods" to the black women of the South. I wish to see large numbers of practical Christian women, women of intelligence and piety; women well trained in domestic economy; women who combine delicate sensibility and refinement with industrial acquaintance—scores of such women to go South; to enter every Southern State; to visit "Uncle Tom's Cabin;" to sit down with "Aunt Chloe"[14] and her daughters; to show and teach them the ways and habits of thrift, economy, neatness, and order; to gather them into "Mothers' Meetings" and sewing schools; and by both lectures and "talks" guide these women and their daughters into the modes and habits of clean and orderly housekeeping.

There is no other way, it seems to me, to bring about this domestic revolution.—We can not postpone this reformation to another generation. Postponement is the reproduction of the same evils in numberless daughters now coming up into life, imitators of the crude and untidy habits of their neglected mothers, and the perpetuation of plantation life to another generation. No, the effort must be made immediately, in *this* generation, with the rude, rough, neglected women of the times.

And it is to be done at their own homes, in their own huts. In this work all theories are useless. This is a practical need, and personal as practical. It is emphatically a personal work. It is to be done by example. The "Sister of Mercy," putting aside all fastidiousness, is to enter the humble and, perchance, repulsive cabin of her black sister, and gaining her confidence, is to lead her out of the crude, disordered, and miserable ways of her plantation life into neatness, cleanliness, thrift, and self-respect. In every community women could be found who would gladly welcome such gracious visitations and instructors, and seize with eagerness their lessons and teachings. Soon their neighbors would seek the visitations which had lifted up friends and kinsfolk from inferiority and wretchedness. And then, erelong, whole communities would crave the benediction of these inspiring sisterhoods, and thousands and tens of thousands would hail the advent of these missionaries in their humble cabins. And then the seed of a new and orderly life planted in a few huts and localities, it would soon spread abroad, through the principle of imitation, and erelong, like the Banyan-tree, the beneficent work would spread far and wide through large populations. Doubtless they would be received, first of all, with surprise, for neither they nor their mothers, for two hundred years, have known the solicitudes of the great and cultivated for their domestic comfort. But surprise would soon give way to joy and exultation. Mrs. Fanny Kemble Butler, in her work, "Journal of a Residence on a Georgian Plantation in 1838–39," tells us of the amazement of the wretched slave women on her husband's plantation when she went among them, and tried to improve their quarters and to raise them above squalor; and then of their immediate joy and gratitude.[15]

There is nothing original in the suggestion I make for the "Sisters of Mercy." It is no idealistic and impractical scheme I am proposing, no new-fangled notion that I put before you. The Roman Catholic Church has, for centuries, been employing the agency of women in the propagation of her faith and as dispensers of charity. The Protestants of Germany are noted for the effective labors of holy women, not only in the Fatherland but in some of the most successful missions among the heathen in modern times. The Church of England, in that remarkable revival which has lifted her up as by a tidal wave, from the dead passivity of the last century, to an apostolic zeal and fervor never before known in her history, has shown, as one of her main characteristics, the wonderful power of "Sisterhoods," not only in the conversion of reprobates, but in the reformation of whole districts of abandoned men and women. This agency has been one of the most effective instrumentalities in the hands of that special school of devoted men called "Ritualists."[16] Women of every class in that Church, many of humble birth, and as many more from the ranks of the noble, have left home and friends and the choicest circles of society, and given up their lives to the lowliest service of the poor and miserable. They have gone down into the very slums of her great cities, among thieves and murderers and harlots; amid filth and disease and pestilence; and for Christ's sake served and washed and nursed the most repulsive wretches; and then have willingly laid down and died, either exhausted by their labors or poisoned by infectious disease. Any one who will read the life of "Sister Dora" and of Charles Lowder,[17] will see the glorious illustrations of my suggestion. Why can not this be done for the black women of the South?

(b) My *second* suggestion is as follows, and it reaches over to the future. I am anxious for a permanent and uplifting civilization to be engrafted on the Negro race in this land. And this can only be secured through the womanhood of a race. If you want the civilization of a people to reach the very best elements of their being, and then, having reached them, there to abide as an indigenous principle, you must imbue the *womanhood* of that people with all its elements and qualities. Any movement which passes by the female sex is an ephemeral thing. Without them, no true nationality, patriotism, religion, cultivation, family life, or true social status is a possibility. In *this* matter it takes *two* to make one—mankind is a duality. The *male* may bring, as an exotic, a foreign graft, say of a civilization, to a new people. But what then? Can a graft live or thrive of itself? By no manner of means. It must get vitality from the *stock* into which it is put; and it is the women who give the sap to every human organization which thrives and flourishes on earth.

I plead, therefore, for the establishment of at least one large "INDUS-TRIAL SCHOOL" in every Southern State for the black girls of the South. I ask for the establishment of schools which may serve especially the *home* life of the rising womanhood of my race. I am not soliciting for these girls scholastic institutions, seminaries for the cultivation of elegance, conservatories of music, and schools of classical and artistic training. I want such schools and seminaries for the women of my race as much as any other race; and I am glad that there are such schools and colleges, and that scores of colored women are students within their walls.

But this higher style of culture is not what I am aiming after for *this* great need. I am seeking something humbler, more homelike and practical, in which the education of the hand and the use of the body shall be the specialties, and where the intellectual training will be the incident.

Let me state just here definitely what I want for the black girls of the South:

1. I want boarding-schools for the *industrial training* of one hundred and fifty or two hundred of the poorest girls, of the ages of twelve to eighteen years.

2. I wish the *intellectual* training to be limited to reading, writing, arithmetic, and geography.

3. I would have these girls taught to do accurately all domestic work, such as sweeping floors, dusting rooms, scrubbing, bed making, washing and ironing, sewing, mending, and knitting.

4. I would have the trades of dressmaking, millinery, straw-platting, tailoring for men, and such like, taught them.

5. The art of cooking should be made a specialty, and every girl should be instructed in it.

6. In connection with these schools, garden plats should be cultivated, and every girl should be required, daily, to spend at least an hour in learning the cultivation of small fruits, vegetables, and flowers.

I am satisfied that the expense of establishing such schools would be insignificant. As to their maintenance, there can be no doubt that, rightly managed, they would in a brief time be self-supporting. Each school would soon become a hive of industry, and a source of income. But the *good* they would do is the main consideration. Suppose that the time of a girl's schooling be limited to *three,* or perchance to *two* years. It is hardly possible to exaggerate either the personal family or society influence which would flow from these schools. Every class, yea, every girl in an outgoing class, would be a missionary of thrift, industry, common sense, and practicality. They would go forth, year by year, a leavening power into the houses, towns, and villages of the Southern black population; girls fit to be the thrifty wives of the honest peasantry of the South, the worthy matrons of their numerous households.

I am looking after the domestic training of the MASSES; for the raising up women meet to be helpers of *poor* men, the RANK AND FILE of black society, all through the rural districts of the South. The city people and the wealthy can seek more ambitious schools, and should pay for them.

Ladies and gentlemen, since the day of emancipation millions of dollars have been given by the generous Christian people of the North for the intellectual training of the black race in this land. Colleges and universities have been built in the South, and hundreds of youth have been gathered within their walls. The work of your own Church in this regard has been magnificent and unrivaled, and the results which have been attained have been grand and elevating to the entire Negro race in America. The complement to all this generous and ennobling effort is the elevation of the black woman. Up to this day and time your noble philanthropy has touched, for the most part, the male population of the South, giving them superiority, and stimulated them to higher aspirations. But a true civilization can only then be attained when the life of woman is reached, her whole being permeated by noble ideas, her fine taste enriched by culture, her tendencies to the beautiful gratified and developed, her singular and delicate nature lifted up to its full capacity; and then, when all these qualities are fully matured, cultivated, and sanctified, all their sacred influences shall circle around ten thousand firesides, and the cabins of the humblest freedmen shall become the homes of Christian refinement and of domestic elegance through the influence and the charm of the uplifted and cultivated black woman of the South!

# 7.

## *Excellence, an End of*
## *the Trained Intellect*

In "The Black Woman of the South," Crummell was concerned with a particular problem, namely the "home life" of the freedwomen. Whatever others
may have thought,[1] he was not against academic instruction for black women
and quite openly endorsed (black) female seminaries, conservatories, and
schools of classical and artistic training. Crummell's interest in the black
female intellect is made clear in this address, delivered to the graduating
class of the high school in Washington, D.C., on June 6, 1884.

YOUNG LADIES: Two nations of antiquity have often in your school life been
brought before you, distinguished respectively, the one for excellence
and the other for practicality. The Greeks stand for in human history pre-
eminently as the type of culture and refinement. The Romans, down to our
day, are the standard of the practical, the people who surpassed all others in
the expression of the principle of utility.

These two ideas may be taken as representing the two prime ends of
human training and education.

You are now on your passage from the High School to the broader field
and the more responsible duties of the Normal School. So well have you
acquitted yourselves in this lower plane of study that the officers of these
schools are glad to tender you the cordial invitation—"Come up higher!"
And so the doors of a higher Academy stand open before you, its accomplished Principal both anxious and ready to welcome you. And here you

will find the many facilities for gaining a wider acquaintance and a more advanced cultivation.

At just this stage of life it seems to me both fit and advisable, to call your attention to the fact, that excellence and utility are the special objects of your school life; and also to point out to you their relative place and importance.

I shall dwell but briefly upon the principle of utility, for the reason that it is not just now the immediate end of your training. There is a time for everything, and the wisdom of man in all ages has made *youth* the time of preparation as a means to a distant end.

If we wish to make our existence a full, complete, and rounded thing it becomes us to have everything in its own order. School life is first in order, a preparatory stage, which is both designed and fitted to reach over to active duty, by and by, in the relations of life. And although it is inevitable that we shall, please God we live, be busy workers in the trades, crafts, callings, service of human life, the very first thing for young people, is the proper moulding and fashioning of their nature and the training of their faculties, that they may gain such suppleness, force and endurance as may fit them for any and all the demands of duty and responsibility.

You will remember just here that utility, though somewhat crude and homely, compared with excellence, is the end and object of life. For doing duty, accomplishing work, applying knowledge to useful ends, carrying on enterprises in the world; all this is *the* work of life. And it is something wider, broader and higher than culture, grand, necessary and beautiful as culture is. For utility in life is that which *must* be, even if we have to dispense with culture. And hence we see that although excellence is more beautiful, and has indeed the primary place, yet utility is the grander, for it is the necessary, nay the absolute, object of our being. Excellence is a means, an instrument. Excellence is that which gives finish, majesty, glory and strength to life in all its relations. But men can live without it. Men *have* lived without it; nay men have lived mightily, masterly, yes, even prodigiously without it. The colossal empires of the ancient world wrought without it, and made grand contributions to the sum of human good. Human history would be incomplete without the annals of such barbaric States as Assyria, Babylon and Egypt in the old world and the Aztecs in this. So, too, great men, devoid of excellence, men uncivilized and rude, have done nobly the work of life and left behind them abiding influences and lasting results. Great would have been the loss to humanity if such men as Constantine and Charlemagne and Peter the Great, and Toussaint L'Ouverture had never lived.

And so you see that culture and refinement, although they be most valuable things, are not entirely indispensable to human achievement.

Nevertheless who will compare crude Babylon with the accomplished Greece? Who will put austere and unadorned Sparta beside polished Athens? Who will name El-Mahdi of the Soudan with Gladstone[2] or our George William Curtis?[3]

We cannot then reject utility. We cannot disregard the practical, for it contains the substance and reality of our life. Nevertheless we must extol, cherish and reach forth for excellence, not so much for itself, as for the facile use of powers it gives us in the duties of life; for the completeness which it bestows upon our being; for the skill it imparts to our faculties; for the finish, grace, and polish with which it will invest our life.

I have spoken in such general terms of excellence that perchance some may desire something more of definiteness concerning it. What, you demand, what do you mean by excellence?

Let me set before you the idea that fills my own mind in speaking of it. I mean by excellence that training by which the intellectual forces are harmoniously developed, and reason and imagination are given their rightful authority. I mean that discipline which enables one to command his own powers, and then to use them with ease and facility. I mean that style of education which puts us in the centre, and affords the soul the widest circumference of nature and humanity, of knowledge and letters. I mean that instruction which gives the faculties strength and skill, sharpness and dexterity, force and penetration. I mean that schooling which puts disdain within us for the gross and ignoble, and saturates our whole being with burning desires for things that are noble, lofty, and majestic.

The elements of this quality of excellence are *self-possession, exactness, facility, taste*.

I use the word *self-possession* more in its literal meaning than in the sense of usage. I mean by it that power which a true education gives one of holding, using, and managing his own faculties with a like facility with which a horseman uses his bridle, or a sailor the helm. Multitudes of well-learned people have neither the knowledge of their capacity nor command of their powers. Well freighted indeed with learning, they have never gained a clear acquaintance with their own forces nor of their fitness to definite ends. It is one of the highest of accomplishments for men to know their own inward resources; to know what they can do with those resources; to know just the way to do the work set before them; and to know how to do that work with skill and effect.

When I speak of *exactness* I refer to veraciousness. There is, it is true, no such thing as perfectness or infallibility of intellect. "Homerus dormit," says Horace.[4] Shakespeare committed the greatest of anachronisms. Milton was slipshod in both his Scripture and theology.[5] Even the accurate Macaulay made mistakes.[6] Nevertheless all true scholarship ends in truth, from the simple recital of the numeration table by a five-year-old youngster to the calculations of an Adams or a Leverier.[7] Accuracy and precision in your intellectual ventures are not only scholarly traits; they are virtues. They give assurance of character. Wherever they discover themselves people feel they can rely upon their possessors. It is not a matter of importance that you should remember everything, for that is an impossibility for both angel and man. But if you will determine to know a few things, and to know them thoroughly, down to the point of nicety and precision, you will do a most masterly thing for your intellect, and you will be made effective in influence upon the minds of men. You will do well, therefore, to learn at an early day the value of accuracy. If you work out a problem see that it is done strictly in accordance with rule. If you memorize a poem, give it precisely as it was written, taking no liberties with the text. If you make an historical reference quote from the most truthful history. Be sure of your numbers in giving statistics. Strive to be accurate in dates. If you are studying science see that you are grasping facts, and not rely upon speculation and fancy. Don't come forth at any time slatternly, with a torn gown and slippers down at heel. Be neat, tidy and thorough in all your intellectual duties.

Next in importance to accuracy comes *facility*. For, in this busy, stirring world where nobody waits for his neighbor, it is desirable that you should aim at a certain measure of quickness and celerity. Error moves with swift feet; and hence truth should never be lagging behind. She should always be first in the field. Cultivate, as much as possible, together with the habit of exactness, the other habit of promptness and speed. You *can* do it; any one can do it; for it depends not so much upon breadth and weight of intellect, as it does upon application and practice. Besides it is the nature of the mind to be alert in all its movements. The mind of man is instinctively, and by the laws of its being, a Pegasus. It is then a work *not* against, but most strictly in *accordance with* nature, to carry on our mental operations with zeal and alacrity. The lines of Cowper are simple ones, but true and significant:—

> "How swift is a glance of the mind!
>   Compared with the speed of its flight,
> The tempest itself lags behind
>   And the swift-winged arrows of light."[8]

And what Shakespeare says of the poet is true of every craft of the intellect:

> "The poet's eye, in a fine frenzy rolling,
>   Doth glance from heaven to earth, from earth to heaven."[9]

This is equally the case with the philosopher, the painter, the scholar, the sailor, the soldier, with *man* in all the estates of human life. Mind naturally is quick, rapid, lightning like in all its movements.

With self-possession and facility I join *taste* as another element in the quality of excellence. And by taste I mean that "exquisite sense," to use the words of Greville, "which instantly discovers and extracts the quintessence of every flower, and disregards all the rest of it."[10]

Taste is nothing more or less than a sensitive disdain of the rude and gross, and the deliberate and constant choice of grace and beauty, wherever they discover themselves. And this discovery is open to every one of us; but on the one condition, namely, that the mind itself is pure; for then its vision instinctively will fall upon the fair, the bright, and pleasing. Taste is the aptitude of the soul for fitness; its craving for the perfect; its desire for the beautiful. It is both a natural and a cultivated gift; and hence it is an acquisition within the reach of every sensitive and aspiring soul.

I beg, young ladies, to press upon you all, the opportunities to secure excellence now in this fit time, which is given you in the days of your school life. This time comes once, and never comes again. Amid the busy whirl of life you cannot turn aside to get it. You know we would all laugh at the soldier who should run from the thick of battle, to sharpen his sword. You can, indeed, do without the grace and finish of your powers; you can be rude, rough, unskilled women, yet be brave and good women too. But you can do better, everywhere in life, by the attainment of excellence. It is Blakie who says: "Beauty, which is the natural food of a healthy imagination, should be sought after by every one who wishes to achieve the great end of existence—that is to make the most of himself."[11]

Strive to make something of yourselves; and then strive to make *the most of yourselves*: not in selfishness; not for vain display in society or in the world; but for a grand reason which I will at once declare to you. It is this: Because you have great powers. I don't know the capacity of any one of you girls. I have never heard, from any quarter, your standing as scholars. But you are human beings; and therefore I can say, if even you were the humblest of our kind, that you have great powers. You are responsible both for your powers of mind, and responsible for the training of them.

Therefore I say cultivate your powers. Bring them under discipline. Give them strength. Try and get for them elasticity and promptitude. Set Truth—whether in fundamental ideas, great generic principles, or grand axioms—set truth, most distinctly before you, as the proper food of the mind. Use books, literature, science, as the instruments and agents of the intellect; mindful, however, that our inborn faculties are greater than all the facilities of culture. For "studies," as Lord Bacon says, serve mainly "to perfect nature."[12]

Join to this the remembrance that there is no essential divorce of the reason from the imagination; and while it is our duty to grasp everything solid and substantial for the intellect, yet

> "Beauty——a living presence of the Earth"——pervades the universe;
> "Waits upon our steps;
> Pitches her tents before us as we move
> An hourly neighbor——;"[13]

is one of the most glorious gifts of God to our nature:—— beauty as we see it at this glorious season, in clear skies, in trees, in flowers, in the emerald verdure of green fields, in laughing, running streams; beauty in art and culture and poetry; beauty deep in the human soul and in all its faculties; and that it is our privilege and rightful prerogative as immortal creatures to take it up wherever we find it, as our heritage and rightful prerogative, and to incorporate it with every element of our being; giving the glory and the adornment of it to every relation of life.

I congratulate you, young ladies, on your advancement to this stage of your studies. I beg to cheer and encourage you in the onward step you are about taking from this evening; and you have my warmest good wishes that superiority may attend you in this later period of your school life, and that in all after days grace, excellence and efficiency may be the fruits of your entire life.

# 8.

## *The Need of New Ideas and New Aims for a New Era*

Crummell's increasing concern with labor, morals, and the status of the black family found most coherent expression in this address, delivered to the graduating class of Storer College, Harpers Ferry, West Virginia, in May 1885. Here again, the emphasis was on the need to develop "character," but the address is also significant because in it Crummell articulated the need for an educated gentry, a notion that was central to his nationalistic vision of racial renaissance and reinvigoration. Equally telling is Crummell's insistence that blacks should guard against the "constant *recollection*" of slavery, advice rejected by Frederick Douglass, who was in the audience on this occasion.[1]

I TAKE it for granted that the young men and women who close their pupilage here to-day are thinking not only of their own personal life desires, but, also, of the destinies of the people with whom they are connected. In such a place as this, full of the most thrilling memories in the history of our race, it seems impossible that any of you could possibly pass over such thoughts. The very hills here seem breezy with the memories and the purposes of old John Brown. And so tragic and so august are those memories and purposes, so vivid, too, is the imagination of man, that there is danger not only that the youthful, but even the elder, mind should be carried back with constant and absorbing interest, especially in those memories and purposes.

But let me remind you here that, while indeed we do live in two worlds, the world of the past and the world of the future, DUTY lies in the future. It is in life as it is on the street: the sentinel DUTY, like the policeman, is ever bidding man "Pass on!" We can, indeed, get inspiration and instruction in the *yesterdays* of existence, but we cannot healthily live in them. We can send back sorrows and repentances to the past. We can, by the magic touch of Fancy, summon the tragedies and commedies of by-gone days; but the sense of obligation, the ideas of responsibility, all pertain to the time to come. It is on this account that I beg to call your attention to-day, to—"THE NEED OF NEW IDEAS AND NEW AIMS FOR A NEW ERA."

The subject divides itself in two heads:—

1st. The *need* suggested, and 2nd, the *aims for a new era,* which shall meet the need.

I choose this topic because it seems to me that there is an irresistible tendency in the Negro mind in this land to dwell morbidly and absorbingly upon the servile past. The urgent needs of the present, the fast-crowding and momentous interests of the future appear to be forgotten. Duty for to-day, hope for the morrow, are ideas which seem oblivious to even leading minds among us. I fear there is a general incapacity to reach forward to a position and the acquisitions which are in advance of our times. Enter the schools, and the theme which too generally occupies the youthful mind is some painful memory of servitude. Listen to the voices of the pulpit, and how large a portion of its utterances are pitched in the same doleful strain! Send a man to Congress, and observe how seldom possible it is for him to speak upon any other topic than slavery. We are fashioning our life too much after the conduct of the children of Israel. Long after the exodus from bondage, long after the destruction of Pharaoh and his host, they kept turning back, in memory and longings, after Egypt, when they should have kept both eye and aspiration bent toward the land of promise and of freedom.[2]

Now I know, my brethren, that all this is natural to man. God gave us judgement, fancy and memory, and we cannot free ourselves from the inherence of these or of any other faculty of our being. But the great poet tells us that "man is a being who looks before and after."[3] There is a capacity in human nature for prescience. We were made to live in the future as well as in the past. The qualities both of hope and imagination carry us to the regions which lie beyond us. But both hope and imagination are qualities which seem dismissed from the common mind among us; and many of our leaders of thought seem to settle down in the dismal swamps of dark and distressful memory.

And nothing can be more hurtful for any people than such a habit as this. For to dwell upon repulsive things, to hang upon that which is dark, direful, and saddening, tends, first of all, to morbidity and degeneracy. Accustom this race to constant reminiscence of its degradation and its sorrow, bring before your own minds or the minds of the rising generation, as a perpetual study and contemplation, the facts of servitude and inferiority, and its mind will, of necessity, be ever

"Sickled o'er with the pale caste of thought;"[4]

and there will be a constant tendency to

"Nurse the dreadful appetite of death!"[5]

And next to this comes the intellectual narrowness which results from a narrow groove of thought. For there are few things which tend so much to dwarf a people as the constant dwelling upon personal sorrows and interests, whether they be real or imaginary. We have illustrations of this fact both at home and abroad. The Southern people of this nation have given as evident signs of genius and talent as the people of the North.

If we go back to Colonial times, if we revert to the early history of the nation, we see in them, as conspicuous evidence of intellectual power, in law, in capability of government, in jurisprudence, in theology, in poetry, and in art, as among their more northern brethren. But for nigh three generations they gave themselves up to morbid and fanatical anxieties upon the subject of slavery. To that one single subject they gave the whole bent and sharpness of their intellect. And history records the direful result. For nigh sixty years have "laws and letters, art and learning,"[6] died away; and we can hardly discover the traces of any conspicuous genius or originality among them. So, too, the people of Ireland. For a century and more they have been indulging in the expensive luxury of sedition and revolution. As a portion of the great Celtic people of Europe, they are an historic race, alike in character and in genius. They are mercurial, poetic and martial, and in some of the lands of their heritage they have shown large powers for governmental control. But in Ireland, sterility has been a conspicuous feature of their intellectual life. The mind of the whole nation has been dwarfed and shriveled by morbid concentration upon an intense and frenzied sense of political wrong, and an equally intense and frenzied purpose of retaliation. And commerce, industry, and manufactures, letters and culture, have died away from them. And while, indeed, shrieking constantly for freedom, their idea of freedom has become such an impracticable and contemptuous thing that it has challenged the sneer of the poet, who terms it

"The school-boy heat,
The blind hysterics of the Celt."[7]

If men *will* put themselves in narrow and straightened grooves, if they will morbidly divorce themselves from large ideas and noble convictions, they are sure to bring distress, pettiness, and misery into their being; for the mind of man was made for things grand, exalted, and majestic.

For 200 years the misfortune of the black race has been the confinement of its mind in the pent-up prison of human bondage. The morbid, absorbing and abiding recollection of that condition—what is it but the continuance of that same condition, in memory and dark imagination? Dwell upon, reproduce, hold on to it with all its incidents, make its history the sum and acme of thought, and then, of a surety, you put up a bar to progress, and eventually produce that unique and fossilated state which is called "arrested development."[8] For it is impossible for a people to progress in the conditions of civilization whose thought and interest are swallowed up in morbid memories, or narrowed to the groove of a single idea or purpose. I am asked, perchance, would you have us as a people forget that we have been an oppressed race? I reply, that God gave us memory, and it is impossible to forget the slavery of our race. The memory of this fact may ofttimes serve as a stimulant to high endeavor. It may act, by contrast, as a suggestive of the best behests of freedom. We are *forced,* not seldom, to revert to our former servile state in defence of the race, against the unreasoning traducers who, not unfrequently, impute to us a *natural* inferiority, which is simply the result of that former servile state. What I would fain have you guard against is not the memory of slavery, but the constant *recollection* of it, as the commanding thought of a new people, who should be marching on to the broadest freedom of thought in a new and glorious present, and a still more magnificent future. You will notice here that there is a broad distinction between memory and recollection. Memory, you will observe, is a passive act of the mind. It is the necessary and unavoidable entrance, storage and recurrence of facts and ideas to the understanding and the consciousness.

*Recollection,* however, is the actual seeking of the facts, is the painstaking endeavor of the mind to bring them back again to consciousness. The natural recurrence of the idea or the fact of slavery is that which cannot be faulted. What I object to is the unnecessary recollection of it. This pernicious habit I protest against as most injurious and degrading. As slavery was a degrading thing, the constant recalling of it to the mind serves, by the law of association, to degradation. Words are vital things. They are always generative of life or death. They cannot enter the soul as passive and inoperative things. Archbishop Trench, referring to the brutal poverty of the language of the savage, says—"There is nothing that so effectually tends to keep him in the depth to which he has fallen. You cannot impart to any man more than the words which he understands either now contain, or can be made, intelligibly to him, to contain. Language is as truly on one side *the limit and restraint of thought,* as on the other side that which feeds and unfolds it."[9] My desire is that we should escape "the limit and restraint" of both the *word* and the *thought* of slavery. As a people, we have had an exodus from it. We have been permitted by a gracious Providence to enter the new and exalted pathways of freedom. The thought, the routine, the usages, and calculations of that old system are dead things; absolutely alien from the conditions in which life presents itself to us in our disenthralled and uplifted state. We have new conditions of life and new relations in society. The great facts of family, of civil life, of the Church, of the State, meet us at every turn; not lightly and as ephemeral things, but as permanent and abiding realities; as organic institutions, to be transmitted, in our blood to live, to the latest generations. From these relations spring majestic duties which come upon us

"With a weight—
Heavy as death, and deep almost as life."[10]

These changed circumstances bring to us an immense budget of new thoughts, new ideas, new projects, new purposes, new ambitions, of which our fathers never thought. We have hardly space in our brains for the old conditions of life. God "has called into existence a new world," to use the language of CANNING, "to redress the balance of the old."[11]

We have need, therefore, of new adjustments in life. The law of fitness comes up before us just now with tremendous power, and we are called upon, as a people, to change the currents of life, and to shift them into new and broader channels.

Says an old poet:—

"The noble soul by age grows lustier,
    Her appetite and her digestion mend;
We cannot hope to feed and pamper her
    With women's milk and pap unto the end!
    Provide you manlier diet!"[12]

I have thus attempted to show the need "of new ideas, new aims and new ambitions for the new era" on which we have entered.

2. And now, in the second place, allow me to make the attempt to suggest some of these new ideas which I think should be entertained by us.

Before passing to them, let me say that it is hardly possible to ignore one or two of the especial ambitions which now-a-days command wide attention in certain classes among us, and in which I fear we are making great mistakes. I do lament the political ambitions which seem the craze of very many young minds among us. Not, indeed, because I expect the continuance of that caste in politics, which is the extension of that social caste which is the disgrace of American society; but because I dislike always to witness a useless expenditure of forces. For, for a long time, the political ambitions of colored men are sure to end in emptiness. And, if so, men will waste energies and powers which might be expended profitably in other directions. I expect, I desire, and when the fitting time arrives, it will be ours to demand *all* the prerogatives and *all* the emoluments which belong to American citizenship, according to our fitness and our ability; and without let or hindrance, because of race or former condition. At the same time, I must remind you here that no new people leap suddenly and spontaneously into Senatorial chairs or Cabinet positions. So narrow have been the limitations of our culture, so brief, too, the period of our opportunity, that it is impossible, if even we had the highest genius, that we should mount the high rounds of the ladder of judicial or statesmanlike capacity. There is no such thing possible as intuitive apprehension of state-craft or the extemporaneous solution of the intricate problems of law. The road by which a people reach grand administrative ability is a long road, now full of deep ruts, and now formidable with its steep acclivities, jagged and rugged in all its pathways, and everywhere obstructed with thorns and briers.

The only means by which its formidable difficulties may be overcome are time, and arduous labor, and rugged endurance, and the quiet apprenticeship in humble duties, and patient waiting, and the clear demonstration of undoubted capacities. All these I am certain the black man of this country can eventually present as racial qualities. But it is well to remember that they are not the product of a day; that they cannot be made to spring up, gourd-like, in a night season. And hence, you will take no offense if I venture to say that you can leave, for a *little while* at least, all idea of being President of the United States, or even of being sent as Minister to the Court of St. James.

Equally skeptical am I as to the manifest desire which I see in many quarters for addiction to aesthetical culture as a special vocation of the race in this country. It is an aptitude, I acknowledge, constitutional to the race, and it cannot be ignored. After two hundred years' residence in the higher latitudes, we are still a tropical race; and the warmth of the central regions constantly discovers itself in voice and love of harmonies, both those which appeal to the eye by color, and those which affect the sensibilities through the ear. Such an aboriginal quality is not to be disregarded, and I do not disregard it. All I desire to say is that there is something higher in life than inclination, however indigenous it may be. Taste and elegance, albeit natural cravings, are always secondary to the things absolute and necessary.

There are circumstances constantly occurring wherein we are bound to ignore the strongest bent of nature and yield to the manifest currents of Providence. There are, moreover, primal duties in life, to which all other things must give way. Art and culture must yield to these needs. It is not necessary that we should debase our natural qualities. But style and beauty are secondary to duty and moral responsibility. Men cannot live on flowers. Society cannot be built up upon the strength which comes from rose-water. While I have the firmest conviction that the black race in this country will, eventually, take rank among the very highest in the several spheres of art, I am equally convinced that the great demand of *this* day is for the homely industries among us; that a premature addiction to it will be morally disastrous, that, as a people, we should be careful to avoid a useless expenditure of our strength and our resources.

What, then, are the special needs of this race? What are the grand necessities which call for the earliest recognition and solicitude?

We find our answer to these queries in the discovery of the deadliest breaches made in the character of our people. We all recognize the evident harm we have suffered in the times of servitude; and hence arises the duty of seeking reparation for them. But to this end we must single out the sorest calamities and the deadliest wounds these injuries have left behind.

Now I do not ignore the intellectual evils which have fallen upon us. Neither am I indifferent to the political disasters we are still suffering. But when I take a general survey of our race in the United States I cannot avoid the conclusion,

1st. That there are evils which lie deeper than intellectual neglect or political injury; and 2d, that to pass over the deeper maladies which destroy a man or a people, to attend to evils less virulent in their effects, shows the greatest unwisdom. "That the soul should be without knowledge is not good;"[13] but wide attention *is* given to the schooling and instruction of the black population of the land; and there need be no fear that the race can relapse into its former ignorance and benightedness. And next, with regard to political rights,—they are grand prerogatives, and to be highly prized. But do not forget that manhood has been reached even under great civil deprivations. Even in the times of the Caesars, St. Paul could exhort men in "the city of God"—"Quit ye like men, be strong!"[14] And the first Christians, under greater disabilities than ours, were the grandest of their kind.

The *three* special points of weakness in our race at this time are, I apprehend:—

1. THE STATUS OF THE FAMILY.
2. THE CONDITIONS OF LABOR.
3. THE ELEMENT OF MORALS.

It is my firm conviction that it is our duty to address ourselves more earnestly to the duties involved in these considerations than to any and all other considerations.

## 1st. THE STATUS OF THE FAMILY.

I shall not pause to detail the calamities which slavery has entailed upon our race in the domain of the family. Every one knows how it has pulled down every pillar and shattered every priceless fabric. But now we have begun the life of freedom, we should attempt the repair of this, the noblest of all the structures of human life. For the basis of all human progress and of all civilization is the family. Despoil the idea of family, assail rudely its elements, its framework and its essential principles, and nothing but degeneration and barbarism can come to any people. Just here, then, we have got to begin the work of reconstruction and up-building. Nothing, next to religion, can compare with the work which is to be done in this sphere. Placed beside this, all our political anxieties are but a triviality. For if you will think but for a moment all that is included in this word *family*, you will see at once that it is the root idea of all civility, of all the humanities, of all organized society. For, in this single word are included all the loves, the cares, the sympathies, the solicitudes of parents and wives and husbands; all the active industries, the prudent economies and the painful self-sacrifices of households; all the sweet memories, the gentle refinement, the pure speech and the godly anxieties of womanhood; all the endurance, the courage and the hardy toil of men; all the business capacity and the thrifty pertinacity of trades and artisanship and mechanism; and all the moral and physical contributions of multitudinous habitations to the formation of towns and communities and cities, for the formation of states, commonwealth, churches and empires. All these have their roots in the family. Alas! how widely have these traits and qualities been lost to our race in this land! How numerous are the households where they have never been known or recognized! How deficient in manifold quarters, even now, a clear conception of the grandeur of the idea of family! And yet this is the beginning of every people's true life. See where the forerunner of the Christian system aimed to plant the germs of the rising faith of Jesus—"And he shall turn the heart of the fathers to the children, and the heart of the children to the fathers."[15] For the beginning of all organized society is in the family! The school, the college, the professions, suffrage, civil office, are all valuable things; but what are they compared to the FAMILY?

Here, then, where we have suffered the greatest of our disasters, is a world-wide field for thought and interest, for intellectual anxieties and the most intelligent effort.

## 2d. The Conditions of Labor.

Turn to another and, in its material aspects, a kindred subject. I refer to the *industrial conditions* of the black race in this nation. No topic is exciting more interest and anxiety than the labor question. Almost an angry contest is going on upon the relations of capital to labor. Into this topic all the other kindred questions of wages, hours of labor, co-operation, distribution of wealth, all are dragged in, canvassed, philosophized upon in behalf of the labor element of the country. All the activity of the keenest intellects is employed in this regard; but *all,* I may say exclusively, for the *white* labor of this great nation.

And yet here is the fact, that this white labor is organized labor, it is intelligent labor, it is skilled labor, it is protected labor, protected in a majority of the States by legislative enactments. It is labor nourished, guarded, shielded, rooted in national institutions, propped up by the suffrage of the laboring population, and needs no extraordinary succors. And yet here is the fact, that this immense system of labor, with all its intelligence and its safeguards, is dissatisfied, querulous and complaining; and everywhere, and especially in the great centres of industry, agonistic and belligerent, because it is fretting under a deep sense of inequality, wrong, and injustice. But, my friends, just look at the *black* labor of this country, and consider its sad conditions, its disorganized and rude characteristics, its almost servile status, its insecure and defenseless abjectness.

What gives labor, in any land, dignity and healthiness? It is the qualities of skill and enlightenment. It is only by these qualities men can work in the best manner, with the least waste, for the largest remuneration, and with the most self-command. Where the laborer is crude, blind, uninformed and merely mechanical in his work, there he knows labor somewhat as an animal does; and he is led almost blindly to the same dull, animal-like endurance of toil, which is the characteristic of the beast of the field. His work, moreover, is not self-directed; for it has no inward spring. It is not the outcome of the knowing mind and the trained and cunning hand. It is labor directed by overseeing and commanding skill and knowledge. Multitudes in every land under the sun know labor precisely in the same way domestic animals do. They know the mere physical toil. They know the severest tasks. They know the iron routine of service. They know the soulless submission of drudgery. But, alas! they have never come to know the dignity of labor; never been permitted to share its golden values and its lofty requitals.

Now, if I do not make the very greatest of mistakes, *this* is the marked peculiarity of the black labor of this country. I am not unmindful of the fact that the black man *is* a laborer. I repel the imputation that the race, as a class, is lazy and slothful. I know, too, that, to a partial extent, the black man, in the Southern States, *is* a craftsman, especially in the cities. I am speaking now of aggregates. I am looking at the race in the mass; and I affirm that the sad peculiarity of our labor in this country is that our labor is rude, untutored, and debased. Let any man examine the diverse crafts of labor in the multitudinous businesses in which men are employed; the almost numberless trades; the heterogeneous callings and the multiform manufactures, which go to make up the industrial civilization of this vast nation; and then see the scores, nay, hundreds, of these careers from which the black man is purposely and inexorably excluded; and *then* you will take in the fact, that the black labor of this land is, of necessity, crude, unskilled, and disorganized labor. And remember here that I am speaking of no less than two millions of men, and women and children; for, to a large extent, black women and children are the laborers of the South, and still work in field and factory.

Join to this the thought of its sad conditions, its servile status and its defenceless abjectness. Here is the fact that tens of thousands of men and women of our race are toiling, have been toiling for years, for men who never think of paying them the worth and value of their toil,—men who systematically "keep back the hire of the laborer by fraud;" men who skillfully and ingeniously, at the close of every year, bring their ignorant laborers into debt to themselves; men who purposely close the portals of all hope, and "shut the gates of mercy"[16] upon the victims of their fraud, and so drive hundreds and thousands of our people into theft and reckless indifference, and many thousands more into despair and premature graves!

Here, then, is a great problem which is to be settled before this race can make the advance of a single step. Without the solution of this enormous question, neither individual nor family life can secure their proper conditions in this land. *Who* are the men who shall undertake the settlement of this momentous question? How are they to bring about the settlement of it? I answer, first of all, that the rising intelligence of this race, the educated, thinking, scholarly men, who come out of the schools trained and equipped by reading and culture; they are the men who are to handle this great subject. Who else can be expected to attempt it? Do you think that men of other races will encourage *our* cultivated men to parade themselves as mere carpet knights upon the stage of politics, or, in the saloons of aestheticism, and they, themselves, assume the added duty of the moral and material restoration of our race? Wherever has philanthropy shown itself thus overofficious and superserviceable? Never in the history of man has it either assumed superfluous cares or indulged a people in irresponsible diversions. The philanthropists of the times expect every people to bear somewhat the burdens of their own restoration and upbuilding; and rightly so. And *next,* as to the other question—How this problem of labor is to be settled? I reply, in all candor, that I am unable to answer so intricate a question. But this I do say, (1) that you have got to bring to the settlement of it all the brain-power, all the penetration, all the historical reading and all the generous devotedness of heart that you can command; and (2) that in the endeavor to settle this question that you are not to make the mistake, *i. e.,* that it is *external* forces which are chiefly to be brought to bear upon this enormity. No people can be lifted up by others to grand civility. The elevation of a people, their thorough civilization, comes chiefly from *internal* qualities. If there is no receptive and living quality *in* them which can be evoked for their elevation, then they must die! The emancipation of the black race in this land from the injustice and grinding tyranny of their labor servitude is to be effected mainly by the development of such personal qualities, such thrift, energy and manliness, as shall, in the first place, raise them above the dependence and the penury of their present vassalage, and next, shall bring forth such manliness and dignity in the race as may command the respect of their oppressors.

To bring about these results we need intelligent men and women, so filled with philanthropy that they will go down to the humblest conditions of their race, and carry to their lowly huts and cabins all the resources of science, all the suggestions of domestic, social and political economies, all the appliances of school, and industries, in order to raise and elevate the most abject and needy race on American soil. If the scholarly and enlightened colored men and women care not to devote themselves to these lowly but noble duties, to these humble but sacred conditions, what is the use of their schooling and enlightenment? Why, in the course of Providence, have they had their large advantages and their superior opportunities?

3. I bring to your notice one other requirement of the black race in this country, and that is *the need of a higher plane of morality.* I make no excuse for introducing so delicate and, perchance, so offensive a topic—a topic which necessarily implies a state of serious moral defectiveness. But if the system of slavery did not do us harm in every segment and section of our being, why have we for generations complained of it? And if it *did* do us moral as well as intellectual harm, why, when attempting by education to rectify the injury to the mental nature, should we neglect the reparation of the *moral* condition of the race? We have suffered, my brethren, in the whole domain of morals. We *are* still suffering as a people in this regard. Take the sanctity of marriage, the facility of divorce, the chastity of woman, the shame, modesty and bashfulness of girlhood, the abhorrence of illegitimacy; and there is no people in this land who, in these regards, have received such deadly thrusts as this race of ours. And these qualities are the grandest qualities of all superior people. You know, as well as I do, how these qualities are insisted upon in Holy Scripture, and there is no need of my referring to it. But some

of you here are scholars. You have moistened your lips with the honey of the classics. You have perchance, strengthened your powers with the robustness of Tacitus; and you may remember how he refers, in plaintive, melancholy tones, to the once virile power of Roman manhood, and the chaste beauty and excellence of its womanhood, and mourns their sad decline.[17] And, doubtless, you have felt the deepest interest in the simple but ingenious testimony he bears to the primitive virtues of the Germanic tribes, pagan though they were, and which have proven the historic basis of their eminence and unfailing grandeur. And these are lessons to us, by which we may be taught that the true grandeur of a people is not to be found in their civil status, in their political franchises, in armaments and navies, not even in letters and culture. More than one are the histories which may be found where people had all these; and then, even in the height of their renown, were standing on the brink, whence they were precipitated into ruin! Other histories, however, may be found in which we can see that people simple, untrained and unadorned have been robust and virtuous; have bred brave and truthful men and chaste and beauteous women; have carefully preserved the purity of their families, the simplicity of their manners and reverence for law. And these excellencies have not only shown "their wisdom and understanding in the sight of the nations,"[18] but have also made them immortal!

This moral elevation should be the highest ambition of our people. *They* make the greatest mistakes who tell you that money is the master need of our race. *They* equally err who would fain fasten your attention upon the acknowledged political difficulties which confront us in the lawless sections of the land. I acknowledge both of these grievances. But the one grand result of all my historic readings has brought to me this single and distinct conviction, that

"By the soul only the nations shall be free."[19]

If I do not greatly err, I have made it evident to-day that a mighty revolution is demanded in our race in this country. The whole status of our condition is to be transformed and elevated. The change which is demanded is a vaster deeper one than that of emancipation. *That* was a change of state or condition, valuable and important indeed, but affecting mainly the *outer* conditions of this people. And that is all a civil status can do, how beneficent soever it may be. But outward condition does not necessarily touch the springs of life. That requires other, nobler, more spiritual agencies. How true are the words of Coleridge:—

"I may not hope from outward things to win
  The passion and the life, whose fountains are within."[20]

What we need is a grand *moral* revolution which shall touch and vivify the inner life of a people, which shall give them dissatisfaction with ignoble motives and sensual desires, which shall bring to them a resurrection from inferior ideas and lowly ambitions; which shall shed illumination through all the chambers of their souls, which shall lift them up to lofty aspirations, which shall put them in the race for manly moral superiority.

A revolution of this kind is not a gift which can be handed over by one people, and placed as a new deposit, in the constitution of another. Nor is it an acquisition to be gained by storm, by excitement or frantic and convulsive agitation, political, religious or other.

The revolution I speak of is one which must find its primal elements in qualities, latent though they be, which reside *in* the people who need this revolution, and which can be drawn out of them, and thus secure form and reality.

The basis of this revolution must be character. *That* is the rock on which this whole race in America is to be built up. Our leaders and teachers are to address themselves to this main and master endeavor, viz., to free them from false ideas and injurious habits, to persuade them to the adoption of correct principles, to lift them up to superior modes of living, and so bring forth, as permanent factors in their life, the qualities of thrift, order, acquisitiveness, virtue and manliness.

And who are the agents to bring about this grand change in this race?

Remember, just here, that all effectual revolutions in a people must be racial in their characteristics. You can't take the essential qualities of one people and transfuse them into the blood of another people, and make them indigenous to them. The primal qualities of a family, a clan, a nation, a race are heritable qualities. They abide in their constitution. They are absolute and congenital things. They remain, notwithstanding the conditions and the changes of rudeness, slavery, civilization and enlightenment. The attempt to eliminate them will only serve to make a people factitious and unmanly. It is law of moral elevation that you must allow the constant abidance of the essential elements of a people's character.

And, therefore, when I put the query— *Who* are to be the agents to raise and elevate this people to a higher plane of being? the answer will at once flash upon your intelligence. It is to be affected by the scholars and philanthropists which come forth in these days from the schools. *They* are to be the scholars; for to transform, stimulate and uplift a people is a work of intelligence; it is a work which demands the clear induction of historic facts and their application to new circumstances,—a work which will require the most skillful resources and the wise practicality of superior men.

But these reformers must not be mere scholars. The intellect is to be used, but mainly as the vehicle of mind and spiritual aims. And hence, these men must needs be both scholars and philanthropists; the intellect rightly discerning the conditions, and the gracious and godly heart stimulating to the performance of the noblest duties for a people.

Allow me, in conclusion, to express the hope that, mingled with the sweet melodies of poetry, the inspiring voices of eloquence and the mystic tones of science, you will have an open ear to hear the voice of God, which is the call of duty. And may he who holds the hearts of all men give you the spirit to forget yourselves, and live for the good of man and the glory of God. Such a field and opportunity is graciously opened to you in the conditions and needs of our common race in this country. May you and I be equal to them!

# 9.

# *Common Sense in*
# *Common Schooling*

In "Common Sense in Common Schooling," preached at St. Luke's in September 1886, Crummell turned his attention to another aspect of the labor question, namely, the competing claims of higher education. Of course, Crummell was not opposed to higher education; on the contrary, he was quick to stress the need for a class of trained and superior men and women. The problem was "disproportion." Lamenting the tendency to indulge and overeducate black youth, Crummell advised parents to use higher education only in "fit and exceptional circumstances." A child of ordinary ability, he argued, should be taken from school and put to work.

> *That the soul should be without knowledge is not good.*
> *—Prov.9:12.*[1]

TO-MORROW morning we shall witness the reopening of the public schools and the beginning of another year's school session. As the training and instruction of our children is a matter of very great interest and importance, I am glad of the opportunity to say a few words upon the whole subject of Common-School education.

I need not pause to explain the special significance of the text. It is so plain and apparent that even the youngest can readily take it in, and you, who are their elders, have years ago become familiar with its point and power.

It has had during the last few years a special and peculiar influence upon *us* as a people. Rarely in the history of man has any people, "sitting in the region and shadow of death"[2]—a people almost literally enveloped in darkness— rarely, I say, has any such people risen up from their Egyptian darkness with such a craving for light as the black race in this country. It has been almost the repetition of the Homeric incident:—

> Dispel this gloom—the light of heaven restore—
> Give me to see, and Ajax asks no more.[3]

Almost universal ignorance was the mental condition of the race previous to emancipation. Out of millions of people, not more than 30,000 were allowed an acquaintance with letters. To-day, hundreds of schools are in existence, and over a million of our children are receiving the elements of common-school education.

The point of interest in this grand fact is that this intellectual receptivity was no tardy and reluctant faculty. Albeit an ignorant people, yet we did not need either to be goaded or even stimulated to intellectual desire. There was no need of any compulsory laws to force our children into the schools. No; the mental appetite of the Negro was like the resurrection of nature in the spring-time of the far northern regions. To-day, universal congelation and death prevail. Tomorrow, the icy bands of winter are broken and there is a sudden upheaval of dead, stolid rivers. The living waters rush from their silent beds and sweep away formidable barriers, and spread abroad over wide and extensive plains.

This craving of the appetite for letters and knowledge knows no abatement. Everywhere throughout the nation there still abides this singular and burning aptitude of the black race for schools and learning.

I am proud of this vast and ardent desire of the race; for the brain of man is the very first instrument of human achievement. Given, a cultivated and elastic brain, and you have the possibility of a man, and, with other qualifications and conditions, the probability of almost a demi-god. Take away the trained and cultivated intellect, and you get the likelihood of an animal, and, possibly, of a reptile.

But while I rejoice in the wide spread of lettered acquaintance among us, I cannot close my eyes to a great evil which has been simultaneous with the increase of our knowledge. This evil is becoming so alarming that I feel it a duty to call the attention of both parents and children to it. The evil itself I call Disproportion! It is that which we mean when we have an excess of somewhat that is pleasing, with a loss of what is convenient and substantial. We are all apt then to say that it is *"too much of a good thing."* The like one-sidedness discovers itself among us in our common-school education. Too many of our parents are ruining their children by this error.

They crave an excess of one kind of education, and at the same time neglect important elements of another and quite as important a kind. This sad fact suggests as a theme for consideration to-day "COMMON SENSE IN COMMON SCHOOLING." The subject presents itself in the two topics, *i. e.,* the *excess* and the *defect* in the training of our youth.

(1) Education as a system in our day divides itself into two sections, which are called, respectively, the higher and the lower. The former pertains to classical learning, *i. e.,* Latin and Greek, Science, and Art, in which latter are included music, drawing, and painting. It is with regard to the higher education that I feel called upon to express my fears and to give my counsel.

I fear we are overdoing this matter of higher learning. Everywhere I go throughout the country I discover two or three very disagreeable and unhealthy facts. I see, *first* of all, (*a*) the vain ambition of very many mothers to over-educate their daughters, and to give them training and culture unfitted for their position in society and unadapted to their prospects in life. I see, likewise, too many men, forgetful of the occupations they held in society, anxious to shoot their sons suddenly, regardless of fitness, into literary characters and into professional life. This is the first evil. (*b*) Next to this I have observed an ambition among the youth of both sexes for aesthetical culture; an inordinate desire for the ornamental and elegant in education to the neglect of the solid and practical. And (*c*), thirdly, to a very large extent school children are educated in letters to a neglect of household industry. Scores of both boys and girls go to school. That is their life business and nothing else; but their parents neglect their training in housework, and so they live in the streets, and during the first twelve or fourteen years of their life are given to play and pleasure. And (*d*), lastly, our boys and girls almost universally grow up without trades, looking forward, if they do look forward, many of them, to being servants and waiters; and many more, I am afraid, expecting to get a living by chance and hap-hazard.

Doubtless some of you will say that the colored people are not the only people at fault in these respects; that the American people, in general, are running wild about the higher culture—are neglecting trades and mechanism, and are leaving the more practical and laborious duties of life to foreigners. Grant that this is the case; but it only serves to strengthen the allegation I make that we, in common with American people, are running into an excessive ambition for the higher culture to the neglect of industrial arts and duties. I go into families. I ask parents what they are preparing their children for, and the answer I frequently receive is: "Oh, I am going to send my son to college to make him a lawyer, or the daughter is to go to the East or to Europe to be made an accomplished lady." Not long ago I met an old acquaintance, and, while talking about the future of her children, I inquired: "What are you going to do with—I will call him 'Tom?'" Tom is a little fellow about fourteen years old; by no means a genius; more anxious about tops and taffy and cigarettes than about his books; never likely, so far as I can see, to set the Potomac on fire. Her answer was that his father proposed sending him to college to make him a lawyer. On another occasion I was talking to a minister of the Gospel about his daughters, and *he* was anxious to send his two girls to Belgium to be educated for society! Not long ago an acquaintance of mine told me that his sons should never do the work he was doing. He was going to educate one to be a doctor, another to be a lawyer, and the third he hoped to make a minister. I must give him the credit that when I had pointed out the danger of ruining his sons by this over-education, and that this sudden rise from a humble condition might turn them into lazy and profligate spendthrifts, he listened to me, and I am glad to say he took my advice. He is now giving them his own trade, and I think they are likely to become quiet and industrious young men.

Let me not be misunderstood. I am not only *not* opposed to the higher culture, but I am exceedingly anxious for it. We *must* have a class of trained and superior men and women. We *must* have cultured, refined society. To live on a dead level of inferiority, or to be satisfied with the plane of uniform mediocrity, would be death to us as a people.

Moreover we need, and in our blood, the great molders and fashioners of thought among us. To delegate the thinking of the race to any other people would be to introduce intellectual stagnation in the race; and when thought declines then a people are sure to fall and fade away.

These, then, are the most sufficient reasons for a large introduction among us of the highest training and culture. But this is no reason or excuse for disproportion or extravagance. Culture *is* a great need; but the greater, wider need of the race is industry and practicality. We need especially multitudinous artizans, and productive toil, and the grand realizations of labor, or otherwise we can never get respect or power in the land.

And this leads me next to the other topic viz., the employments and occupations of industrial life. Here we encounter one of the most formidable difficulties of our civil life in this country. The state of things in this regard is an outrage upon humanity! And I protest, with all my might, against the mandate of the "Trades' Unions," which declare "You black people must be content with servant life!" I say that this race of ours should demand the right to enter every avenue of enterprise and activity white men enter. They should cry out, too, against our exclusion from any of the trades and businesses of life. But with all this remember that no people can *all*, or even many of them, become lawyers, doctors, ministers, teachers, scholars! No people can get their living and build themselves up by refined style and glittering fashion or indulgence in bellelettres.

No people can live off of flowers, nor gain strength and robustness by devotion to art.

And it is just this false and artificial tendency which is ruining colored society almost everywhere in the United States. It is especially so in the large cities. The youth want to go to school until they are nineteen or twenty years of age. Meanwhile, the book-idea so predominates that duty and industry are thrown into the shade. Mothers and fathers work hard to sustain their children. After awhile the children look with contempt upon their unlettered, hard-handed parents, and regard them as only born for use and slavish toil. Is this an exaggeration? Have you not seen some of those fine young ladies, whose mothers sweat and toil for them in the wash-tub or cook in the kitchen, boasting that they can't hem a pocket handkerchief or cook a potato? Have not you seen some of these grand gentlemen who forget the humble parents who begot them, forget the humble employments of those parents, turn up their noses at the ordinary occupations of the poor race they belong to, and then begin the fantastic airs of millionaires, while they don't own ground enough to bury themselves in?

You say, perchance, "Such girls and boys are 'sillies,'" and that their brainless folly is no reason why the higher education should not be given in all the schools. It is just here I beg to differ with you. I maintain that parents should exercise discrimination in this matter. They have no right to waste time and expense upon incapable girls and boys. They have no right to raise up a whole regiment of pretentious and lazy fools to plague society and to ruin themselves. They have no right to send out into the world a lot of young men and women with heads crammed with Latin, Greek, and literature; with no heart to labor; with hands of baby softness; interested only in idleness, and given to profligacy and ruinous pleasure. And just this, in numerous cases, is the result of this ambitious system of education in this land. We are turning out annually from the public schools a host of fine scholars, but not a few of them lazy, inflated, senseless, sensual! Whole shoals of girls bating labor, slattern in habits, and at the same time bespangled with frippery, devoted to dress, and the easy prey of profligate men! And lots of young men utterly indifferent to the fortunes of their families and the interests of their race; not thoughtless and heedless, like foolish girls, but scores of them thoroughly unprincipled and profligate!

They live for to-day, but the life they live is for sensual delight, and the culture they have gained is spent in skillful devices to administer to the lusts of the flesh. This I am constrained to say is the result of the higher education in well nigh half of the colored youth who graduate from high schools and colleges, and it is ruinous to our people.

You ask me the remedy of this great evil. My answer is by avoidance of the excess which I have pointed out and the adoption of the ordinary common-school education. Shun disproportion. Hold on to the higher education, but use it only in fit and exceptional cases. If you have a son or a daughter burning with the desire for learning, give that child every possible opportunity. But you see the condition I present, viz., that it *burns* with intellectual desire. But how often is this the case? The difficulty in the matter is that parents themselves are to blame for the miscarriage of their children's education. Everybody now-a-days is crazy about education. Fathers and mothers are anxious that their children should shine. However ordinary a boy or girl may be, the parents want them to be scholars. The boy may be a numbskull, the girl a noodle. The fond parent thinks the child a prodigy; stimulates its ambition, gives it indulgence, saves it from labor, keeps it at school almost to its majority, and then, at last, it finds out that the child has no special talent, dislikes labor, is eager for pleasure, dress, and display, is selfish and cruel to its parents, unable to earn its own living, and expects father and mother to drudge for its support and vanity. I am sure that you all know numerous cases of such failure and ruin.

And it all comes from a neglect of a few plain common-sense rules which belong naturally to the subject of education.

Let me briefly set before you some of these rules:

First of all, secure for your children an acquaintance with reading, writing, arithmetic, and geography. When well grounded in these studies, which is ordinarily at 12 or 13, then ascertain whether your children are fitted for the higher branches. If you yourself are educated, form your own judgement; if not, get the advice of a well-qualified friend, or the opinion of your minister, or take counsel of the child's schoolmaster. If convinced that the child gives promise of superiority, keep it at school, give it the best opportunities, and labor hard to make your child a thorough scholar.

(2) On the other hand, if you find your child has but ordinary capacity, take it from school and put it at an early day to work. If you don't you will not only waste time but you are likely to raise up a miserable dolt or a lazy dandy. Such a child, brought up to fruitless inactivity, dawdling for years over unappreciated culture, will, likely as not, never want to work for his living, may turn out a gambler or a thief, and in the end may disgrace your name or break your heart. Don't keep your children too long at school; don't think too much about the book and so little about labor. Remember that the end of all true education is to learn to do duty in life and to secure an honorable support and sustenance.

And here (3) let me press upon you the importance of training your children in industrial habits *at home* during the period of their school life. Going to school should never prevent a girl from learning to sew, to cook, to sweep, bed-making, and scrubbing the floor; nor a boy from using a hammer, cleaning the yard, bringing in coal, doing errands, working hard to help his mother, or to assist his father. Home work, moreover, is the natural antidote to the mental strain, and ofttimes the physical decline which, in these days, comes from the excess of study, which is the abnormal feature of the present school system.

From labor health, from health contentment flows.[4]

If you begin your child's school life by the separation of books and learning from manual labor, then you begin his education with poison as the very first portion of his intelligent life! He had better a deal be ignorant and industrious than lettered and slothful, and, perchance, a beggar! Laziness and learning are as incongruous as a "jewel in a swine's snout,"[5] and few things are so demoralizing to the young. Witness the large numbers of lettered youth and young men, fresh from schools, academies, and colleges, who fill the jails and prisons of the country, and then think of the large and more skillful numbers outside who ought, in justice, to be companying with those *within*. Nothing is more contemptible than the crowds of these dandaical "Clothes-bags,"—for they deserve no better title, one sees in our large cities, who have, indeed, the varnish of the schools and literature, but who lack common sense, full of vanity and pretense, poisoned with lust and whisky, and, while too proud and too lazy to work, get their living by vice and gambling. This abuse of learning, however, is not confined to men. Alas! that it must be acknowledged, we have all over the land scores of cultured young women in whose eyes labor is a disgrace and degradation, who live lives of lazy cunning or deception, or plunge determinedly into lust and harlotry. And the poor old fathers and mothers who toiled so painfully for their schooling, and hoped such great things for their daughters, have been cast down to misery and despair, or else have died broken-hearted over their daughters' shame and ruin. And in every such case how sad the reflection: "O, that I had been wise with my child! O, that I had scouted her false notions about style and elegance! O, that I had been more anxious to make her industrious and virtuous! Then all this anguish and distress would never have fallen upon me!" Such cases of folly have their lessons for all of us who are parents. May Almighty God make us both wise in our generation, and prudent and discreet with our children.

The words I have spoken this day have sprung from two or three deep convictions which I am sure are thoroughly scriptural and true, and which, I think, may rightly close this discourse:

1. The first of these is that children are neither toys nor playthings, such as are embroidery and jewels and trinkets. They are moral and spiritual beings,

endowed with conscience and crowned with the principle of immortality. You may toy and play with your trinkets, but you are accountable to God for the soul, the life, the character, and the conduct of your child. Hence duty and responsibility are the two paramount considerations which are to be allied with the entire training of your children, whether at home or in their school life.

2. Children are trusts for the good and health of society and the commonwealth. The law don't allow you to poison the air with filth and garbage, and for the simple reason that as a householder you are a trustee for your fellow-creatures. But in the regards of your children you are, in a far higher sense, a trustee for your fellow-creatures around you. What right have you to send forth from your threshold a senseless fool, full of learning it may be, but with no sense, no idea of responsibility for anybody, impudent to old people, a rowdy in God's Church, a rioter, a gambler, a rake? Ought not the culture you have toiled to give him serve to make him modest, a mild-mannered man, a stay to his humble toilsome parents, a useful man in society, a thrifty and productive citizen in the community? And was it not your duty, all his life long, to strive to realize such a large and high-souled being as the fruit of your family life and training?

Or, perchance it is a girl, what right have you to send forth into the world a lazy, impertinent creature, bedecked and bejeweled indeed; full, perchance, of letters and accomplishments, but with no womanly shame; brazen with boldness; lazy as a sloth, and, yet, proud, pretentious, crazy for ruinous delights; swept away by animal desires; alien from domestic duties, and devoted to pleasure? Go to, now. Is this the fruit of your vineyard? When God and man, too, look that it should bring forth grapes, will you only thrust upon us such wild grapes?[6]

You have no such right! You are a trustee for society, and you should take a pride in rearing up ornaments for society—"Sons," as the psalmist describes them, "who may grow up as the young plants;" "daughters, as the polished corners of the temple."[7] Just such, I am proud to say, as I see in many of your own families in this church, whose children are intelligent, scholarly, and, at the same time, virtuous, modest, obedient, and industrious. God's holy name be praised for such children, such parents, such godly families! May God, for Jesus' sake, multiply them a hundred fold in all our communities!

3. Join to this, thirdly, the most solemn of all considerations, *i. e.,* that your children are the servants of the most high God. "All souls are mine,"[8] says the Almighty. God made them and sent them into the world. He it is who places living souls in the family, in human society, in the nation, in the church, for His own honor and glory. Not for mere pastime, for trifling, or for pleasure are human beings put amid the relations of life. We are all God's

property— our children and ourselves—for God's service and His praise. Beloved, accept this grand prerogative of your human existence; train your children for godly uses in this world; train their minds by proper schooling; their bodies by industry; their immortal souls by teaching, catechising, and family devotion, so that they may glorify God in their bodies and their spirits; and then God will give you family order and success in this world; your children honor and blessing by the Holy Ghost; and everlasting light shall be the inheritance of your seed, and your seeds' seed from generation to generation on earth; and glory, honor, and peace, at the last, in the Kingdom of Heaven above!

## 10.

---

## Right-Mindedness: An Address before the Garnet Lyceum, of Lincoln University

Crummell's faith in the ideas of race and intellect was made abundantly clear in this address, delivered to the Garnet Lyceum of Lincoln University, c.1886. Adopting an elevated and self-consciously learned tone, Crummell attacked what he described as the "aesthetical" tendency evident among cultivated African-Americans—a love of the beautiful, elegant, and ornamental—and called for greater mental vigor. It was not aesthetics that the race and its leaders needed but "tenacity," "endurance," and "persistence," qualities associated with intellectual strength and discipline.

GENTLEMEN: It gives me no little pleasure to come to this school of learning, and to see such a number of young men assembled here for the purposes of study. For I presume that the main and most inspiring impulse which has drawn you hither from so many quarters, has been your personal desire for knowledge. Not, I judge, from the impulses of pride, not from the stimulus of mere ambition, but, as I have every reason to believe, from that enthusiasm for letters which is a characteristic of your period of life; and, from strong devotion to your race, have you been brought to these halls and placed yourselves under these masters. And most fortunate do I regard it for any young men who find the current of their sensibility running in the stream of thought or imagination, or noble purpose.

Temporal and transitory regards sweep away the thousands. With multitudes, your period of life is one of mere passion. But how felicitous is *their* lot whose being is inspired by promptings which spring from the intellect!

Happy the youth, I say, whose minds are inflamed by all the glowing aspirations which are excited by Poetry, Eloquence, History, and Scholarship! Happy the youth who prefer the simplest sip from the fount of intellectual delight, to the largest draughts of passion. The tiniest rill of literature is preferable to the broadest, strongest stream of delight and voluptuousness.

But even at the risk of seeming paradox, I wish to suggest to you, who are now, at the beginning of a scholar's life, that you have a long course to run; that on that course albeit you may find many a beauteous blossom, many a gorgeous flower, yet on the other hand, you will surely encounter many a rugged hill, and meet multitudinous thorns and briers. And therefore you will, at the start of life, make a serious, if not a fatal mistake if you suppose that the passionate desire, of even a literary nature, will remain a constant and abiding stimulus. I have not a word to say in disparagement of the enthusiasm of letters. I have already commended it. Nay more,—I would say to every one of you, hold on, as long as you can, to every stimulating impulse of your intellectual being; fan the flames of your mental desire as long as a single spark remains, vital and aglow. For all the passions of your nature have their place, and serve legitimate ends. But at the same time bear well in memory that zeal and enthusiasm are not primary qualities; that their functions are only secondary in the work of life; and that in their very nature, they are but transitory and ephemeral in their force and influence. At times when their importance is exaggerated; or when we are carried along impulsively, under their spell; we find on our recovery, how delusive is their nature; and that if allowed full mastery over us—"They serve to bewilder and dazzle to blind."[1] Gentlemen, all the great things in life come from a deeper source than the passions or sensibilities. When we seek physical growth, we turn to the muscle and fibre of our bodies, and try to feed and develope both. When we aim at moral strength we seek a basis in the most solid and abiding region of our nature. Even so it is with the intellectual life. Your aim I apprehend is the upbuilding of your mental faculties. You desire especially to strengthen and invigorate the endowments of mind which God has given you; for the specific value of such faculties, as also for the advantages which the processes of training may afford you. With these convictions of your purposed life, it is possible that I may somewhat serve you, to-day, if I attempt to point out the great truth that you can't depend upon mere impulse for these grand ends. Besides enthusiasm you need other higher qualities. To one of these I wish to call your attention to-day. I refer to that grasp upon one's intellectual powers which gives men facility and command in the spheres of life. I venture to call it "Right-mindedness." As there are conditions of our physical powers, which fit us for large activities and which we call health; as there is such a thing in the moral life, as rectitude, so we may assume that there is such a thing as the rectitude and integrity of our intellectual faculties, and which I may call RIGHT-MINDEDNESS. How may we attain it?

First of all, then, I would suggest that you accustom yourselves to fall back upon the mind itself as a main instrument and agency to the end desired.

Many are disposed to seek the aids and facilities for mental growth in objects external to themselves. In our day, especially, lectures, magazines, the newspapers, and books, are the common reliance of most intelligent people. Perhaps it is no exaggeration to say that the vast majority of persons who have a reputation for sense and acquaintance have thrown their minds implicitly upon authority. We see this dependence more especially in the use of books. It is a very rare thing to find persons whose master convictions have been evolved out of their own inward experience, or from the anxious struggles of their own minds. Most of the ideas we find afloat in society, come from the printed pages of some noted and sometimes *inferior* authors. What with the mere delight of reading: with the stores of information they bring us; with the facial facilities of memory; what wonder that the mind, almost imperceptibly to itself, strives to avoid the strain and tug of its own muscle; and to rest content in the flimsiest self-satisfaction, and in effortless repose! What wonder then if the tendency becomes an abiding one to run away to this seeming fountain of excellence, to that deposit of fancied wealth; instead, first of all, falling back upon, and looking deeply (to use the lines of Wordsworth,)

> "Into our minds, into the mind of men
> Our haunt and the main region of my song."[2]

It is not a legitimate inference from this that we are to repudiate these various means of culture, and give up the use of books. The proper conclusion would seem to be that, in the training of the intellect, we should put things in their proper order. The natural, manifestly is the first in order. Our own forces were antecedent to all the supplementary agencies of culture.

The inference, without doubt, is that while we use all available facilities for our mental upbuilding, it is the part of wisdom to depend chiefly, upon the natural powers with which we are gifted.

It is for these reasons, if I do not err, that mental science ranks so high in the schools: especially because it helps to set before us the anatomy of our intellectual being; and aids us, by introspection, to a view of the whole apparatus of our faculties. Some way or other we must secure this knowledge; or, otherwise, there is no possibility of effectiveness in the work of life. You know that in the handicraft of society, the very first step to efficiency is the conscious possession of powers. Not a trade can be plied without this; not a business be carried on. If you wish to make a carpenter, or a blacksmith, out of your apprentice, he must, first of all, be aware of having hands; and *then,* of their capacity; of their adaptedness to specific ends; and then get a knowledge of his tools, and of their uses. It is precisely so with regard to that other higher craft of the brain, to which, as students, you are more especially called. In this vocation one prime endeavour must be to know yourselves; know your faculties; know their quality; know their functions. Brains, is the first knowledge; brains as a power, and instrument; *before* books.

This is the starting point of all intellectual enterprise. You must know your grandest implement. "It is in me and it shall come out" was the cry of Sheridan,[3] after a miserable failure in the House of Commons. Here was that possession and consciousness of power which, was a real thing within him; and which is the very beginning of all successful endeavour. It is hardly possible to overvalue this conviction and assurance. Observation of the widest kind *is* a necessity. The grasp of every sort of knowledge is desirable. Learning and erudition are grand appliances: but neither science however profound, nor learning however accurate, nor erudition however deep; nor observation however wide can suffice for that inward spirit of intelligence which at once vitalizes, measures, and interprets all the facts and realities which come to the consciousness of man.

These other acquisitions have their uses; but I apprehend that the force and impress of men in this world come from the direct energy of their own native powers; and that all real success in life springs from that inward might which we exert upon society. They may have had learning; but this has been the aliment on which they have fed for the nourishment of inward powers; the agents they have used to strengthen living faculties. It is personal force which tells; it is the man himself who is felt in every real work which is undertaken in this world; not only in the spheres which are purely intellectual; but also in those too which meet the sense; whether it is building a Church, or, erecting a fort; or, uprearing, solidly and enduringly a colossal dock. Men do indeed need the advantages of culture in all the vocations of life; but your master need is yourself; the consciousness, *not* overconsciousness of your own powers and capacity; the thorough apprehension that you are able to gauge the work before you; and that your forces are superior to the accidents which hang around them. And this quality of intellectual selfhood, is to be mingled with all your work, and should be its main characteristic.

It is this personal element which differences the abiding things from the merely factitious and ephemeral. When you examine the lives and works of the great men whose names shine upon the historic page this characteristic is observable. We may divide these names into two classes, *i. e., (a)* the names of men not so much distinguished for learning, as for intellectual might; and then *(b)* a large class, brilliant, as well, for the richness and the vastness of their acquirements, and the glow of their refinement. Such men as Homer, Socrates, and Plato, stand most pre-eminent among the former. The age in which they lived shut them off from the almost boundless realm of letters which printing in our day yields even to excess. It is evident nevertheless that their names rank as high as any of the grand thinkers in more modern times. Everywhere in literature, among statesmen, philosophers, orators, scientific men and poets, we see their influence, impress, and power. Everywhere they are spoken of as authority; they tower above ordinary men, as kings.

And yet their one main characteristic is that strong personal element, which permeates everything they wrote. When we read, for instance, the Dialogues of Plato, or the History of Tactitus,[4] or the grand Poems of Homer, we are struck with the freshness and power in them. We feel the force of great original might. It is somewhat as though some strong personal force was acting upon our inward nature, a force which we could not possibly resist, and which indeed we would be loath to escape, or, in any way to separate from us.

Then, next, when we turn to the very eminent men whose rich, original genius is everywhere made resplendent by the opulence of their learning, and studded with the pearls and diamonds of the grandest scholarship; when we look, I say, upon *their* brilliant pages; that which more especially shows the brilliancy of letters, shows still more that force of inward might to which I have been referring.

In reading, for instance, the works of great modern literatures, poets, scholars, critics, orators; such men as Dante,[5] Milton, Southey,[6] Coleridge or Ruskin,[7] or, Burke;[8] the largess of scholarly wealth, the prodigality of learning is as much a surprise as a delight. But far more surprising is the SPIRIT of such writers. Their works seem a revelation of their very soul-life. And indeed all the great and lasting works of men get their characteristic, not so much from learning; but from the element of individuality which permeates them. Learning and culture are great factors; but personal power is *the* force which gives reputation and authority.

2. Another great auxiliary to the integrity of your intellectual being is DISCIPLINE. It is, moreover a corrective to all mere impulse or spontaneity. You will find it also a grand instrumentality to both self-mastery and all effectual endeavour.

"I keep under my body," says Saint Paul.[9] By this, doubtless the Apostle meant, that as a helmsman stands at the wheel, and holds under his mastery, the bulky vessel beneath his feet, with all her prodigious freight and cargo;—turning her, with ease, whithersoever he wishes; so he kept his body, with its appetites and passions under command. The like authority is possible, and is a necessity over our intellectual faculties.

The true scholar should endeavour to get the same control of his mental endowments, which a well-organized and highly-trained man has over his body. For our minds are instruments as well as our physical members. The intellect is not the man. Back of all our faculties, physical, mental and moral, resides one great commanding, central quality, man's personality; which regulates and uses all the powers of our nature, whether inward or outward, for its own ends.

"My mind to me a kingdom is,"[10]

is the line of a well known poem, but the man himself is the sovereign in that kingdom. One great purpose of the training of educational institutions, is to give us this sway over our powers. And that training is the best which is at once so facial and effectual that it puts us in possession of our several capacities. The process by which this is effected is termed—discipline.

This discipline may be regarded in two aspects. First, in the light of control and subjection of our will.

And doubtless you have observed men of ordinary capacity, as well as those endowed with extraordinary gifts, who held their faculties under their control; who possessed themselves, and were not possessed by any of their powers. On the other hand, we have all seen, at times, even geniuses who were deficient in this attainment. The result in their respective cases has been as marked, as the broad contrast between their abilities. Your clever maladroit, undisciplined genius, most commonly proves a failure, albeit, richly freighted with endowments. On the other hand, your ordinary character, well trained and regulated, plods on with system, to superiority, perchance to eminence. The difference arises from the fact that the one man, largely gifted, lacked the mastery of his powers; the other, with but moderate forces, has learned to possess himself.

It is this mastery of our faculties which is one half of achievement in life. There can be no right-mindedness without it. No man, without it, save as a matter of mere luck, can look forward to success. It is in our mental struggles, as it is in our physical; everything depends upon the skillful, nay almost unconscious handling of the muscles and sinews.

I remember an incident that took place once in London. A young sprig of fashion from the West End, tall, slender, almost boyish in his build; was insulted by a great burly coal-heaver,—a man over 6 feet in height; weighing more than 200 lbs. and carrying a fist as big as an ox's hoof. The young dandy put the reins of his horse into his servant's hands; jumped from his Gig, and pitched into the giant. Everyone thought the gentleman would have been killed. If the coal-heaver could have closed in with him, he would have eaten him up in a moment. But in as brief time as I have been telling the story, the gentleman had smashed the fellow's face to pieces, and left him sprawling, on the ground. I believe you young gentlemen call that sort of thing *science*.

The secret of his success lay in the force of an Aphorism of Dr. Arnold—"Discipline is superior to enthusiasm." You will find it, with a most interesting illustration, in his "Lectures on History;" a volume, which you will do well to possess yourselves of, and to read with care and diligence.[11]

Now the practical bearing of my words may be taken, in this way:— Some of our faculties are naturally stronger than others. In some persons, imagination preponderates; in others, Reason or Judgement. Some have a mathematical tendency; and others again linguistic. Our natural proclivities incline to our taste and tendency, and lead to the cultivation of the more masterful powers. And this you will observe is itself a proneness to that spontaneity, which though easy and agreeable to inclination, makes us rather the creatures of propensity; instead of giving us self-control. Now I say that we should guard ourselves against the abnormal, and absorbing self-concentration of any single faculty.

We should seek the training and education of our whole nature. That is not a true real system of education which is one-sided. I would therefore urge upon you that *that* mental training is defective which leaves entirely neglected certain distinct provinces of the intellect. Unfortunately this is not unseldom the case. Men with one idea; men mastered by special and peculiar theories; men swept away by prodigious acquisitions in one single line, but babes, in even some of the simpler elementary branches, are met with in all circles, and in all countries. There are more Dominie Sampsons[12] in real life than were ever begotten in fiction.

Now while it is evident that there can be but few of the princes of learning, the men who with eagle glance sweep the whole horizon of letters and science, who with equal ease and facility, turn at will, and with masterful power, to any department of learning or erudition; yet we should remember that we all possess, in a measure, precisely the same faculties which the grandest geniuses have owned; that there is no redundancy and prodigality in the gifts of God to man; that the possession of powers always involves a commission to use them.

Such gifted men as I have referred to are the rarest. Such extraordinary capacity as they exhibited is exceptional. Even to attempt the dizzy heights where they climbed, and to tread the lofty plains where they walked with composure, would be only to exhibit our folly, and to ensure our ruin.

And yet, in one respect, they *are* examples to us. Within certain limitations we may imitate them: for they show certain possibilities of the intellect which every man is bound to recognize; they discover to our view the wide range of human capacity; they evidence the amazing power of cultivation; they exemplify the duty of cultivating the whole group of faculties with which God has endowed us. While therefore you will recognize your inability to tread the highest planes of achievement; while you may elect to ascertain your own special aptitudes in the field of study; be careful to bend yourself to the cultivation, in some degree, of *every* power and every faculty. There is nothing superfluous in the make-up of our intellectual being. Every talent is by nature, a necessity to the completeness and integrity of your system. Neglect of any gift is sure to beget anomaly and dissonance in your mental organization. All disproportion is sure to produce weakness and awkwardness.

The harmonious development of your capacities is the surest means for the attainment of that inward magistracy and rule; which puts a man at his ease; serves him with a quiet self-sufficing assurance and enables him to tread the path of life with undoubted strength and capacity.

Some of you perchance have a greater line of mathematical studies, with a distaste to languages. Some prefer Mental Science. And some again have a thirst for languages; and turn with aversion, from both classics and science. We have various and diverse aptitudes. These aptitudes of men are valuable and suggestive. They are sign boards of duty. They are indications that these are naturally our special callings, the right arm of accomplishment, in our respective cases.

But don't be mastered by them, cultivate the very study you dislike. Bend your powers to the attainments to which you feel yourselves averse. Bridle your more masterful faculties. Put a rein upon mere self-asserting qualities; and stimulate to active duty the tardy and reluctant members, which lurk sluggish and inert, in dark and sequestered unconsciousness. No matter if your talents be small and meager; it is a matter of first-rate importance, that you should have them all at your disposal. For the mind, to use St. Paul's most apt imagery "is not one member but many,"[13] and those members which seem to be more feeble, are necessary. And those members which we think to be less honourable, upon these we bestow more abundant honour; and our uncomely parts have more abundant comeliness. For our comely parts have no need.[14]

So in our intellectual system. All our faculties are, in some way, valuable and essential. They are all helps to usefulness, health and vigour; the less prominent and powerful, as well as the most commanding; and therefore more regard and pains should be spent upon the faculties which are lame, inert and of slender texture.

So shall you secure freedom and superiority in the region of the understanding.

I commend one further facility and expedient to the attainment of the
rectitude of your intellectual powers. You will find all through life that both
tone and elevation of mind will be your constant acquisitions, by accus-
toming yourselves to aims and objects of the highest character. No matter
what may be your sphere in life; keep before you the ultimate ends, in the
domain of thought. Habituate your intellect to the primary truths which
appertain to the mind; and you will find, that not only will the narrow and
trivial become foreign to your thought, but that strength will be your constant and increasing gain.

For it is, in intellectual concerns, as it is in the sphere of religion and
spirituality, the ultimate and the highest is the most ennobling. The Christian
man has indeed to attend to all the petty and minute concerns of every day
life. Things of the most ordinary character are the daily duties which he has
to meet. But observe how the Church seeks ever to have her children mastered by a divine idea; and enjoins upon them to carry that idea, and to
intermingle it, with the commonest affairs of life. "*Sursum Corda*"[15] has been
the call of the church, to her children from the earliest centuries. And in
that branch of it, in which it is my privilege to minister, these two simple
words, in the vernacular, are repeated every day at thousands of her altars;
calling upon the faithful, not indeed to turn a deaf ear to duty, "stern daughter of the voice of God:"[16]—not indeed to step aside in pride and self-
importance from the state of life into which it has pleased God to call us;
but to meet every obligation, and to answer every responsibility; but even,
"as in our great Taskmaster's eye."[17] And so I say to you, if you wish to become men of might and effectiveness,—"Lift up your minds." However
humble any of us may be, however ordinary and common-place in mind, our
nature is prefigured after the universal; all the cardinal facts of the universe
are the common heritage of humanity; all the prime ideas which pertain to
the Godhead and to humanity, all the ground ideas and principles which
abide in the realms of mind and spirit! The inferiority and degradation of
the masses of men lie mostly in the fact that they are content to be unduly
pressed by the laws of their lower nature.

If we are content with the earthly and the carnal, if we are engrossed with
the sensible and material, then we shall surely eschew the heavens above,
and lose sight of the stars of glory. But yet there remains for us all; man, the
soul of man; the progress of humanity; the destiny of the race; the great
unsettled questions of the spirit; the grand moral entities; the yet untried
possibilities of culture; and far above these the majesty and eternity of God.
No matter who or what you are, these themes are the prerogative of no

exclusive aristocracy of intellect. They belong to man! They are always, in one way or another, forcing themselves upon the attention of man. It is only by closing the ears of the soul, or, by listening too intently to the clamors of sense, that we become oblivious of their utterances; and suffer thereby the greatest soul-loss. If we only endeavour to lift ourselves up to these grand themes, and abide by them, small men indeed we may be, by nature; yet we shall, nevertheless, enlarge the measure of our own souls; we shall get a light which never streamed from stars or sun; and a power shall come into our innermost being, fitting us for the grandest purposes of existence.

> —"These rules regard;
> These helps solicit; and a steadfast seat
> Shall then be yours among the happy;
> Few who dwell on earth, yet breathe Empyreal air,
> Sons of the morning!"[18]

I have ventured to present this special train of thought, because you are coloured young men; and, as such, allied to a people whose special need, for a long while, will be strength. All history shows that when a new people come on the stage of action and commence the career of manhood, there is, and for no short period either, a very large demand made on them for union, for combination, for effective force, for demonstrated manhood, for manifest and indubitable strength. The conditions under which they commence the race of life imply weakness; and consequently they must needs husband all their resources, and be covetous of all possible might. And, for the simple reason that they themselves have got to work out their own salvation, to raise themselves to that equality, far in the future, which your dreamers would fain persuade you is a present possibility and an existent reality.

Your work then in life, young gentlemen, is most serious, and most burdensome. You have got to organize a people who have been living nigh 200 years, under a system of the most destructive mental, moral, and physical disorganization the world has ever seen. You have got to train a people to solid, sober and persistent thought; a people who have been accustomed for generations, to every seductive, sensual inducement which might banish thought, and dissipate all the sober processes of the intellect. You have got to deliver from the thraldom of the flesh a vast population, who, for centuries, have been given over to the domain of the sense, and the instincts of animal passion.

If any of you suppose you can enter on such a work as if it were the jousts of a tournament; as though your activities were to be like the tilting of Carpet Knights; then you have made one of the most serious of all possible mistakes; and you need an instant and most radical reconstruction of your convictions.

I have one other reason for the topic which I have presented to your consideration. I see, especially in the large cities, in many and wide circles, a strong tendency to cultivation and refinement. I see much accumulation of property, and the rising of a new generation of educated and cultivated persons. The youth of the present day are very many years in advance of their fathers. One marked and dangerous peculiarity however constantly betrays itself: the stream of tendency among cultivated coloured Americans is too exclusively *aesthetical*. There is a universal inclination to that which is pleasing, polished and adorning. Where there is cultivation, it is mainly in poetry, music, fiction, private theatricals, the Opera. There is much elegance and real taste in house decoration; and dress is everywhere, and in a true sense of the term, a Fine Art. The mind of our people seems to be a hot-bed of rich, precocious, gorgeous and withal genuine plants:—and, if I mistake not, I discover in it all, that permanent *tropical* element which characterizes all the peoples whose ancestral homes were in the southern latitudes; and who may be called "children of the sun." I find no fault with this tendency. I regard it one of the most natural outgrowths from the soil of our African nature. Believe me there is nothing more abiding, nothing more persistent than race, and race peculiarities.

No people can be regarded as wise who look upon these tendencies as weeds; and who will strive rudely to pluck them up, and destroy them.

Whatever is natural, is, in its due measure, healthy and elevating. The aesthetical tendency is a grand and opulent capital wherewith to commence the work of responsible life and duty.

It serves, up to a certain point, to deliver a people from the control of the gross and vulgar. It gives, very considerably, the fine aptitudes, for the super-sensual. And without doubt this same tendency, has been a large element in all human progress and development.

> "These polished arts have civilized mankind,
> Softened the rude and calmed the boisterous mind."

At the same time, I must say, that this love of the beautiful among our people shows all the signs of being but a mere possession. It looks like tendency; and but little else. I see, nowhere, any counterbalance of the hardier studies, and more tasking scholarship, which serve to give vigor, hardihood and robustness to a race. I discover nowhere distinctive end or aim in it.

> "The river windeth as its own sweet will."[19]

It is, so far as I can see, mere, unrestrained spontaneity; and spontaneity, valuable as it is, requires restraints and limitations; which can only be furnished by the imperial faculties of the moral and mental nature, the Conscience and Reason. Just as the Mississippi with its vast volume and its boundless riches, flows on toward the Ocean; diffusing fertility through many a long league, and through broad far-reaching Empires; and yet, from the Prairie lands to the Ocean, has to be watched and guarded and kept within bounds; now, to be banked up; and now, to be drained of redundant waters; and now to be guided into new channels; and all, least the prodigality of its flow should serve to sweep away the gift of its own riches or bring on devastation in the very centres where it has given opulence and glory!

Now, young gentlemen, if you are to be leaders, teachers and guides among your people, you must have strength. No people can be fed, no people built up on flowers. Aesthetics, while indeed they give outward adornment, and inward delicate sensibility, tend but little, in the first place, to furnish that hardy muscle and strong fibre which men need in the stern battle of life; nor, next, do they beget that tenacity, that endurance, that positive and unwavering persistence, which is the special need of a new people, running a race which they have never before entered upon; and undertaking civilizing achievements, from which their powers and capacities have been separate for long centuries.

Every thing in this work is new; and believe me, as *severe* as it is new. The past is forever gone; and it has no teachings either for the present or the future. Nowhere in our *American* history can you light upon any instructive antecedents. What was supposed to be fit and suitable to our Race under a past regime, we know now was but chaff and sawdust! Since then the breeze of nature has stirred within their souls; and now, life in all its departments, domestic, civil, political, religious and educational has stimulated a prodigious appetite which will brook neither denial nor delay. Their mental voracity will surely make the most enormous demands upon you; and if you trifle away your time here, or are pleased with a mental gewgaw or a silly rattle, when you go out in life, you will sink to the dimensions of a dwarf, and you will fall helpless and imbecile, before even the broken lance of a true knight.[20]

I congratulate you, Young Gentlemen of the "Garnet Lyceum," on the grand opportunities of this University; I commend you most earnestly to a prudent, punctual, and most earnest cultivation of your advantages; and I trust that when you enter upon the active duties of life you may be found possessed of so great self-command and such large resources, that you may tell powerfully, in your day and generation, for the elevation of your race, for the progress of science and learning; and for the glory of God!

## 11.

# The Best Methods of Church Work
# among the Colored People

As the foremost black Episcopal minister of his day, Crummell had a vested interest in the future of black Episcopalianism, not least in the South. In this paper, read before the Episcopal clergy of Washington, D.C., on March 14, 1887, Crummell outlined his vision for the future, an ambitious plan involving not only a black ministry, an essential part of Crummell's romantic racialism, but a new black theological seminary in the Southwest, in either Mississippi or Arkansas, and the setting up of strong and effective black ministries in those cities (principally in the South) with large concentrations of black inhabitants. Needless to say, much of this would have been anathema to Episcopal church leaders in the South.

IT IS IMPOSSIBLE to reach just conclusions upon this subject unless we consider, first of all, the formidable hindrances which encompass it on every side. If we leave these hindrances unnoticed, the Church[1] is sure, in the future as in the past, to go on hanging blindly around narrow and obscure angles, instead of moving on broad and noble circles.

For the actual religious condition of the black race in the United States has originated serious, not to say prodigious, difficulties, which, if not rightly gauged, may postpone the effective work of the Church a half-century.

First of all is the fact of magnitude,—i.e., that this people are not only multitudinous in number (fully seven millions of souls), but, so far as the

Christian system is concerned, they form a negro solidarity almost universally controlled and regulated by racial influence and authority. There are two religious bodies which absorb, almost entirely, this race in America, —the Baptists and Methodists. The ministry of the Baptists number four thousand five hundred and ninety. The ministry of the African Methodists number, in three sections, four thousand five hundred.[2]

The black preacher, moreover, is the creation of the people. Even in a state of servile ignorance the people craved and sought for the spiritual leadership of their own kinsmen, and thus it came that the field-preacher was the fruit of the plantation religion of the slave era.

Since emancipation this demand has everywhere increased. When freedom came, the emancipated class, by one common impulse, rushed from the chapels provided by their masters,— deserted in multitudes the ministry of white preachers,—in search of a ministry of their own race.

In South Carolina, for instance, there were, previous to emancipation, not less than *thirty* colored chapels under white lay-readers and ministers.

When compulsory attendance fell to the ground, these chapels were left vacant, and now black attendants by hundreds are to be found in Baptist and Methodist chapels, ministered to by black preachers.[3]

From these general facts we may get suggestions pertaining to the subject before us.

The first of these relates to the agents to be employed in the work of the Church; the second will pertain to localities; the third, to various instrumentalities.

First, then, we begin with the ministry as the prime agency in methods of Church work among colored people, for the reception of the Gospel is conditioned on its heralding. But who are to be the heralds of the Cross to this new and ready race? What methods shall the Church pursue in this prime department of her labors? Will she fall back upon the heretofore universal principle of missionary venture,—viz., the employment of an indigenous agency,—or, on the other hand, will she attempt a novel and a revolutionary step in getting hold of and incorporating this people into her fold?

There is no possibility of avoiding this question, for it stands out at the very entrance upon this work. Already has a school of opinion risen in our Church which says, "No negro priests or deacons. Let this work be carried on by white men. The Roman Church has no black priests. Why need we have them?" The Roman Church has no black priests, it is true, and her methods may be satisfactory in this and other respects to a class of churchmen; but, in the light of results, is her system and policy to be followed by us? Take the two States,— *i.e.,* Maryland and Louisiana. Once the black race in these two States was almost entirely under her control. Where are they now? Multitudes have slipped through her fingers, and are now to be found in the Baptist and Methodist Churches, and her authority over them has gone forever.

At the time of emancipation crowds of black Romanists came from Roman Catholic households and plantations to Baltimore and Washington. There is the strongest probability to-day that more than one-third of them in each city are now under the control and direction of colored Baptists and Methodists. Precisely the same thing has taken place with hundreds of black church-people. Emancipation came, and with it came full freedom of choice in religious matters, and at once came, likewise, the drift to the black preacher.

All this is an inevitability. Every race of people has its special instincts, carries in its blood its distinctive individuality. This peculiar element is its own and exclusive possession, and is incapable of transference. To seize upon this quality, to give it natural expression, to use it with forceful power, is a spontaneity in men native to the race; but, on the other hand, it is a clumsy and crooked imitation with alien and foreign natures. Out of this springs the strong and urgent need of a negro ministry, *if* the Church is to work with skill and effect in the negro race in the United States. The teachers of *any* race of men must possess the genius of the race; must carry with them the full stuff of the race; must glow with the temperament of the race; and then they become surcharged with power to act upon the reason, to stir the sensibilities, to move the hearts, and to control the affections of their kinsmen; and, further, they are thus fitted and enabled to make the most of the powers and abilities of their people, and to put them to the best uses. This is a conspicuous fact in all human history, discoverable especially in the propagation of the Gospel. That Gospel is handed over, *first* of all, by an agency exotic in blood and lineage; but it is made to inhere in a people, as a thing of life and heredity, by an indigenous training and influence.

This racialism is not, be it noticed, simply a matter of language. A missionary may know the language of a people,—know it, scientifically, better than the people themselves,—but he needs something more than this. He needs the spirit, the sensibilities, the home sympathies, the special desires, the native peculiarities, the crude experiences, the agonized history,—nay, even the prejudices,—of that people in order to speak to their hearts and to address himself to their needs. There is a vernacular of sympathy as well as a vernacular of speech among all peoples. And it is this vernacular which it is the most difficult of all things for alien blood to acquire.

It is mainly by adherence to this principle of Gospel propagation that the Church will be able to make progress in her work among the colored people of the land. The principle has already asserted itself, crudely indeed, in the masses of black preachers which have been called forth as ministers to this race in the past. But the indication is a clear and distinct, an historic and racial, a positive and determined one in the black race. All the tendency of things seems to fix the conclusion that no church organization can change it. So far as a ministry for the negro is concerned, it is seemingly *this,* or else almost universal divorcement of this race from the Church.

2. But, secondly, what fields should the Church especially choose for effective service in this work? Where shall she concentrate her forces and her resources in carrying on this work of souls? And here again it is well to observe another trend of the negro mind, and to get the practical wisdom therefrom which it gives us. The African race is constitutionally gregarious. From time immemorial, on its native soil, in Africa, the race has been accustomed to live in clustering towns and large cities. This tendency was fostered by the plantation system. The slaves were generally gathered in large numbers on great estates. This proclivity still maintains in the race, and since emancipation they have flocked in multitudes to the great towns and the large cities of the South and the Southwest.

These cities and large towns, then, are the radiatory spots towards which everything points, towards which everything important should naturally converge, and from which power and influence should flow in an easy and inartificial manner. A strong, effective force should be brought to bear upon the great centres of the black population, so as to take captive for Christ and His Church the masses of the humble and uncared-for, and also the *leaders* of colored society, who the unthinking are wont to follow and to imitate.

In this connection, it is well to remember that the great need of the black race, in their present state of freedom, is a new religion. "Young Africa," everywhere, trained more or less for twenty years in public schools, is just like "young Ireland,"[4]—restless, ambitious, free-thinking, self-sufficient,— and, while clinging to the religion of the fathers, demands a new and a higher spiritual system. It was only last week that Dr. Hartzell,[5] at the anniversary of the "Methodists Freedman's Aid Society," remarked, "We had to take the best preachers we could get at first. Our bishops in the South have ordained hundreds of men who could not read. I have seen *one* reading the hymn with the book upside-down. We put men in the pulpit, and almost all they could do was to shout and pound the Bible. But now they must have better preachers, and they must be educated in the schools of this society."

Whence comes this demand? "The schoolmaster" is abroad, and the rising generation of black youth, educated in the schools, in court-houses, in political caucuses, and by political harangues, won't tolerate the old plantation style, with its frenzy and its hysteria. Young Africa demands a new religion.

This demand comes especially from the large cities, not, indeed, to the neglect of crowded country populations, where, indeed, it is often as great and as urgent, but the cities are the great centres. And the Church now, in the prosecution of this large and important work for a new race, must needs do as she did in Apostolic times,—plant herself with strength at the very heart of society, in the sections where the race is massed in the largest numbers. The advantage of the cities, as centres of widespread influence, may be seen in this wise: The cities have their roots in the rural districts. The cities are the overflow of the towns and villages and hamlets of the land. Almost every city man is the representative, not simply of the family from whence he sprung, but of many households with which he is connected by kinship, family ties, friendship, association, and influence. The cities, moreover, are the criterion of life, the index of manners, the type of fashion and of style, and the standard of morals. As go the cities, so go the towns; as go the towns, so go the villages; as go the villages, so go the hamlets and houses and farms and the country people in general.

It is, therefore, a matter of the vastest importance in methods of church work among colored people that the Church should seat herself with force and with strong demonstrations of power in the great centres of negro population,—the large cities of the South.

The cities of Washington, Richmond, New Orleans, Baltimore, Charleston, Savannah, and St. Louis are notable for population, position, and influence, and in some cases resources. They stand, for the most part, in the centre of large surrounding populations of colored people. The case of Washington is an illustration. It is at once the capital of the nation and the centre of the large negro population of Maryland, Pennsylvania, and Delaware [*i.e.,* 263,479 persons] on the one side, and of Virginia, West Virginia, and Ohio [576,054] on the other, while its own colored population is 63,000. The same conditions, but with larger force, maintain with respect to most of the other six cities referred to.

The work of the Church in these great centres should be carried on with full force, with much impressment, with much beneficence, with fervent spiritual power, with visitations of mercy to both the bodies and souls of men.

These great cities, moreover, should be made the bases of effort in the large towns contiguous to them. By large towns I mean, with judicious reservations, places or communities with from twenty to twenty-five thousand inhabitants.

3. But *how* shall church work be carried on under these conditions? In the answer to this question important features of policy and method may here be brought forward:

(*a*) And, first of all, the effort to plant the Church at a great central point should be a strong effort, and *not* a weak one. It had better not be made at all than to begin with feebleness, hesitancy, and doubt.

It *should be strong in its ministry.* This is the way work for Christ was always begun by the Apostles in every great centre. No one man, singly and alone, should be called upon to cope with the needs of forty or fifty thousand people, with, perchance, the opposition of ten or twenty Baptist and Methodist ministers, to be stuck up in a miserable, dingy, out-of-the-way hall, and in the midst of a low white population who hate and sneer at "niggers," the minister himself meanwhile living in a state bordering on raggedness, and almost starving, day by day, at his lean and beggarly table.

To put a black clergyman in a city or in a crowded district, and then to give him the scantiest living, to leave him "tremendously alone," to pronounce upon him in *act,* if not by word, the vulgar sentence, "root, hog, or die,"[6] to make him a perpetual beggar for his salary and his chapel-rent, to bring to bear upon him a score of lofty clerical telescopes, scrutinizing his despairing, starveling work, and then, with haughty mien and uplifted nose, to spurt out the scornful utterance, "Oh, these black ministers are good for nothing!" is nothing short of an atrocity.

"All work is badly done by people in despair," says Pliny. And what but despair can be the fruit of such straitened, beggarly, pauperized circumstances upon a lone, needy, single-handed man in a large city and with opposition on every side.

Our church work at the great centres, however simple, should be strong. Every priest should have his deacon or catechist, or both; a woman worker, whether called sister or mother; a good industrial school, and, when possible, a hospital. Whenever practicable, parochial schools should be established, where daily morning and evening service should be a marked feature of the training of the pupils and for the blessedness of adults.

No one lone man can carry on such a work in a large city. He needs the help, as likewise the society, of an associate and assistant.

(*b*) For immediate service of this character it will be necessary that the Church should avail herself of the labors of what are called in the Church of England "catechists."

The black population of the United States is increasing at the rate of five hundred souls a day. For this work, then, an immediate, if extemporaneous, agency is needed at once. If the Church waits until she can send forth large corps of learned priests and deacons, she will do about as much effective work in *this* age for the race as the dropping of a tear would add to the volume of the Potomac.

The Church of England began her use of an indigenous agency in India, Africa, and the West Indies by the mission of pious and intelligent catechists.[7] These catechists in towns and villages might unite the duties of masters in parochial schools with reading the service, visiting the sick, and burying the dead, under the direction of a priest or the archdeacon of a district.

In Sierra Leone many of the catechists showed so much cleverness, aptitude, and spiritual devotedness that, after several years' service, they were made deacons. In special cases a few were made priests. Bishop Crowther, of the Niger, sprang from this class. The colored Episcopal churches now in existence could furnish this day fifty men—men, too, of no inferior capacity—who could thus serve the Church and their race with as much force and efficiency as many deacons.

(*c*) It is impossible to pass over, at this point, the query, How shall men be prepared for the work of ministers or catechists?

We have two special schools for the theological training of colored men,—one at Raleigh, N.C., and the other at Petersburg, Va.,—and both neighboring the Atlantic seaboard. *One* more is needed, and only *one more,* which may be established in the Southwest, in either Mississippi or Arkansas. The multiplication of such schools should be carefully avoided. Two or three divinity schools, well-officered, made strong by concentration of funds and forces, will prove more effective and useful than a number of weak and puerile institutions.

One point, however, is indispensable. The course of study in these institutions should be as thorough as at Nashotah, or Berkeley, or Gambier.[8] No colored man should be priested with inferior qualifications. The time has passed for anything approaching the old plantation style of ministry. The colored Methodists and Baptists repudiate it. They have no less than twenty-two theological schools, and are sending forth annually scores of well-trained men. The time has been when the handful of colored Church ministers in the North were the most learned and cultivated ministers in America, and in the common parlance of those days were called by their people "larned black preachers." That day has passed away forever. There are Methodist, Presbyterian, Baptist, and Congregational colored pastors at the present not only equal, but some superior, in learning, to colored clergymen in our own ranks. All comparisons of this kind in the future will be death to our work. If we send inferior men into the field, we shall soon find no people to follow them; for, besides the ministerial aspect of the matter, there is the added fact, viz., that the *pew,* in many places, is fully up to the pulpit in training and knowledge.

(*d*) These schools, moreover, should be, largely as possible, under the control of colored professors and teachers. Institutions of divers kinds, industrial, academical, collegiate, founded, governed, and taught by colored men, are springing up all through the South. These institutions spring from the demands of the race. The people wish their children to be taught by men of their own blood. This tendency is a growing one, and it is irresistible. Since emancipation they have demanded colored teachers, colored doctors, colored lawyers, colored editors and newspapers to the number of one hundred, colored colleges and professors, and colored preachers, and they have got them. Such a craving and aspiration of a whole race is neither to be ignored nor despised. It is idle for any man or any organization to suppose they can start a backward revolution which will ever put this whole race, or any large section of them on this soil, under any other than racial training. Whether from weal or woe, the tendency of the black race in the South, in education, in social life, in societies and fraternities, and in religion, is to racial autonomy and racial self-training. It will be well and wise for our Church to notice and observe this tendency. If she does not, she may gather under her wings a pitiful brood of black adherents, but the masses will stand aloof from her portals. The great leaders of the race will resort to the fold where the PEOPLE gather together, and the large black organizations already in existence will use every possible device, through the race-feeling, to keep our churches empty and to make our influence a nullity!

These, then, are some of the methods needed to carry forward with success and blessedness our church work among the colored people:

(1) A racial ministry.

(2) This ministry planted especially at the great centres of the black population.

(3) This ministry strongly aided by assistants, woman-workers, industrial and parochial schools, and hospitals.

(4) A large reinforcement of catechists.

(5) The supply of ministers from three theological schools in the South and Southwest.

(6) The agency of colored professors and teachers, in moulding and preparing men for the ministry.

Other important topics, such as church edifices, funds, the episcopate, need to be considered; but I cannot venture further.

# 12.

# The Race-Problem in America

Fiercely proud of his black skin and his pure African ancestry, Crummell opposed anything which diluted either race feeling or race loyalty. In "The Race Problem in America," read before the Protestant Episcopal Church Congress at Buffalo, New York, in November 1888, he set out to defend these beliefs against the assimilationist ideas of George Rawlinson and, more controversially, Josiah Strong, whose *Our Country: Its Possible Future and Its Present Crisis* was published in 1885. Not surprisingly, Crummell rejected amalgamation as a solution to the race problem in the United States. Instead, he put his faith in the doctrine of human rights and the progress of the democratic spirit.

THE RESIDENCE of various races of men in the same national community, is a fact which has occurred in every period of time and in every quarter of the globe. So well known is this fact of history that the mention of a few special instances will be sufficient for this occasion.

It took place in earliest times on the plains of Babylon. It was seen on the banks of the Nile, in the land of the Pharaohs. The same fact occurred again when the barbarian hosts of the North fell upon effete Roman society, and changed the fate of Europe. Once more we witness the like fact when the Moors swept along the banks of the Mediterranean, and seated themselves in might and majesty on the hills of Granada and along the fertile slopes of Aragon and Castile.[1] And now, in the nineteenth century, we have the largest illustration of the same fact in our own Republic, where are gathered together, in one national community, sixty millions of people of every race and kindred under the sun. It might be supposed that an historical fact so large and multiform would furnish a solution of the great race-problem, which now invites attention in American society. We read the future by the past.[2] And without doubt there are certain principles of population which are invariable in their working and universal in their results. Such principles are inductions from definite conditions, and may be called the laws of population. They are, too, both historical and predictive. One cannot only ascertain through them the past condition of States and peoples, but they give a light which opens up with clearness the future of great commonwealths.

But, singular as it may seem, there is no fixed law of history by which to determine the probabilities of the race-problem in the United States. We can find nowhere such invariability of result as to set a principle or determine what may be called an historical axiom.

Observe just here the inevitable confusion which is sure to follow the aim after historical precedent in this problem.

The descendants of Nimrod and Assur, people of two different stocks, settled in Babylon; and the result was amalgamation.[3]

The Jews and the Egyptians under the Pharaohs inhabited the same country 400 years; but antagonism was the result, and expulsion the final issue.

The Tartars overran China in the tenth century, and the result has been amalgamation.

The Goths and Vandals poured into Italy like a flood, and the result has been absorption.

The Celts and Scandinavians clustered like bees from the fourth to the sixth centuries in the British Isles, and the result has been absorption.

The Northmen and Gauls have lived side by side in Normandy since the tenth century, and the result has been absorption.

The Moors and Spaniards came into the closest contact in the sixth century, and it resulted in constant antagonism and in final expulsion.

The Caucasian and the Indian have lived in close neighborhood on this continent since 1492, and the result has been the extinction of the Indian.

The Papuan and the Malay have lived side by side for ages in the tropical regions of the Pacific, and have maintained every possible divergence of tribal life, of blood, government, and religion, down to the present, and yet have remained perpetually and yet peacefully separate and distinct.[4]

These facts, circling deep historic ages, show that we can find no definite historical precedent or principle applicable to the race-problem in America.

Nevertheless we are not entirely at sea with regard to this problem. There are certain tendencies, seen for over 200 years in our population, which indicate settled, determinate proclivities, and which show, if I mistake not, the destiny of races.

What, then, are the probabilities of the future? Do the indications point to amalgamation or to absorption as the outcome of race-life in America? Are we to have the intermingling of our peoples into one common blood or the perpetuity of our diverse stocks, with the abiding integrity of race, blood, and character?

I might meet the theory which anticipates amalgamation by the great principle manifested in every sphere, viz: "That nature is constantly departing from the simple to the complex; starting off in new lines from the homogeneous to the heterogeneous";[5] striking out in divers ways into variety; and hence we are hedged in, in the aim after blood-unity, by a law of nature which is universal, and which excludes the notion of amalgamation.

But I turn from the abstract to history. It is now about 268 years since the tides of immigration began to beat upon our shores. This may be called a brief period, but 268 years is long enough to fix a new type of man. Has such a new type sprung up here to life? Has a new commingled race, the result of our diverse elements, come forth from the crucible of our heterogeneous nationality?

We will indulge in no speculation upon this subject. We will exclude even the faintest tinge of the imagination. The facts alone shall speak for themselves.

First of all is the history of the Anglo-Saxon race in America. In many respects it has been the foremost element in the American population; in largeness of numbers, in civil polity and power, in educational impress, and in religious influence. What has become of this element of our population? Has it been lost in the current of the divergent streams of life which have been spreading abroad throughout the land?

Why, every one knows that in New England, in Virginia, in the Far West, along the Atlantic Seaboard, that fully three-fifths of the whole American population are the offspring of this same hardy, plodding, common-sense people that they were centuries ago, when their fathers pressed through the forests of Jamestown or planted their feet upon the sterile soil of Plymouth.

Some of you may remember the remark of Mr. Lowell, on his return in 1885 from his mission to England. He said that when English people spoke to him of Americans as a people different from themselves, he always told them that in blood he was just as much an Englishman as they were;[6] and Mr. Lowell in this remark was the spokesman of not less than thirty-six millions of men of as direct Anglo-Saxon descent as the men of Kent or the people of Yorkshire.

The Celtic element came to America in two separate columns. The French entered Canada in 1607. They came with all that glow, fervor, gallantry, social aptitudes, and religious loyalty which, for centuries, have characterized the Gallic blood, and which are still conspicuous features on both sides of the Atlantic.

The other section of the Celtic family began their immigration about 1640; and they have almost depopulated Ireland to populate America; and their numbers now are millions.

One or two facts are observable concerning the French and Irish, viz: (1) That, although kindred in blood, temperament, and religion, they have avoided both neighborhood of locality and marital alliance; and (2) so great has been the increase of the Hibernian family that in Church life and political importance, they form a vast solidarity in the nation.

The German, like the Celtic family, came over in two sections. The Batavian stock came first from Holland in 1608, and made New York, New Jersey, and Pennsylvania their habitat. The Germans proper, or High Germans, have been streaming into the Republic since 1680, bringing with them that steadiness and sturdiness, that thrift and acquisitiveness, that art and learning, that genius and acumen, which have given an elastic spring to American culture, depth to philosophy, and inspiration to music and to art.

And here they are in great colonies in the Middle and Western States, and in vast sections of our great cities. And yet where can one discover any decline in the purity of German blood, or the likelihood of its ultimate loss in the veins of alien people?

The Negro contingent was one of the earliest contributions to the American population. The black man came quickly on the heel of the Cavalier at Jamestown, and before the arrival of the Puritan in the east. "That fatal, that perfidious bark"[7] of Sir John Hawkins, that "ferried the slave captive o'er the sea"[8] from Africa, preceded the Mayflower one year and five months.

From that small cargo and its after arrivals have arisen the large black population, variously estimated from 8 to 10,000,000. It is mostly, especially in the wide rural areas of the South, a purely Negro population. In the large cities there is a wide intermixture of blood. This, by some writers, is taken as the indication of ultimate and entire amalgamation. But the past in this incident is no sign of the future. The gross and violent intermingling of the blood of the Southern white man cannot be taken as an index of the future of the black race.

Amalgamation in its exact sense means the approach of affinities. The word applied to human beings implies will, and the consent of two parties. In *this* sense there has been no amalgamation of the two races; for the Negro in this land has ever been the truest of men, in marital allegiance, to his own race.

Intermixture of blood there has been—not by the amalgamation, which implies consent, but through the victimizing of the helpless black woman.

But even this has been limited in extent. Out of 4,500,000 of this race in the census of 1861, 400,000 were set down as of mixed blood. Thousands of these were the legitimate offspring of colored parents; and the probability is that not more than 150,000 had white fathers. Since emancipation the black woman has gained possession of her own person, and it is the testimony of Dr. Haygood and other eminent Southerners that the base process of intermixture has had a wide and sudden decline, and that the likelihood of the so-called amalgamation of the future is fast dying out.[9]

And now, after this survey of race tides and race life during 268 years, I repeat the question: "Has a *new* race, the product of our diverse elements, sprung up here in America? Or, is there any such a probability for the future?"

Let me answer this question by a recent and striking reference.

Dr. Strong, in his able, startling, striking Tractate, entitled *"Our Country,"* speaks, in ch. 4, p. 44, of the Helvetian settlement in southern Wisconsin.[10] He deprecates the preservation of its race, its language, its worship, and its customs in their integrity. In this, you see, he forgets the old Roman adage that "though men cross the seas they do not change their nature."[11] He then protests (and rightly, too) against the perpetuation of race antipathies, and closes his criticism with the suggestion, similar to that of Canon Rawlinson,[12] of Oxford, viz., that the American people should seek the solution of the race-problem by universal assimilation of blood.[13]

Dr. Strong evidently forgets that the principle of race is one of the most persistent of all things in the constitution of man. It is one of those structural facts in our nature which abide with a fixed, vital, and reproductive power.

Races, like families, are the organisms and the ordinance of God; and race feeling, like the family feeling, is of divine origin. The extinction of race feeling is just as possible as the extinction of family feeling. Indeed, a race *is* a family. The principle of continuity is as masterful in races as it is in families—as it is in nations.

History is filled with the attempts of kings and mighty generals and great statesmen to extinguish this instinct. But their failures are as numerous as their futile attempts; for this sentiment, alike subtle and spontaneous, has both pervaded and stimulated society in every quarter. Indeed, as Lord Beaconsfield says, "race is the key to history."[14] When once the race-type gets fixed as a new variety, then it acts precisely as the family life; for, 1st, it propagates itself by that divine instinct of reproduction, vital in all living creatures, and next, 2nd, it has a growth as a "seed after its own kind and in itself,"[15] whereby the race-type becomes a perpetuity, with its own distinctive form, constitution, features, and structure. Heredity is just as true a fact in races as in families, as it is in individuals.

Nay, we see, not seldom, a special persistency in the race life. We see families and tribes and clans swept out of existence, while race "goes on forever." Yea, even nations suffer the same fate. Take, for instance, the unification of States now constantly occurring. One small nation after another is swallowed up by another to magnify its strength and importance, and thus the great empires of the world become colossal powers. But it is observable that the process of unification leaves untouched the vitality and the persistency of race. You have only to turn to Great Britain and to Austria to verify this statement. In both nations we see the intensity of race cohesion, and at the same time the process of unification. Indeed, on all sides, in Europe, we see the consolidation of States; and at the same time the integration of race: Nature and Providence thus developing that principle of unity which binds the universe, and yet at the same time manifesting that conserving power which tends everywhere to fixity of type. And this reminds us of the lines of Tennyson:

> "Are God and nature, then, at strife,
>  That nature lends such evil dreams?
>  So careful of the type she seems,
> So careless of the single life."[16]

Hence, when a race once seats itself permanently in a land it is almost as impossible to get rid of it as it is to extirpate a plant that is indigenous to its soil. You can drive out a family from a community. You can rid yourself of a clan or a single tribe by expulsion. You can swallow up by amalgamation a simple emigrant people.

But when a RACE, *i. e.,* a compact, homogeneous population of one blood, ancestry, and lineage—numbering, perchance, some eight or ten millions—once enters a land and settles therein as its home and heritage, then occurs an event as fixed and abiding as the rooting of the Pyrenees in Spain or the Alps in Italy.

The race-problem, it will thus be seen, cannot be settled by extinction of race. No amalgamating process can eliminate it. It is not a carnal question—a problem of breeds, or blood, or lineage.

And even if it were, amalgamation would be an impossibility. How can any one persuade seven or eight millions of people to forget the ties of race? No one could *force* them into the arms of another race. And even then it would take generations upon generations to make the American people homogeneous in blood and essential qualities. Thus take one single case: There are thirty millions of Negroes on the American *continent* (eight or more millions in the United States of America), and constantly increasing at an immense ratio. Nothing but the sheerest, haziest imagination can anticipate the future dissolution of this race and its final loss; and so, too, of the other races of men in America.

Indeed, the race-problem is a moral one. It is a question entirely of ideas. Its solution will come especially from the domain of principles. Like all the other great battles of humanity, it is to be fought out with the weapons of truth. The race-problem is a question of organic life, and it must be dealt with as an ethical matter by the laws of the Christian system. "As diseases of the mind are invisible, so must their remedies be."

And this brings me to the one vast question that still lingers, *i. e.,* the quesiton of AMITY. Race-life is a permanent element in our system. Can it be maintained in peace? Can these races give the world the show of brotherhood and fraternity? Is there a moral remedy in this problem?

Such a state of concord is, we must admit, a rare sight, even in christendom. There is great friction between Celt and Saxon in Britain. We see the violence of both Russ and German against the Jew. The bitterness is a mutual one between Russia on the one hand and Bulgaria and the neighboring dependent principalities on the other, and France and Germany stand facing one another like great fighting cocks.

All this is by no means assuring, and hence we cannot dismiss this question in an off-hand and careless manner.

The current, however, does not set all one way. There is another aspect to this question.

Thus, the Norman and the Frank have lived together harmoniously for centuries; the Welsh, English, and Scotch in England; the Indian, the Spaniard, and Negro in Brazil, and people of very divergent lineage in Spain.

And now the question arises: What are the probabilities of amity in a land where exists such wide divergence of race as the Saxon on the one hand and the Negro on the other?

First of all, let me say that the social idea is to be entirely excluded from consideration. It is absolutely a personal matter, regulated by taste, condition, or either by racial or family affinities; and there it must remain undisturbed forever. The Jews in this land are sufficient for themselves. So are the Germans, the Italians, the Irish, and so are the Negroes. Civil and political freedom trench in no way upon the domestic state or social relations.

Besides, there is something ignoble in any man, any class, any race of men whining and crying because they cannot move in spheres where they are not wanted.

But, beyond the social range there should be no compromise; and this country should be agitated and even convulsed till the battle of liberty is won, and every man in the land is guaranteed fully every civil and political right and prerogative.

The question of equality pertains entirely to the two domains of civil and political life and prerogative.

Now, I wish to show that the probabilities tend toward the complete and entire civil and political equality of all peoples of this land.

1st. Observe that this is the age of civil freedom. It has not as yet gained its fullest triumphs; neither yet has Christianity.

But it is to be observed in the history of man that, in due time, certain principles get their set in human society, and there is no such thing as successfully resisting them. Their rise is not a matter of chance or hap-hazard. It is God's hand in history. It is the providence of the Almighty, and no earthly power can stay it.

Such, pre-eminently, was the entrance of Christianity in the centre of the world's civilization, and the planting of the idea of human brotherhood amid the ideas in the laws and legislation of great nations. *That* was the seed from which have sprung all the great revolutions in thought and governmental policies during the Christian era. Its work has been slow, but it has been certain and unfailing. I cannot pause to narrate all its early victories. We will take a limited period. We will begin at the dawn of modern civilization, and note the grand achievements of the idea of Christian brotherhood.

It struck at the doctrine of the Divine Right of Kings, and mortally wounded it. It demanded the extinction of Feudalism, and it got it. It demanded the abolition of the Slave Trade, and it got it. It demanded the abolition of Russian Serfage, and it got it. It demanded the education of the masses, and it got it.

In the early part of the eighteenth century this principle of brotherhood sprouted forth into a grander and more consummate growth, and generated the spirit of democracy.

When I speak of the spirit of democracy I have no reference to that spurious, blustering, self-sufficient spirit which derides God and authority on the one hand, and crushes the weak and helpless on the other. The democratic spirit I am speaking of is that which upholds the doctrine of human rights; which demands honor to all men; which recognizes manhood in all conditions; which uses the State as the means and agency for the unlimited progress of humanity. This principle has its root in the Scriptures of God, and it has come forth in political society to stay! In the hands of man it has indeed suffered harm. It has been both distorted and exaggerated, and without doubt it needs to be chastised, regulated, and sanctified. But the democratic principle in its essence is of God, and in its normal state it is the consummate flower of Christianity, and is irresistible because it is the mighty breath of God.

It is democracy which has demanded the people's participation in government and the extension of suffrage, and it got it. It has demanded a higher wage for labor, and it has got it, and will get more. It has demanded the abolition of Negro slavery, and it has got it. Its present demand is the equality of man in the State, irrespective of race, condition, or lineage. The answer to this demand is the solution of the race-problem.

In this land the crucial test in the race-problem is the civil and political rights of the black man. The only question now remaining among us for the full triumph of Christian democracy is the equality of the Negro.

Nay, I take back my own words. It is NOT the case of the Negro in this land. It is the nation which is on trial. The Negro is only the touch-stone. By this black man she stands or falls.

If the black man cannot be free in this land, if he cannot tread with firmness every pathway to preferment and superiority, neither can the white man. "A bridge is never stronger than its weakest point."

> "In nature's chain, whatever link you strike
> Tenth or ten-thousandth, breaks the chain alike."[17]

So compact a thing is humanity that the despoiling of an individual is an injury to society.

This nation has staked her existence on this principle of democracy in her every fundamental political dogma, and in every organic State document. The democratic idea is neither Anglo-Saxonism, nor Germanism, nor Hibernianism, but HUMANITY, and humanity can live when Anglo-Saxonism or any class of the race of man has perished. Humanity anticipated all human varieties by thousands of years, and rides above them all, and outlives them all, and swallows up them all!

If this nation is not truly democratic then she must die! Nothing is more destructive to a nation than an organic falsehood! This nation cannot live— this nation does not deserve to live—on the basis of a lie!

Her fundamental idea is democracy; and if this nation will not submit herself to the domination of this idea—if she refuses to live in the spirit of this creed—then she is already doomed, and she will certainly be damned.

But neither calamity, I ween, is her destiny.

The democratic spirit is of itself a prophecy of its own fulfillment. Its disasters are trivialities; its repulses only temporary. In this nation the Negro has been the test for over 200 years. But see how far the Negro has traveled this time.

In less than the lifetime of such a man as the great George Bancroft,[18] observe the transformation in the status of the Negro in this land. When *he* was a child the Negro was a marketable commodity, a beast of the field, a chattel in the shambles, outside of the pale of the law, and ignorant as a pagan.

Nay, when I was a boy of 13, I heard the utterance fresh from the lips of the great J. C. Calhoun, to wit, that if he could find a Negro who knew the Greek syntax he would then believe that the Negro was a human being and should be treated as a man.[19]

If he were living to-day he would come across scores of Negroes, not only versed in the Greek syntax, but doctors, lawyers, college students, clergymen, some learned professors, and *one* the author of a new Greek Grammar.[20]

But just here the caste spirit interferes in this race-problem and declares: "You Negroes may get learning; you may get property; you may have churches and religion; but this is your limit! This is a white man's Government! No matter how many millions you may number, we Anglo-Saxons are to rule!" This is the edict constantly hissed in the Negro's ear, in one vast section of the land.

Let me tell you of a similar edict in another land:

Some sixty years ago there was a young nobleman, an undergraduate at Oxford University, a youth of much talent, learning, and political ambition; but, at the same time, he was *then* a foolish youth![21] His patrician spirit rose in bitter protest against the Reform Bill of that day, which lessened the power of the British aristocracy and increased the suffrages of the Commons. He was a clever young fellow, and he wrote a brilliant poem in defense of his order, notable, as you will see, for its rhythm, melody, and withal for its— silliness! Here are two lines from it:

> "Let Laws and Letters, Arts and Learning die;
> But give us still our old Nobility."[22]

Yes, let everything go to smash! Let civilization itself go to the dogs, if only an oligarchy may rule, flourish, and dominate!

We have a blatant provincialism in our own country, whose only solution of the race-problem is the eternal subjection of the Negro, and the endless domination of a lawless and self-created aristocracy.

Such men forget that the democratic spirit rejects the factious barriers of caste, and stimulates the lowest of the kind to the very noblest ambitions of life. They forget that nations are no longer governed by races, but by ideas. They forget that the triumphant spirit of democracy has bred an individualism which brooks not the restraints of classes and aristocracies. They forget that, regardless of "Pope, Consul, King," or oligarchy, this same spirit of democracy lifts up to place and power her own agents for the rule of the world; and brings to the front, now a Dane as King of Greece, and now a

Frenchman as King of Sweden; now a Jewish D'Israeli as Prime Minister of England, and now a Gallatin and a Schurz as cabinet ministers in America.[23] They forget that a Wamba and a Gurth in one generation, whispering angry discontent in secret places, become, by the inspiration of democracy, the outspoken Hampdens[24] and Sydneys[25] of another. They forget that, as letters ripen and education spreads, the "Sambos" and "Pompeys" of to-day will surely develop into the Touissants and the Christophes, the Wards and the Garnets of the morrow, champions of their race and vindicators of their rights. They forget that democracy, to use the words of De Tocqueville, "has severed every link of the chain" by which aristocracy had fixed every member of the community, "from the peasant to the king."[26]

They forget that the Church of God is in the world; that her mission is, by the Holy Ghost, "to take the weak things of the world to confound the mighty,"[27] "to put down the mighty from their seats, and to exalt them of low degree;"[28] that now, as in all the ages, she will, by the Gospel, break up tyrannies and useless dynasties, and lift up the masses to nobleness of life, and exalt the humblest of men to excellence and superiority.

Above all things, they forget that "the King invisible, immortal, eternal"[29] is upon the throne of the universe; that thither caste, and bigotry, and race-hate can never reach; that He is everlastingly committed to the interests of the oppressed; that He is constantly sending forth succors and assistances for the rescue of the wronged and injured; that He brings all the forces of the universe to grind to powder all the enormities of earth, and to rectify all the ills of humanity, and so hasten on the day of universal brotherhood.

By the presence and the power of that Divine Being all the alienations and disseverances of men shall be healed; all the race-problems of this land easily be solved; and love and peace prevail among men.

# 13.

## *Incidents of Hope for the Negro Race in America*

Crummell never lost his faith in the ability of blacks to cast off the heritage of slavery and fulfill their own unique destiny. In this sermon, delivered in Washington, D.C., on November 26, 1895, he once again drew attention to the vitality of the race and the mental and spiritual progress it had made since emancipation. The parallels with "A Defence of the Negro Race in America" are obvious, but there was a new note of urgency, reflecting Crummell's growing concern that if left unchecked, industrial education threatened to impede black progress in the United States. Reacting angrily to the idea of placing any sort of limit on the black intellect, he reiterated his call for "common sense in common schooling," demanding that African-Americans should be allowed to find their own place in the "scale of nature."

Ps. CVII; Vs. 13–16.

13. Then they cried unto the LORD in their trouble, *and* he saved them out of their distresses.

14. He brought them out of darkness and the shadow of death, and brake their bands in sunder.

15. Oh that *men* would praise the Lord *for* his goodness, and *for* his wonderful works to the children of men!

16. For he hath broken the gates of brass, and cut the bars of iron in sunder.[1]

THE PSALMS OF David are, for the most part, songs of praise and thanksgiving for the gifts and mercies of the Almighty. The special peculiarity of this 107th Psalm is, that it is a continuous utterance of adoration for the deliverance of the children of Israel from the land of bondage; for their protection from their enemies in the wilderness; for their rescue from divers dangers and misfortunes, by flood and field; from drought and famine.

The sense of gratitude was so vivid and so glowing that the Psalmist bursts forth, not once or twice, but over and over again, into the exclamation,— "O that men would praise the Lord for His goodness, and declare the wonders that He doeth for the children of men."

So similar, in several ways, has been the providence of the Almighty in the history of our race in this country, that I have chosen the text just announced, as the base of remarks pertaining to the future prospects stretching out before us. My subject to-day is—"INCIDENTS OF HOPE FOR THE NEGRO RACE IN AMERICA."

The trials and sufferings of this race have been great for centuries. They have not yet ceased. They are not likely to cease for a long time to come. It may take two or three generations for the race to get a firm and assured status in the land.

Nevertheless there are, I maintain, underlying all the past, present and future attritions and tribulations of our condition, certain large and important incidents, which are pregnant with hope, and which are fitted to serve as stimulants to high ambition and indomitable energy.

There is need, just now, for such encouragements. For, in some quarters, there seems to be despondency; as though the car of progress was tardy in its movements; many forgetting that it is impossible to extemporize a full civilization for any people; impossible to leap, at a spring, into a lofty elevation. Hence the dark cloud of despair which overhangs a moody group, leading almost to repudiation of their race. And then, from another section, come the insensate screeching and screaming tones which call upon us to flee to Africa.[2]

For my own part I regret these views as idle and unreasoning. Not blind, indeed, to numerous difficulties, I see, nevertheless, gracious providences in our case; and I am anxious to set before you what I deem some sound and solid grounds of Hope.

1. Consider, first of all, the fact of Negro vitality as an important factor in his destiny. There must be a physical basis, a material substratum for the mental and moral life of man. "A sound mind in a sound body" is an old adage, applied to a promising individual. The adage recognizes the relation of mind to body; the correlation of flesh and spirit; the connection of the soul of man with animal conditions; which shows itself in all the masterful

peoples in human history. Grand intellectuality in the races of men, has been generally connected, more or less, with robustness, life-tenacity, and strong vital forces. Weak people, for the most part, are weak in both body and mind; run a short race; have but a slight hold upon life, and soon vanish away.

It is a characteristic of the Negro race that it seems, everywhere, to have a smack of the immortal. Amid the rude conditions of the fatherland, shut out for ages from the world's civilization, fecundity and vital powers were immemorial qualities. Never, until the ravages of the slave-trade, was there known a disturbance of this vital feature.

During the last two hundred or more years, a large section of the race has been in a captive state, on the continent and the islands of America. But not even the severest conditions of bondage have been able to bar out this quality. The Negro, everywhere, is a productive factor on American soil. The slave-trade was, for the most part, put an end to, in 1809. The slave populations of the West Indies, of the American States, of Brazil and the other South American States, at the time of the great Emancipations which have taken place in this century, were less than half of their present numbers under freedom; and hence our increase, under the British, American, and Brazilian flags, cannot be attributed to the supplies and reinforcements of the slave-trade.

And yet here is the fact, that this race, under the unsettled and abnormal conditions of a new freedom, has gone on increasing, at, at least, as rapid a rate as any people on the continent.[3]

In the West Indies, the white race, in many quarters, decreases. By the census of 1880 the rate of *our* increase, i. e. in the United States, was said to be fully 6 per cent greater than that of the whites. That census report has since been repudiated as incorrect. Nevertheless the last returns of the Census Bureau, though placing us considerably below that of the white population of the land, sets forth the fact of an *actual* increase of our numbers; though, relatively, less than that of white Americans. The disparity, however, can easily be accounted for by the unsettled conditions of a newly emancipated and antagonized people.[4]

Here then is the fact of persistent vitality, under the difficulties of poverty, bitter repulsion, and political suffering. It is not a fact which stands separate and apart from ideas. Vital force has always some potent underlying principles. There must be thrift, or economy, or a measure of family virtue; or conscious, or unconscious Hope; some, or most of these; or otherwise, a people,—any people,—will die out. Spiritual ideas do, more or less, attend the persistent life of the humblest classes. The Negro lives and grows; because vitality, in his case, springs from internal sources.

The averment may be made—"Your increase is only an evidence of the sheerest animality. It has no relation to the *inner* life, which is the true criterion of manhood, the only promise of futurity."

2. But this taunt is easily refuted. It is refuted first, by a view of its *intellectual* aspect; and I will take up its spiritual phase later on.

*Now I maintain that the mental progress of the Negro has run parallel with its persistent and vital continuity.*

The special point to be considered, just here, is the fact that in all the places of our servitude every effort has been put forth, by legislation, to shut out the light of letters from the intellectual eye of the black man. The Statute books, in every State and Nation, on this Western Continent, bristle with the laws which interdict the teaching of the Negro; which forbid, with severe penalties, his instruction in letters. And yet intellectual aspiration has characterized the race in all the lands of their servitude. The laws themselves testify the fact. And, thus, for two hundred years there has been a struggle for the Alphabet; the Primer; the Newspaper, and the Bible.[5]

"Put out the light; and then put out the light"[6] has been the common cry of slavery; in Virginia, in the Carolinas; in Mexico, in Peru, and in Brazil; in Jamaica and in Bermuda.

But the answering cry has gone up from multitudinous plantations, during the entire reign of slavery—"Light! Light!" And so, through murky darkness, despite law and penalties, in cane brake, in slave hut, in the seclusion of the forest; in the deep of night by the embers of dying fire-light; thousands of slaves have clandestinely groped, and stumbled, and plodded on; struggling to emerge from the darkness of ignorance, to attain, if possible, the ability to read, and the illumination of letters.

Thus it came to pass that even in the darkest days of slavery, not seldom, whole groups of men reached, dimly, to light of letters. Right from the gloomiest precincts of servitude sprung such geniuses as Phillis Wheatley, Banneker, Ward, and Garnett and others. Some, without doubt, were encouraged in their intellectual desires by generous, liberal-minded masters and mistresses. But even thus, the proffer of a gift is a nullity if there be no glad receptivity in the taker. The receptive, yearning faculty was in the Negro; and hence the anxiousness which constantly disclosed itself, in the domain of slavery, for light; and which everywhere met with the effort to reach it!

Just go back with me, a moment, to the year 1620. Stand up beside me, and look at that unfortunate captive! He is the *first* victim of the slave-trade; just landed on American soil. He is a naked pagan! For thousands of years, his ancestors, on the soil of Africa, have lived in a land of ignorance and benightedness; their intellectual life, never, during the ages, stirred by a breeze or a breath of mental inspiration from the world of letters. Through him, the race he represents, is now for the first time, brought into the neighborhood of cultivation, placed in juxtaposition with enlightened civilization.

It is two hundred years and more since this civilizing influence began; and you must remember that it has been only incidental; it has been unintentional; always tardy and reluctant; that it has been carried on under the severest and narrowest limitations.

Join to this another fact. It is indeed a fact of contrast, but it has its special significance.

At the time when the black man came in contact with the civilization of the Western World, there was a large group of nations, tribes, and peoples, on the Continent and in the Pacific and Atlantic seas, mostly, in precisely the same semi-barbarous condition as the Negro; with not a few, however, on a higher plane of elevation. There were the American Indians. There were the aboriginal Mexicans and Peruvians, south of the States. There were the Caribs of Hayti, Cuba, and Jamaica. There were the Maoris of New Zealand. There were the Gauches of the Canaries. There were the divers tribes of Australia. All these people were, nevertheless, crude and uncivilized peoples at the time of the discovery of America.

All were then, touched, for the first time, with the rising rays of civilization. And so it happens that we, with them, have run the same difficult course of enlightenment, which has been so grudgingly given the ruder peoples of the world.

How do we stand today, relatively, in the problem of attainment and of progress? I challenge any man to the comparison.

Go back again with me to that untrained, mind-shrouded, and naked African, a captive and a stranded slave on these shores.

Turn back again, on the instant, to his descendants, in the West Indies, and on this American soil. What is the sight which meets your eyes?

Here, remote from the land of their forefathers, is a race, numbering nigh thirty millions of people;[7] a people to a large extent lettered and enlightened; thousands of them cultured persons; in some of the lands of their captivity, merchants, planters, scholars, authors, magistrates, rulers. And, in *two* of the provinces of their former servitude, masters of the situation; having driven out their former owners; and, wresting from them the staff of authority, have become, in their own race and blood, Rulers of the land.[8]

Within the period of these two hundred years this same Negro race, despised, trodden upon, sold as beasts and cattle, oft-times murdered by overwork and cruelty, has, nevertheless, by almost superhuman energy, risen above their crushing servitude; and in the very lands of their oppression, produced historic names and characters. Out from the very limitations and agonies of slavery have come cultured civilians, accomplished gentlemen,

Physicians, Lawyers, Linguists, Mathematicians, Generals, Philosophers; and from the Coast of Africa men eminent in attainments, in great Universities; not seldom holding professorships in the great schools of Europe. Among these—Henry Diaz, an experienced and commanding officer in Brazil; Hannibal, Lieutenant-General in Russia; Don Juan Lateno, Latin Professor, at Saville; Anthony William Arno, Doctor of Philosophy of the University of Wittenburg.[9]

How stands the case with the divers races and peoples, living in Pagan isolation at the time of the discovery of America? Why, the breath of European civilization seemed too strong for nearly all of them! Down they went, tribe after tribe, race after race, to utter oblivion! Some of them are utterly extinct! Once I was shown a Bible in the Library of Andover Seminary, translated, by Elliott,[10] into the tongue of a New England tribe of Indians. There is not a man living on earth who can read it! The tribe has utterly perished!

Not so with the Negro. Not one of the then humbler races has stood the ordeal as he has. Terrible as has been the ordeal, through the murderous invasion of slave-traders, on the coast of Africa; by the horrors of the Mid-passage; and through the sufferings of slavery in the lands of our exile; still the Negro lives!

Neither have these other peoples surpassed this race in progress! Not one of them has pressed through direful agonies, up to the hopeful attainments and the promising destiny which seems clearly opening before us.

3. Allied to this intellectual outgrowth, is another incident of hope for the race,—*its moral and spiritual perception.*

I do not pretend angelic qualities for our race. Such a claim would be ludicrous. The common human depravity is our heritage with all the rest of humanity. Moreover slavery has brought forth its fruitful progeny of special enormities for the depravation of the Negro.

But it is a difficult thing to obliterate aboriginal qualities. The history of man shows how *innate* tendencies abide in a people, notwithstanding the most adverse, and even deteriorating circumstances. It is thus, through this peculiarity, that the Negro has held on to those special moral qualities, to those high spiritual instincts which were recognized by ancient Pagan writers as qualities of the Hamitic family; and which have been noticed by discerning Christian philosophers and philanthropists in all subsequent times.

Back of all the moral infirmities of nature and of the special vices bred of ignorance and servitude, there are certain constitutional tendencies in the race which are, without doubt, unique and special. A high moral altitude is a primitive quality, antecedent to the coming of Christianity; and which has developed into more positive forms, in Christian lands, under the inspiration of Christian teaching.[11]

The race is essentially religious. Even in his pagan state the *spiritual* instinct always has had the ascendency. Homer perceived this quality; for he speaks of the Gods visiting and feasting with

"Ethiopia's blameless race."[12]

The great African travellers of modern times speak of the same moral characteristic. The testimony of Adamson who visited Senegal in 1754 chimes in with that of Homer. "The Negroes," he says, "are sociable, humane, obliging and hospitable; and they have generally preserved an estimable simplicity of domestic manners. They are distinguished by their tenderness for their parents, and great respect for the aged."[13] In similar terms speaks the other great travellers into Africa: Mungo Park; Livingston; the great Stanley of our own day; that extraordinary personage, Mrs. Sheldon French, and others.[14] Kinmont, in his "Lectures on Man," says "that the sweet graces of the Christian religion appear almost too tropical and tender plants, to grow in the soil of the Caucasian mind; they require a character of human nature of which you can see the rude lineaments in the Ethiopian."[15] Dr. Wm. Ellery Channing, many years ago, declared—"We are holding in bondage one of the best races of the human family. . . . His nature is affectionate, easily touched; and hence is more open to religious impressions than the white man. . . . When I cast my eyes over our Southern region, the land of bowie knives, lynch law and duels—of chivalry, honor and revenge,—and when I consider that Christianity is declared to be 'charity, which seeketh not her own, is not easily provoked, thinketh no evil and endureth all things'—can I hesitate in deciding to which of the races in that land, Christianity is most adapted, and in which its noblest disciples are most likely to be reared?"[16]

It will be a great mistake to regard these native qualities of the race as merely *negative* qualities, divorced from strength and robustness. It was first here, if I mistake not, our friend, Dr. Blyden, erred in his learned and interesting Lecture, the other evening.[17] He seemed to think that *passivity* is the normal, aboriginal quality of the race. The Negro, however, is brave as well as gentle; courageous as well as amiable; a gallant soldier as well as a patient sufferer and an enduring martyr. The quiet and submissive qualities of the race have been, not seldom, the butt of ridicule and the sneer of the jester. How constant, down to the present day, is the purpose, in the common American mind, to make the term Negro the equivalent of a ludicrous *Simian*! One instance is quite conspicuous. If you visit the east corridor of the Capitol, on the Senate side, you will see there a noted picture of the naval battle on Lake Erie.[18] That picture is one of the most disgraceful prostitutions of Art in modern times! It is an attempt to stamp a libel and a lie on the dark brow of an innocent, a suffering, but a brave race.[19] There, the

Negro is represented as a frightened grimace and coward;[20] whereas we have the record of his prowess, and the eulogy of his bravery, in this very battle, in the archives of this Government. This picture is not only disgraceful to the vulgar creature who painted it; but it is disreputable to a nation which fastens, emblazons and perpetuates a gross mendacity upon the very walls of its National Capitol!

Moreover the fact is historic that, in the Revolutionary war, and in every conflict of this Nation with a foreign or domestic foe, the black man, whether as soldier or sailor, has been a hero; eulogized by Generals and Commodores for his prowess.[21] General Lord Wolsely, next to Von Moltke, the greatest Captain of the age, declares that "the Negro makes one of the bravest soldiers in the world."[22]

No one who has read the history of St. Domingo and the grand struggle of the brave Haytiens, under Touissant, can do otherwise than concur with Lord Wolseley's opinion. Where, elsewhere, in the annals of War, a grander martial spirit can be discerned, than under the mighty chief of Hayti, I know not. Nobody will deny the burning, blazing prowess of the black troops in our late civil war in the South. That prowess led to the enrolment of Negroes in the standing army of the Nation: and, year by year, we are receiving the reports of American Generals, of the grand qualities of the Negro Cavalry; whether in action, in conflict with the Indians; or in camp, in order, discipline, and high soldierly bearing.

These moral and manly qualities are indications of a noble future. Moral qualities are prophecies. Their predictive elements are strengthened by the facts of progress and of mental advancement which I have brought to your notice; and by the persistent vitality which itself reaches over to the future.

I say therefore that we have every reason to thank God and to take courage. That we have not gone up like sky-rockets, at once, to the highest Empyrean, in the brief period of a generation, is no cause for surprise in our own ranks, nor for the carpings of unthinking critics who delight in disparagement of the Negro. Every thoughtful reader of history knows, thoroughly well, the almost universal fact that the *first,* the almost immediate result of any great revolution, or, any large Emancipation is the decadence of a people. Freedom does not generate a spontaneous elevation, a prompt and extemporaneous development. It always takes an emancipated people TIME to draw themselves together; to get to know themselves, to learn to know their powers and their responsibilities. The children of Israel, after their deliverance from Egypt, went down, down, down for four hundred years; and never became anything until the times of David and Solomon. The modern Greeks, after their bloody severance from Turkish oppression, have had, down to the present, stagnant and unprogressive existence; and today are almost nobodies! See these petty South American Republics! What wonderful things have they done since their Emancipation?

And now I ask—Why should the Negro-haters of America demand a miraculous, a superhuman development in us? *Contrary* to the general trend of history we do show progress; and that should suffice, for just and reasonable men.[23]

At the same time we must remember that we have reached no place where we can say—"Rest and be thankful!" Nor should we forget that our heritage, for an age or more, is repulse and opposition. Great trials are, without doubt, yet before us as a people; long vistas of thorny roadways, we have yet to travel; many wounds, sore lacerations; and the suffering of many martyrdoms!

For a long time you will have to meet the assaults of that large brutal class which would fain sweep us out, as remorsely as they would trample out a nest of ants! And then you will have to resist the insidious influences of that weak *pious* class, which is ever prophesying the failure of the Negro; and then, Jesuitically, strive, by sneers, limitations, and cruel neglects to fulfil their own atheistic prophecy!

But you must never listen to the tones of discouragement, come from whatever quarter they may. Least of all may we give heed to the despairing tones of hopeless men in our own ranks, nor to the scepticism of those who confidently assert the narrowest limitations of Negro capacity.

They may tell you—"You have indeed made progress. We admit that you stand on a higher plane than your ancestors;—but you have gone as far as you *can* go! You are incapable of reaching the higher platforms of human achievement. The place of the Negro is, forever, a secondary and inferior one."

But don't you listen, for a moment, to the delusive dictum of finality. It is all a folly and a snare. You have risen from a most prostrate condition, to freedom. That was *one* step. You have pushed forward from freedom to manhood. That was another and a higher step. You have advanced somewhat from manhood to culture and monetary assistance. And now I ask — "Where, in what section of your constitution has been planted the law of belittling limitation? Into what cell of the Negro's brain has Almighty God dropt the stagnant atom of finality?"

My friends, there are no ascertained bounds to the growth of any active, energetic, hopeful and ambitious race. In the world of Art, Science, Philosophy and Letters, there is no pent up monopoly, which excludes *any* section of the great human family. And no spell has fallen upon the intellect of the Negro which confines *his* capacity to narrow and contracted grooves.

I am drawn to these suggestions by certain oblique tendencies of the day. Just now we are in real danger of being hoodwinked by specious, but unreal teachings, pertaining to the education of the race. Certain pseudo-philanthropists who pity the Negro, but cannot learn to love and to uplift him, are endeavoring to fasten upon his brain the "cordon of narrowness." Their counsel is, in substance, this:—"Keep the Negro in a narrow groove! His brain *is* narrow. Give him but a little learning! Then bind him down to the merest manual exercises! Keep him, perpetually, a clown in the fields!"

No such limitations, however, are suggested for the miserable, ofttimes brutalized immigrants, who, by tens of thousands, are landed upon our shores!

"No pent-up Utica may contract *their* powers."[24] They, debased, not seldom half-paganized as they are, are to enter every avenue of culture in the land; to reach forth for the grandest acquisitions of both erudition and ambition! But the Negro must be kept in the humblest places; must be restrained to the narrowest systems of training!

For my own part I utterly repudiate all this specious policy. It is nothing but CASTE, and that of the most injurious character! I ask indeed that there shall be "common sense, in common schooling;" that there shall be no waste of money, or, of means, upon Incapacity; that a whole host of noodles shall not be sent to Universities or Colleges; that manual labour shall be the duty and the destiny of the ordinary and unaspiring.

But, when you fall upon a Scholar, an Artist, or a Genius, in any line, if even he be black as mid-night, open wide the gates; clear the pathways, for his noblest gait and his swiftest career! He has the right, by virtue of his endowments, to mount to the highest rounds of the ladder! Cheer him on his way! Give him every possible encouragement to reach the levels; and to rival, if possible, the most ambitious intellects of his age, be they as white as snow!

In the world of mind we are to tolerate neither exclusiveness nor caste. In all humanity and with self-restraint we are, as a people, to find our own place in the scale of nature, in the ranks of society, and in the order of the State.

But *we* must find it ourselves: not be forced into it by others! Hence we should resist the arrogance of that whole class of Americans, both in Church and State, who think they have a divine commission to thrust the Negro into a special place, as an underling, in American society.

Meanwhile we must study the situation in all quietness, soberness, with non-disturbance of soul, yea, even with a goodly quantum of stoicism. Withal, however, we must cultivate the spirit of Hope, perseverance, high self-reliance, and unfailing trust in God.

> "Zealous, yet modest, innocent, tho' free,
> Serene amidst alarms, inflexible in faith!"[25]

The great need of our race in this generation is sobriety, a deep sense of imperfection, diligence in all pursuits, simplicity in manners, and a deep and pervasive influence of the religious sentiment.

If this people get crazed by the possession of a little liberty; if they become intoxicated by inebriating and destructive politics; if they get carried away by the attainment of dazzling learning; if they are soon puffed up and made pompous by the grasp of a little wealth or property; and then begin to exaggerate their importance, to disgust their friends, to forget God, and so become blind to the high virtues—all hope for the future departs!

The race, in this country, is still at school. If they can learn to put away lightness, the love of pleasure, and the mere gratification of sense;

> "If they can scorn delights, and live
> Laborious days;"[26]

if they can bring themselves to see that the life of a race, is the same as the life of a family, or the life of a man;—that is, that it is a trust from God, for the noblest purposes of humanity, and for the glory of God; then they are sure to run a glad and a glorious career, if even it be a trying one; to attain the highest excellence of man; to achieve the grandest results in the majestic work which God has committed to the care of his creatures on earth.

*14.*

---

# At Hampton Institute, 1896

Despite the concerns expressed in "Incidents of Hope for the Negro Race in America," Crummell evidently had no qualms about visiting Hampton Institute on January 30, 1896. He gave two addresses on this occasion: the first is an appreciation of General Samuel Armstrong, founder of Hampton and mentor of Booker T. Washington, and the second is a short meditation on man as a constructive being.

### Founder's Day Address

THIS IS THE birthday of General Armstrong; and with reverence and gratitude you are holding it, year by year, in glad commemoration. This day is suggestive of a grand and a beneficent personality, whose works, all around us here, testify to the fact that he still lives, and that that life of his will be perpetuated, not merely in stately, useful buildings, but by living, active, and thankful hearts.

It was doubtless a glad day when General Armstrong was born. We cannot tell exactly, what was the gladness of that sensitive, trembling, tearful, but rejoicing mother, when she first looked upon that little eye-closed, pulling infant, her own flesh and blood, whom God had given to her bosom. But that motherly joy was not a joy single and alone, in that household. There was the joy of the father, the joy of brothers and sisters, the joy of kinsfolk and relatives. The joy of a wide circle, reaching out, I have no doubt, from their island home to distant households and kinsmen, and perchance to foreign lands. And what is true with regard to that one household, is true in innumerable households in all the lands of earth, and in all periods of time, on the birth of a child.

The birth of a child is, with some exceptions, a cause of delight and satisfaction in every quarter of the globe, and in all its divers nations.

What is the ground of joy and rejoicing? It is the principle of hope, or expectation, or assured faith.

What sort of man will this child make? No one can tell with certainty what will be the outcome of this new life and being. But every birth brings into existence expectancy, anticipation, hope. The minds of a whole circle of kinsfolk and friends are stirred, somewhat, by the principle of faith. They are, perchance unconsciously to themselves, thrust into the arena of the future. The thought, in some way, will arise—"This is going to make a man!" or, perhaps the query will arise, as it did in the case of John the Baptist—"What manner of child shall this be?"[1]

Now let me ask—what does all this signify?—Simply this, viz.—That when we come to think about human life, we are at once thrown into the attitude of *looking forward.*

First, it begins, on our coming into the world, by parents and kinsfolk. Then this attitude is taken by teachers and pastors. They with anxiousness begin to look forward for us. By and by, as years and thought come to the personal being, we ourselves rise to deep convictions and begin to look forward for ourselves.

In reading, here and there, detached statements concerning General Armstrong, I have been struck by this attitude of his mind. The tendency to look forward—the disposition to forecast things; the endeavour, by some native, inward impulse, to peer into the future, was a marked tendency of his nature.

Let me pause, just here, for a moment, to dwell upon an incident, in your Founder's life; which will show what I mean by "looking forward." Not only will it show you what I mean:— it will illustrate a marked trait of his character—I mean his foresight.

Here is a sketch of the General's character by your Mr. Howe.[2] I get it from the pages of your own WORKMAN, March 1894:—[Reminiscences given at a meeting of the Armstrong League of Hampton Workers.]

"This is a beautiful spot for the school," he said—"See that knoll over there" (there was a knoll or bluff by the creek where Academic Hall now stands, with a salt marsh between it and the Mansion House). "That's just the place for an Academic Building," he said. "Don't take too much trouble with these barracks. Three years will demonstrate whether we can make teachers out of these colored people. Then we shall want some substantial, lasting buildings. That will be the spot for the Academic Hall, and just here for a building for girls, and a general dining room. We'll call it Virginia Hall."—He gave it the very name it bears now. Then he pointed out sites for boys' cottages—all as you see it now. I sat on a log and just looked at him and laughed. I thought he was a visionary. It came to pass. Nothing was impossible to him—not a thing.

After Academic Hall was begun, we at last had no more money to pay the hands. "How much money do we owe on this building?" said the General to me. The bricks were all made. We footed up all the bills and found we owed $17,000. "Well," said the General, "I'm going North—If I don't get that money, you will never see me again." He went to General Howard[3] and to Mrs. Hemenway[4]—and the money came, as it always did.

Here is another by a Mr. Edward Jones:

[Hampton's first bricklayer and still in the School's employ.]

Now, Mr President, if we all have faith in God, as General Armstrong had, to go and dig out a foundation for an eighty thousand dollar house, without a dollar comparatively speaking, and depend on praying and working for money, which he did and got it every time, this is what I call faith equal to Abraham or anybody else. So if we have that kind of faith in God to believe he will help a good cause, then we may not fear about our League.[5] We will come out all right. All of us together ought to have half as much faith as General Armstrong. If we have it and work, that is all that is necessary. We must use the three W's that I heard Mr. Monroe[6] speak of five or six years ago when he was speaking to the Senior class. He said, "Work, watch, wait." If we work in faith we shall not have to wait very long.

Now this, unless I very greatly err, was a marked and a constantly recurring disposition in General Armstrong. He had, in its minor tones, the prophetical instinct. He could see, both *what* should be done in the future, and had the rare quality likewise, of knowing *how* to do the definite thing that should be done. And the result, under God, is the great "labor university." I called it this, once before, on this very spot, and I venture to give it this title again, to-day.[7]

Looking forward, then, is a great thing; and I purpose making it *the* topic of my speech to-day; because I am convinced that, in doing so, I shall contribute my small portion to the large purpose of this celebration—i.e. the commemoration of your great Founder.

I pause, just here, for a moment, to dwell, in the way of warning, on the opposite of the General's attitude; the antithesis of looking forward is backward. And from this I wish, at the start, to dissuade you. Don't look backward! It is the rarest of instances wherein one finds any advantage in ruminating upon the past. There is so much of error and blindness, of guilt and trangression, in the past, that you had better turn away from it. Even under the very best circumstances, and with the grandest inheritance, there is more or less of weakness, frailty and disaster, in the past, so that a man had better turn his face the other way. If you were the sons of nobles, or kings, or emperors; what good, save in exceptional cases, would the memory of their careers do you? You have got to build up your own characters, to shape your own careers, and make your own fortunes.

But you are not of either kingly or noble heritage. You and I are the inheritors of sorrows and disasters. The painful memories of past servitude are our inheritance! Up they come, thick and fast; the agonies and the wrongs of ancestors, torn from their native land; the horrors of the mid-passage; the long stretch of crushing and benighted slavery, 200 years and more, on the blood-stained soil of America!

What can all these yield but bitterness, melancholy and despair? Human beings are born for destiny! Their lives are given them in order to stretch out, beyond their times, to somewhat above and beyond both selfish and transitory things.

Don't then look backward. There is naught but the dead past *there*. It can give you neither health, nor strength, nor life. The past is the domain of darkness, and distress and melancholy remembrance and brooding pain!

"Let the dead past bury its dead!"[8]

Look forward!

First of all, then, I exhort—look forward with definite aims, plans and purposes. You are all young, I know: but you are, none of you, too young to form a plan of life. You have read the scriptures and you see in them, how not a few of their great men fixed, early in their lives, their ends and objects of pursuit. They did not wait for age, or maturity, ere they decided what they would do, in this busy responsible life which God had given them. In the very freshness of their years, life opened before them its grand opportunities, its lofty duties, and its majestic possibilities. And with clear, open vision they took in, gladly, the glory of life, the beauty of responsibility, the weight of burdensome duty, and leaped forward to the grand summonses of human existence. And thus it has come to pass that, through the prescience, the forecasting of minds as youthful as your own, we have the glorious portraits on the pages of Scripture, of the purity, the uprightness, the straight forwardness of youthful Joseph; the simplicity and piety of Samuel; the heroic fervor of David; the unswerving loyalty of Daniel; the unstained godliness of Timothy; and others who show forth the majesty and the nobleness, of youthful election of the higher ends of living; of an early consecration of soul to the lofty purposes of human existence.

And what you have learned of youthful purpose and aspiration from the

Scripture of God, you have caught, if you have pondered it rightly, from the voluminous pages of secular history.

There you can see, with your own eyes, how numerous are the names of those who, in art, and mechanism, and scholarship and science, and statesmanship planted in almost the boyish periods of life, the high resolves and the noble ambitions, by which in the later years, they reached the highest rounds of the ladder of fame; and honoured their kindred, and gave glory, as well as beneficence, to their nations!

Run down the line of these exalted names. Look at this panorama of noble characters, who began the life of noble activities long before they reached their majority;—began it in the lofty resolves, and the majestic aims which stirred their bosoms while yet in early boyhood.

So do you, I beseech you, magnify and illustrate your boyhood and your girlhood by the objects and the purposes which you set distinctly before you as the ends of your existence.

Don't wait for manhood and womanhood; look before you!

There is, I know, a "tide in the affairs of man which taken at the flow, leads on to fortune."[9] In the first place, don't you wait for it: and in the second, if it comes, don't let the tide take *you*. Do you take *it*. It is your instrument. Look out for it, if it comes your way, and you are sure it can be used for the good of man and the glory of God; and then use it. But don't wait in life, for any tide, or flood. Look before you! For remember that the principle of forecast is a principle of your nature. The prophetic element which we see in Isaiah and Ezekiel, is a natural quality; magnified, in these grand seers to vast proportions, by special divine inspiration. We lesser men must see the more ordinary element in the fortunes and the uses of life. And to do this we must open the eyes God has given us, and look forward.

Look forward, then, to the special personal activities in which you will employ yourselves in life. Choose and elect, at an early day, what you are going to do. Be careful and wise in your choice. Ask advice of parents and elders; but, by all means, reach forward to determinate aims, and at an early day. Don't suffer yourselves to be mere machines in life, looking for something to turn up, like a set of blind Micawbers.[10] Look forward with settled plans; with distinct purposes; with noble and beneficent aims; with indomitable wills; with great courage; and with abiding faith in God!

Remember that life is a two-fold subsistence. The major quantity is, indeed, the Almighty Being who made and governs us. But, vast and stupendous as He is, He wills that man shall be a secondary, but responsible agent in it.

So much then, with regard to the *personal* aspects of the matter.

2. But now arises the query—Are we to live simply for ourselves? Are

we to be absorbed only in our own interests? Are the forecastings of the human soul to pertain mostly to selfish personal ends?

If such were our views, what a travesty would this commemoration of General Armstrong be!

No, my friends, the previsions of human souls, are to reach out from the limitations of our personal being to larger circuits and wider circumferences than our own individualism. The healthiness and integrity of our lives is found in the principle of reproductiveness. We are lofty, noble, and superior in proportion as we can get beyond ourselves, and stretch out in living and saving regards to others. This was the greatness of your great Founder. No one eulogizes him because he took care of himself! No one extends his memory, because he sought mere personal aggrandizement! The praise and honor of his name come from the fact, that, in self-forgetfulness, he lived for others. He is a great man in the regards of men, because, though dead in the body he still lives; by sending down, daily, the beneficence of a large and generous life, to the scores and hundreds of eager minds who gather here, for preparation for the great duties of life.

So too, if *you* would imitate *his* prescience; if you are eager to open the eyes of your soul to noble duty and generous beneficence; you must look out beyond the limitations of your own personal being; and cultivate gracious anxieties for others.

Let me dwell, for a moment or two, upon the solicitudes which are demanded of our souls, beyond the confines of narrow personality.

"No man liveth to himself."[11] Relations of life cluster, like infinitesimal arteries, every where around us. We reach out, every moment, unconsciously to ourselves, to kindred spirits, both visible and invisible, with telling influence and power. But the more conscious and intentional man's influence may be, the higher do we reach in dignity, and the stronger in might.

It is this solicitude for others which is the glory of motherhood; the beauty of patriotism; the excellence of brotherhood; the grace of sisterly devotion. Out of these regards come the forecast and the self-sacrifices of devoted friendship—such as Damon and Pythias,[12] and of Jonathan and David.[13] Let us see then how this sentiment will act in the relations of life.

Doubtless it will lead us to look before us.

First, *for the family;* for our family regards come *first,* in the order of nature, and *primary,* in the evolutions and the outgrowth of human society. You cannot separate your regards and solicitudes from your fellow beings. As you, in your birth and growth, are a part of others who preceded you; so, likewise, you are a section of that constant flow of human life which is rushing up daily into being. We all, are "parts of the tremendous whole."[14]

Think then of the family. Look forward for your own kin. Provide, by generous anticipations and manly zeal, for your own blood.

Remember this, especially, that the idea of family stretches out beyond the limitations of blood and kinship. Don't forget that a *race* is a family; and that solicitudes, anxieties, forethought, and noble zeal, are needed and are *due* to the race with which you are connected; and are as heavy a responsibility as that of family. Very many of you here, to-day, are, as I am, *Negroes*. I speak to such especially;—Do not suffer any advantages, in the present or the future, to lead to forgetfulness of race feeling, and race devotedness! The very abjectness of this race should be a stimulant to every one of you, to the greatest self-sacrifice, and the warmest, heartiest loyalty to, and the most generous zeal for the uplifting of this needy, rising and, I believe, most promising race.

This crystalizing the families of men into races, is manifestly the will and providence of God. It has become a part of the order of nature. By it the Almighty has always been working out special and important ends and there is nothing superfluous in His august plans. Care and interest in your race, makes you a co-worker with God for some noble, albeit unseen purpose in the future. Look forward, then, for your race!

In what I have said to you, this day, I have been anxious to impress the idea:

1st. That things, in this life, have but seldom, greatness in themselves. The greatness of most earthly things springs from their relation to something beyond themselves. All the things of time reach over to invisible and eternal things, and their value resides in something *beyond!* By the very constitution of your being, you *must* act in the present; but remember that the very fact of man's imperfection should force him to constant dissatisfaction with his present imperfect state. And this will surely give him that quality, which we all need—prescience;—the disposition to work for the future. This looking forward is a noble and uplifting attitude. It is a divine instinct. The poet tells us.

> "Man's heart the Almighty to the future set,
> By secret and invisible springs."[15]

And we all should strive to rise to the measurement of our being and our duty, in this regard.

I say, therefore, do not suffer yourselves to be chained to the visible and the transitory. Open your eyes. Look forward. Behold grand futurity! It is no imagination. It is the grand solid reality of our spiritual being, our higher, nobler nature stretched out constantly toward the eternal.

Look forward then. Do not limit your lives by the boundaries of sense. Meet all present duties, but tie the simplest of them on to the future. Do any of you say that this is an impossibility? Why that is surely blindness!

Young men! young women!—Can't you *see?* You do see! You see, I know, these walls; this ceiling; these seats; these men and women around you.

But haven't you too the *other* sight? The sight which sees into the invisible? The sight which looks into the future? Can't you see truth, beauty, and spiritual excellence? Can't you look into futurity? If I thought you could not, I would stand here and pray, as the prophet of old did—"Lord open the eyes of these youth that they may see."[16]

But I will not indulge in any such misgivings. I take it for granted, that, like your great master and benefactor you too are looking forward:—looking forward for the acquisition of learning; looking forward for the capacity for work; looking forward for the opportunities for grand beneficences; looking forward for accumulation of useful wealth; looking forward for rearing noble families; looking forward for the importation of letters and learning into darkened regions; looking forward for the preaching and the triumphs of the Gospel; looking forward for the upbuilding of your race; looking forward for the illumination of light through all the borders of darkened Africa; looking forward for a regenerated nation here on American soil; looking forward for the reign of peace and purity in this sinful world; and then, beyond all, looking forward for that ineffable peace, and that endless light which are promised believers, in the Kingdom of grace and glory above.

## At Evening Prayers, on the Day of Prayer for Colleges

I HAVE GREAT satisfaction, my young friends and brethren, in having the opportunity once again of standing before you, this evening. It is a real privilege; but I shall not speak at great length. I have, however, a specific purpose in what I shall say; and I address myself, at once, to it.

I desire, first of all, to call your attention to the fact that the Almighty has put us into the world to be builders of men. For this end all colleges and schools have been founded.

You and I and all men have, to some extent, the capacity of constructiveness. We have certain inborn faculties, which, rightly cultivated fit human beings, to mould and fashion the souls and characters of other human beings. The schools of nations and society are the places where this education of human powers is carried on, to give us the fitness and facility to build men.

Think for a moment of the faculties God has given us; and you will see, at once, proof of this constructive power in human souls. What is imagination but a creative faculty? What is reason, but a basic element in our nature? What is judgement, but a compacting power? What is the will of man, but a guiding and determining force?

Look, for instance, at the lower nature of man, and you will see somewhat the proof of this constructiveness. Notice the physical powers of the body. Look at the human hand. It can indeed, drag down and destroy. But what is its proper and natural use, in the societies of men and in the work of life? All the concerns of life, all the activities of humanity, in families and states and communities, demonstrate the universal fact, that its proper use is to construct and to build up.

Hence from the development of the exercise of this natural power of the hand come all the several trades of communities. From the proper normal uses of the hand spring carpenters, and blacksmiths and wheelwrights and house-builders and all the other trades of men. We are constructive beings, judged only by our outward and physical nature.

But how more especially, then, is all this true of the inner, the invisible, intellectual and spiritual nature of man! For indeed what is the hand more than the claw of a bird, were it not for the inner unseen power of our be-ing,—the constructive power which lies entirely in the human soul?

Schools then, such schools as this, and all other schools, are the training grounds for just the purpose I am dwelling upon. We send our little children to infant schools, we send our boys and girls to the common schools, we send our young men and maidens to Academies and Colleges, to train their faculties for constructive uses.

To this end we are gathered together here, in this great "Labor University." While here, if you have come to a true knowledge of your work and responsibility in this place, you are in the process of preparation; in order that you may go forth hence, to build up yourselves and others, for the uses of life.

What a wonderful thing it is to build up a human soul! Just close your eyes for a moment, as you sit here; and think of the primitive, barbarous people of the world; such as I have seen in the tribes of Africa; uncivilized, ignorant, mind-shrouded, in some respects like animals; and then contrast them with the great civilized, progressive nations of the earth, such as the English, the German and the French; and you will see that the difference lies in this; viz., that their progress has been brought about by the gradual but persistent training of the youth of these nations, from original barbarism, generation after generation, down to the present.

You may thus see how that this school has for its ultimate end and pur-pose, the training and fashioning men to greatness, power and beneficence. The world would never have had these great nations but for this training and building up of men. It is not an original result; a native inborn quality in any people. It is the result and outgrowth of training and rigid preparation of souls.

So thus it comes to pass that this is the master object of the schools of nations. And nothing powerful, nothing glorious and majestic, nothing good, can be brought about except by the building up of human nature.

And this will come from the training you are getting here in the schoolroom and in the shops. It is the shaping of character to enable you to lift up other men, to make them stand upon their feet, to give the use of their limbs: their *interior* limbs; i.e. the faculties and powers of the soul: to push them upward and onward; to lift them up to glory.

You are builders of human souls! Build them up in truth! Build them up in goodness! Build them up in integrity! Build them up in purity; in firmness; and in godliness! Build them up for the benefit of man, and for the glory of God!

# 15.

## *Civilization the Primal Need*
## *of the Race*

Crummell's growing unease over industrial education, at least as espoused by Booker T. Washington, eventually led to the organization of the American Negro Academy in March 1897. Here, in his inaugural address to the academy, Crummell reaffirmed his faith in the ideas of race and intellect. The special need of the race, he spelled out, was civilization, "not mere mechanism; not mere machinery; not mere handicraft; not the mere grasp on material things; not mere temporal ambitions." Crummell proposed to meet this need through a community of true leaders who would nurture scholars and scholarship and through their publications would teach the crude masses race consciousness and race pride.

GENTLEMEN:—

There is no need, I apprehend, that I should undertake to impress you with a sense either of the need or of the importance of our assemblage here to-day. The fact of your coming here is, of itself, the clearest evidence of your warm acquiescence in the summons to this meeting, and of your cordial interest in the objects which it purposes to consider.

Nothing has surprised and gratified me so much as the anxiousness of many minds for the movement which we are on the eve of beginning. In the letters which our Secretary, Mr. Cromwell, has received, and which will be read to us, we are struck by the fact that one cultured man here and another there,—several minds in different localities,—tell him that this is just the thing they have desired, and have been looking for.

I congratulate you, therefore, gentlemen, on the opportuneness of your assemblage here. I felicitate you on the superior and lofty aims which have drawn you together. And, in behalf of your compeers, resident here in the city of Washington, I welcome you to the city and to the important deliberations to which our organization invites you.

Just here, let me call your attention to the uniqueness and specialty of this conference. It is unlike any other which has ever taken place in the history of the Negro, on the American Continent. There have been, since the landing of the first black cargo of slaves at Jamestown, Va., in 1619, numerous conventions of men of our race. There have been Religious Assemblies, Political Conferences, suffrage meetings, educational conventions. But *our* meeting is for a purpose which, while inclusive, in some respects, of these various concerns, is for an object more distinct and positive than any of them.

What then, it may be asked, is the special undertaking we have before us, in this Academy? My answer is the civilization of the Negro race in the United States, by the scientific processes of literature, art, and philosophy, through the agency of the cultured men of this same Negro race. And here, let me say, that the special race problem of the Negro in the United States is his civilization.

I doubt if there is a man in this presence who has a higher conception of Negro capacity than your speaker; and this of itself, precludes the idea, on my part, of race disparagement. But, it seems manifest to me that, as a race in this land, we have no art; we have no science; we have no philosophy; we have no scholarship. Individuals we have in each of these lines; but mere individuality cannot be recognized as the aggregation of a family, a nation, or a race; or as the interpretation of any of them. And until we attain the role of civilization, we cannot stand up and hold our place in the world of culture and enlightenment. And the forfeiture of such a place means, despite, inferiority, repulsion, drudgery, poverty, and ultimate death! Now gentlemen, for the creation of a complete and rounded man, you need the impress and the moulding of the highest arts. But how much more so for the realizing of a true and lofty *race* of men. What is true of a man is deeply true of a people. The special need in such a case is the force and application of the highest arts; not mere mechanism; not mere machinery; not mere handicraft; not the mere grasp on material things; not mere temporal ambitions. These are but incidents; important indeed, but pertaining mainly to man's material needs, and to the feeding of the body. And the incidental in life is incapable of feeding the living soul. For "man cannot live by bread alone, but by every word that proceedeth out of the mouth of God."[1] And civilization is the *secondary* word of God, given for the nourishment of humanity.

To make *men* you need civilization; and what I mean by civilization is the action of exalted forces, both of God and man. For manhood is the most majestic thing in God's creation; and hence the demand for the very highest art in the shaping and moulding of human souls.

What is the great difficulty with the black race, in this era, in this land? It is that both within their ranks, and external to themselves, by large schools of thought interested in them, material ideas in divers forms are made prominent, as the master-need of the race, and as the surest way to success. Men are constantly dogmatizing theories of sense and matter as the salvable hope of the race. Some of our leaders and teachers boldly declare, now, that *property* is the source of power; and then, that *money* is the thing which commands respect. At one time it is *official position* which is the masterful influence in the elevation of the race; at another, men are disposed to fall back upon *blood* and *lineage,* as the root (source) of power and progress.

Blind men! For they fail to see that neither property, nor money, nor station, nor office, nor lineage, are fixed factors, in so large a thing as the destiny of man; that they are not vitalizing qualities in the changeless hopes of humanity. The greatness of peoples springs from their ability to grasp the grand conceptions of being. It is the absorption of a people, of a nation, of a race, in large majestic and abiding things which lifts them up to the skies. These once apprehended, all the minor details of life follow in their proper places, and spread abroad in the details and the comfort of practicality. But until these gifts of a lofty civilization are secured, men are sure to remain low, debased and grovelling.

It was the apprehension of this great truth which led Melancthon,[2] 400 years ago, to declare—"Unless we have the scientific mind we shall surely revert again to barbarism."[3] He was a scholar and a classic, a theologian and a philosopher. With probably the exception of Erasmus,[4] he was the most erudite man of his age. He was the greatest Grecian of his day. He was rich "with the spoils of time."[5] And so running down the annals of the ages, he discovered the majestic fact, which Coleridge has put in two simple lines:

"We may not hope from outward things to win
The passion and the life whose fountains are within;"[6]

which Wordsworth, in grand style, has declared,

"By the soul only the nations shall be free."[7]

But what is this other than the utterance of Melancthon,—"Without the scientific mind, barbarism." This is the teaching of history. For 2,000 years, Europe has been governed, in all its developments, by Socrates, and Aristotle, and Plato, and Euclid. These were the great idealists; and as such, they were the great progenitors of all modern civilization, the majestic agents of God for the civil upbuilding of men and nations. For civilization is, in its origins, ideal; and hence, in the loftiest men, it bursts forth, producing letters, literature, science, philosophy, poetry, sculpture, architecture, yea, all the arts; and brings them with all their gifts, and lays them in the lap of religion, as the essential condition of their vital permanence and their continuity.

But civilization never seeks permanent abidence upon the heights of Olympus. She is human, and seeks all human needs. And so she descends, re-creating new civilizations; uplifting the crudeness of laws, giving scientific precision to morals and religion, stimulating enterprise, extending commerce, creating manufactures, expanding mechanism and mechanical inventions; producing revolutions and reforms; humanizing labor; meeting the minutest human needs, even to the manufacturing needles for the industry of seamstresses and for the commonest uses of the human fingers. All these are the fruits of civilization.

Who are to be the agents to lift up this people of ours to the grand plane of civilization? Who are to bring them up to the height of noble thought, grand civility, a chaste and elevating culture, refinement, and the impulses of irrepressible progress? It is to be done by the scholars and thinkers, who have secured the vision which penetrates the center of nature, and sweeps the circles of historic enlightenment; and who have got insight into the life of things, and learned the art by which men touch the springs of action.

For to transform and stimulate the souls of a race or a people is a work of intelligence. It is a work which demands the clear induction of world-wide facts, and the perception of their application to new circumstances. It is a work which will require the most skillful resources, and the use of the scientific spirit.

But every man in a race cannot be a philosopher: nay, but few men in any land, in any age, can grasp ideal truth. Scientific ideas however must be apprehended, else there can be no progress, no elevation.

Just here arises the need of the trained and scholarly men of a race to employ their knowledge and culture and teaching and to guide both the opinions and habits of the crude masses. The masses, nowhere are, or can be, learned or scientific. The scholar is exceptional, just the same as a great admiral like Nelson[8] is, or a grand soldier like Caesar or Napoleon. But the leader, the creative and organizing mind, is the master-need in all the societies of man. But, if they are not inspired with the notion of leadership and duty, then with all their Latin and Greek and science they are but pedants, trimmers, opportunists. For all true and lofty scholarship is weighty with the burdens and responsibilities of life and humanity.

But these reformers must not be mere scholars. They must needs be both scholars and philanthropists. For thus, indeed, has it been in all the history of men. In all the great revolutions, and in all great reforms which have transpired, scholars have been conspicuous; in the re-construction of society, in formulating laws, in producing great emancipations, in the revival of letters, in the advancement of science, in the renaissance of art, in the destruction of gross superstitions and in the restoration of true and enlightened religion.

And what is the spirit with which they are to come to this work? My answer is, that *disinterestedness* must animate their motives and their acts. Whatever rivalries and dissensions may divide man in the social or political world, let generosity govern *us*. Let us emulate one another in the prompt recognition of rare genius, or uncommon talent. Let there be no tardy acknowledgement of worth in *our* world of intellect. If we are fortunate enough, to see, of a sudden, a clever mathematician of our class, a brilliant poet, a youthful, but promising scientist or philosopher, let us rush forward, and hail his coming with no hesitant admiration, with no reluctant praise.

It is only thus, gentlemen, that we can bring forth, stimulate, and uplift all the latent genius, garnered up, in the by-places and sequestered corners of this neglected Race.

It is only thus we can nullify and break down the conspiracy which would fain limit and narrow the range of Negro talent in this caste-tainted country. It is only thus, we can secure that recognition of genius and scholarship in the republic of letters, which is the rightful prerogative of every race of men. It is only thus we can spread abroad and widely disseminate that culture and enlightenment which shall permeate and leaven the entire social and domestic life of our people and so give that civilization which is the nearest ally of religion.

# 16.

## The Prime Need of
## the Negro Race

As this essay makes clear, Crummell's disagreement with Booker T. Washington was not over the value of industrial education per se but the "undue or overshadowing exaggeration of it in the case of the Negro." The problem, in other words, was disproportion. Just as Crummell was adamant that higher education should not be wasted on "noodles and numbskulls," he was unwilling to see gifted and intelligent blacks confined to industries, trades, farming, and commerce. "The Prime Need of the Negro Race" was published in the *Independent* for August 19, 1897.

UNFORTUNATELY, men often misconceive some of the larger *incidents* of life for its *problems,* and thus, unconsciously, they hinder the progress of the race.

Just such a mistake, if I err not, has arisen with regard to the solution of the "Negro Problem" in the South. It may be seen in the divergence of two classes of minds: the one maintains that industrialism is the solution of the Negro problem; and another class, while recognizing the need of industrial skill, maintains that culture is the true solution.

The thing of magnitude in the South, all must admit, is the civilization of a new race. The question is, then, how is this civilization to be produced? Is industrialism the prime consideration? Is the Negro to be built up from the material side of his nature?

But industrialism is no new thing in Negro life in this country. It is simply a change in the old phase of Southern Society. It is, in fact, but an incident;

doubtless a large, and in some respects, a vital one. It would be the greatest folly to ignore its vast importance. Yet it is not to be forgotten that the Negro has been in this "school of labor" under slavery in America, fully two hundred and fifty years; and every one knows that it has never produced his civilization. That it was crude, previous to emancipation; that it is to be enlightened labor now, in a state of freedom, is manifestly but an alteration in the form of an old and settled order of life.

When the Negro passed from under the yoke he left a state of semi-barbarism behind him, put his feet for the first time within the domain of civilization, and immediately there sprang up before him a new problem of life. But that problem is not industrialism. That is simply the modification of an old condition; for it is but the introduction of intelligence into the crudeness of the old slave-labor system.

The other question, then, presents itself—is not the Negro's elevation to come from the quickening and enlightenment of his higher nature? Is it to come from below or from above?

It seems manifest that the major factor in this work for the Negro is his higher culture. There is not dispute as to the need of industrialism. This is a universal condition of life everywhere. But there is not need of an undue and overshadowing exaggeration of it in the case of the Negro.

And, first of all, industrialism itself is a *result* in man's civilization, not a cause. It may exist in a people and with much excellence for ages, and still that people may "lie in dull obstruction,"[1] semi-barbarous and degraded. We see in all history large populations moving in all the planes of industrial life, both low and high, and yet paralyzed in all the high springs of action, and for the simple reason that the hand of man gets its cunning from the brain. And without the enlightened brain what is the hand of man more than the claw of a bird or the foot of a squirrel? In fine, without the enlightened brain, where is civilization?

The Negro race, then, needs a new factor for its life and being, and this new factor must come from a more vitalizing source than any material condition. The end of industrialism is thrift, prosperity or gain. But civilization has a loftier object in view. It is to make men grander; it is to exalt them in the scale of being; and its main energy to this end is the "higher culture."

Observe, then, just here, that "every good gift and every perfect gift comes from above."[2] I have no hesitation in using this text (albeit thus abbreviated) as an aphorism. And what I wish to say in its interpretation is this, viz., that all the greatness of men comes from altitudes. All the improvement, the progress, the culture, the civilization of men come from somewhere above. They never come from below!

Just as the rains and dews come down from the skies and fall upon the hills and plains and spread through the fields of earth with fertilizing power, so, too, with the culture of human society. Some exalted man, some great people, some marvelous migration, some extraordinary and quickening cultivation, or some divine revelation, "from above" must come to any people ere the processes of true and permanent elevation can begin among them. And this whole process I call civilization.

If a more precise and definite meaning to this word is demanded, I reply that I use it as indicative of letters, literature, science and philosophy. In other words, that this Negro race is to be lifted up to the acquisition of the higher culture of the age. This culture is to be made a part of its heritage; not at some distant day, but now and all along the development of the race. And no temporary fad of doubting or purblind philanthropy is to be allowed to make "industrial training" a substitute for it.

For, first of all, it is only a dead people who can be put into a single groove of life. And, next, every live people must have its own leaders as molders of its thought and determiners of its destiny: men, too, indigenous to the soil in race and blood.

For it is thought that makes the world—high, noble, prophetic, exalted and exalting thought. It is this that makes races and nations, industries and trades, farming and commerce; and not the reverse of this, i.e., that these make thought and civilization. And without thought, yea, scientific thought, peoples will remain everlastingly children and underlings, the mere tools and puppets of the strong.

And such thought, in these days, comes from the schools. The leaders of races must have wisdom, science, culture and philosophy. One such man has often determined the character and destiny of his race for centuries.

This does not mean that noodles and numbskulls shall be sent to college; nor that every Negro shall be made a scholar; nor that there shall be a waste of time and money upon incapacity. No one can make a thimble hold the contents of a bucket! But what it does mean is this, that the whole world of scholarship shall be opened to the Negro mind; and that it is not to be fastened, temporarily or permanently to the truck-patch or to the hoe, to the anvil or to the plane; that the Negro shall be allowed to do his own thinking in any and every sphere, and not to have that thinking relegated to others. It means that when genius arises in this race and elects, with flaming torch, to push its way into the grand arcanum of philosophy or science or imagination, no bar shall be raised against its entrance; albeit it be incarnated in a form deeply tinged with

"The shadowed livery of the burnished sun."[3]

I submit:

1. That civilization is the foremost, deepest need of the Negro race.

2. That the "higher culture" is its grandest source.

3. That the gift to the Negro of the scientific mind, by Fisk and Clark and Lincoln,[4] and Oberlin and Howard[5] and Yale, and Harvard and other colleges, is of the most incalculable value to the black race.

# 17.

## The Attitude of the American Mind toward the Negro Intellect

As its president Crummell was invited to give the first annual address to the American Negro Academy on December 28, 1897. Fittingly, he chose as his subject the black intellect. In a sweeping survey he described the struggles experienced by African-Americans to acquire intellectual training, setting the late nineteenth-century vogue for "industrialism" in its proper historical context. Reiterating the need for "civilization," Crummell concluded his remarks with an appreciation of the scholarship of W. E. B. Du Bois and Kelly Miller, drawing attention to the work of the American Negro Academy and the intellectual achievements of its members.

FOR THE FIRST TIME in the history of this nation the colored people of America have undertaken the difficult task, of stimulating and fostering the genius of their race as a distinct and definite purpose. Other and many gatherings have been made, during our own two and a half centuries' residence on this continent, for educational purposes; but ours is the first which endeavors to rise up to the plane of culture.

For my own part I have no misgivings either with respect to the legitimacy, the timeliness, or the prospective success of our venture. The race in the brief period of a generation, has been so fruitful in intellectual product, that the time has come for a coalescence of powers, and for reciprocity alike in effort and appreciation. I congratulate you, therefore, on this your first anniversary. To me it is, I confess, a matter of rejoicing that we have, as a people, reached a point where we have a class of men who will come together for purposes, so pure, so elevating, so beneficent, as the cultivation of mind, with the view of meeting the uses and the needs of our benighted people.

I feel that if this meeting were the end of this Academy; if I could see that it would die this very day, I would nevertheless, cry out—"All hail!" even if I had to join in with the salutation—"farewell forever!"[1] For, first of all, you have done, during the year, that which was never done so completely before,—a work which has already told upon the American mind; and next you have awakened in the Race an ambition which, in some form, is sure to reproduce both mental and artistic organization in the future.

The cultured classes of our country have never interested themselves to stimulate the desires or aspirations of the mind of our race. They have left us terribly alone. Such stimulation, must, therefore, in the very nature of things, come from ourselves.

Let us state here a simple, personal incident, which will well serve to illustrate a history.

I entered, sometime ago, the parlor of a distinguished southern clergyman. A kinsman was standing at his mantel, writing. The clergyman spoke to his relative—"Cousin, let me introduce to you the Rev. C., a clergyman of our Church." His cousin turned and looked down at me; but as soon as he saw my black face, he turned away with disgust, and paid no more attention to me than if I were a dog.

Now, this porcine gentleman, would have been perfectly courteous, if I had gone into his parlor as a cook, or a waiter, or a boot-black. But my profession, as a clergyman, suggested the idea of letters and cultivation; and the contemptible snob at once forgot his manners, and put aside the common decency of his class.

Now, in this, you can see the attitude of the American mind toward the Negro intellect. A reference to this attitude seems necessary, if we would take in, properly, the present condition of Negro culture.

It presents a most singular phenomenon. Here was a people laden with the spoils of the centuries,[2] bringing with them into this new land the culture of great empires; and, withal, claiming the exalted name and grand heritage of Christians. By their own voluntary act they placed right beside them a large population of another race of people, seized as captives, and brought to their plantations from a distant continent. This other race was an unlettered, unenlightened, and a pagan people.

What was the attitude taken by this master race toward their benighted bondsmen? It was not simply that of indifference or neglect. There was nothing negative about it.

They began, at the first, a systematic ignoring of the fact of intellect in this abased people. They undertook the process of darkening their minds.

"Put out the light, and then, put out the light!"[3] was their cry for centuries. Paganizing themselves, they sought a deeper paganizing of their serfs than the original paganism that these had brought from Africa. There was no legal artifice conceivable which was not resorted to, to blindfold their souls from the light of letters; and the church, in not a few cases, was the prime offender.[4]

Then the legislatures of the several states enacted laws and Statutes, closing the pages of every book printed to the eyes of Negroes; barring the doors of every school-room against them! And this was the systematized method of the intellect of the South, to stamp out the brains of the Negro!

It was done, too, with the knowledge that the Negro had brain power. There was *then,* no denial that the Negro had intellect. That denial was an after thought. Besides, legislatures never pass laws forbidding the education of pigs, dogs, and horses. They pass such laws against the intellect of *men.*

However, there was then, at the very beginning of the slave trade, everywhere, in Europe, the glintings forth of talent in great Negro geniuses,—in Spain, and Portugal, in France and Holland and England;[5] and Phillis Wheatley and Banneker and Chavis[6] and Peters,[7] were in evidence on American soil.

It is manifest, therefore, that the objective point in all this legislation was INTELLECT,—the intellect of the Negro! It was an effort to becloud and stamp out the intellect of the Negro!

The *first* phase of this attitude reached over from about 1700 to 1820:—and as the result, almost Egyptian darkness fell upon the mind of the race, throughout the whole land.

Following came a more infamous policy. It was the denial of intellectuality in the Negro; the assertion that he was not a human being, that he did not belong to the human race. This covered the period from 1820 to 1835, when Gliddon and Nott and others, published their so-called physiological work, to prove that the Negro was of a different species from the white man.

A distinguished illustration of this ignoble sentiment can be given. In the year 1833 or 4 the speaker was an errand boy in the Anti-slavery office in New York City.

On a certain occasion he heard a conversation between the Secretary and two eminent lawyers from Boston,—Samuel E. Sewell and David Lee Child. They had been to Washington on some legal business. While at the Capitol they happened to dine in the company of the great John C. Calhoun, then senator from South Carolina. It was a period of great ferment upon the question of Slavery, States' Rights, and Nullification; and consequently the Negro was the topic of conversation at the table. One of the utterances of Mr. Calhoun was to this effect—"That if he could find a Negro who knew the Greek syntax, he would then believe that the Negro was a human being and should be treated as a man."

Just think of the crude asininity of even a great man! Mr. Calhoun went to "Yale" to study Greek Syntax, and graduated there. His son went to Yale to study Greek Syntax, and graduated there. His grandson, in recent years, went to Yale, to learn the Greek Syntax, and graduated there. Schools and Colleges were necessary for the Calhouns, and all other white men to learn the Greek Syntax.

And yet this great man knew that there was not a school, nor a college in which a black boy could learn his A. B. C's. He knew that the law in all the Southern States forbade Negro instruction under the severest penalties. How then was the Negro to learn the Greek syntax? How then was he to evidence to Mr. Calhoun his human nature? Why, it is manifest that Mr. Calhoun expected the Greek syntax to grow in *Negro brains,* by spontaneous generation!

Mr. Calhoun was then, as much as any other American, an exponent of the nation's mind upon this point. Antagonistic as they were upon *other* subjects, upon the rejection of the Negro intellect they were a unit. And this, measurably, is the attitude of the American mind to-day:—measurably, I say, for thanks to the Almighty, it is not universally so.

There has always been a school of philanthropists in this land who have always recognized mind in the Negro; and while recognizing the limitations which *individual* capacity demanded, claimed that for the RACE, there was no such thing possible for its elevation save the widest, largest, highest, improvement. Such were our friends and patrons in New England, in New York, Pennsylvania, a few among the Scotch Presbyterians and the "Friends" in grand old North Carolina; a great company among the Congregationalists of the East, nobly represented down to the present, by the "American Missionary Society," which tolerates no stint for the Negro intellect in its grand solicitudes. But these were exceptional.

Down to the year 1825, I know of no Academy or College which would open its doors to a Negro.[8] In the South it was a matter of absolute legal disability. In the North, it was the ostracism of universal caste-sentiment. The theological schools of the land, and of all names, shut their doors against the black man. An eminent friend of mine, the noble, fervent, gentlemanly Rev. Theodore S. Wright,[9] then a Presbyterian licentiate, was taking private lessons in theology, at Princeton; and for his offense was kicked out of one of its halls.

In the year 1832 Miss Prudence Crandall opened a private school for the education of colored girls;[10] and it set the whole State of Connecticut in a flame. Miss Crandall was mobbed, and the school was broken up.

The year following, the trustees of Canaan Academy in New Hampshire opened its doors to Negro youths; and this act set the people of that state on fire. The farmers of the region assembled with 90 yoke of oxen, dragged the Academy into a swamp, and a few weeks afterward drove the black youths from the town.[11]

These instances will suffice. They evidence the general statement, *i.e.* that the American mind has refused to foster and to cultivate the Negro intellect. Joined to this a kindred fact, of which there is the fullest evidence. Impelled, at times, by pity, a modicum of schooling and training has been given the Negro; but even this, almost universally, with reluctance, with cold criticism, with microscopic scrutiny, with icy reservation, and at times, with ludicrous limitations.

Cheapness chracterizes almost all the donations of the American people to the Negro:—Cheapness, in all the past, has been the regimen provided for the Negro in every line of his intellectual, as well as his lower life. And so, cheapness is to be the rule in the future, as well for his higher, as for his lower life:—cheap wages and cheap food, cheap and rotten huts; cheap and dilapidated schools; cheap and stinted weeks of schooling; cheap meeting houses for worship; cheap and ignorant ministers; cheap theological training; and now, cheap learning, culture and civilization!

Noble exceptions are found in the grand literary circles in which Mr. Howells moves—manifest in his generous editing of our own Paul Dunbar's poems.[12] But this generosity is not general, even in the world of American letters.

You can easily see this in the attempt, now-a-days, to side-track the Negro intellect, and to place it under limitations never laid upon any other class.

The elevation of the Negro has been a moot question for a generation past. But even to-day what do we find the general reliance of the American mind in determinating this question? Almost universally the resort is to material agencies! The ordinary, and sometimes the *extraordinary* American is unable to see that the struggle of a degraded people for elevation is, in its very nature, a warfare, and that its main weapon is the cultivated and scientific mind.

Ask the great men of the land how this Negro problem is to be solved, and then listen to the answers that come from divers classes of our white fellow-citizens. The merchants and traders of our great cities tell us—"The Negro must be taught to work;" and they will pour out their moneys by thousands to train him to toil. The clergy in large numbers, cry out—"Industrialism is the only hope of the Negro;" for this is the bed-rock, in their opinion, of Negro evangelization! "Send him to Manual Labor Schools," cries out another set of philanthropists. "'Hic haec, hoc,' is going to prove the ruin of the Negro," says the Rev. Steele, an erudite Southern Savan. "You must begin at the bottom with the Negro," says another eminent authority—as though the Negro had been living in the clouds, and had never reached the bottom. Says the Honorable George T. Barnes,[13] of Georgia—"The kind of education the Negro should receive should not be very refined nor classical, but adapted to his present condition:" as though there is to be no future for the Negro.

And so you see that even now, late in the 19th century, in this land of learning and science, the creed is—"Thus far and no farther," *i.e.* for the American black man.

One would suppose from the universal demand for the mere industrialism for this race of ours, that the Negro had been going daily to dinner parties, eating terrapin and indulging in champagne; and returning home at night, sleeping on beds of eiderdown; breakfasting in the morning in his bed, and then having his valet to clothe him daily in purple and fine linen—all these 250 years of his sojourn in this land. And then, just now, the American people, tired of all this Negro luxury, was calling him, for the first time, to blister his hands with the hoe, and to learn to supply his needs by sweatful toil in the cotton fields.

Listen a moment, to the wisdom of a great theologian, and withal as great philanthropist, the Rev. Dr. Wayland, of Philadelphia. Speaking, not long since, of the "Higher Education" of the colored people of the South, he said "that this subject concerned about 8,000,000 of our fellow-citizens, among whom are probably 1,500,000 voters. The education suited to these people is that which should be suited to white people under the same circumstances. These people are bearing the impress which was left on them by two centuries of slavery and several centuries of barbarism. This education must begin at the bottom. It must first of all produce the power of self-support to assist them to better their condition. It should teach them good citizenship and should build them up morally. It should be, first, a good English education. They should be imbued with the knowledge of the Bible. They should have an industrial education. An industrial education leads to self-support and to the elevation of their condition. Industry is itself largely an education, intellectually and morally, and, above all, an education of character. Thus we should make these people self-dependent. This education will do away with pupils being taught Latin and Greek, while they do not know the rudiments of English."[14]

Just notice the cautious, restrictive, limiting nature of this advice! Observe the lack of largeness, freedom and generosity in it. Dr. Wayland, I am sure, has never specialized just such a regimen for the poor Italians, Hungarians or Irish, who swarm, in lowly degradation, in immigrant ships to our shores. No! for them he wants, all Americans want, the widest, largest culture of the land; the instant opening, not simply of the common schools; and then an easy passage to the bar, the legislature, and even the judgeships of the nation. And they oft times get there.

But how different the policy with the Negro. *He* must have "an education which begins at the bottom." "He should have an industrial education," &c. His education must, first of all, produce the power of self-support, &c.

Now, all this thought of Dr. Wayland is all true. But, my friends, it is all false, too: and for the simple reason that it is only half truth. Dr. Wayland seems unable to rise above the plane of burden-bearing for the Negro. He seems unable to gauge the idea of the Negro becoming a thinker. He seems to forget that a race of thoughtless toilers are destined to be forever a race of senseless *boys;* for only beings who think are men.

How pitiable it is to see a great good man be-fuddled by a half truth. For to allege "Industrialism" to be the grand agency in the elevation of a race of already degraded labourers, is as much a mere platitude as to say, "they must eat and drink and sleep;" for man cannot live without these habits. But they never civilize man; and *civilization* is the objective point in the movement for Negro elevation. Labor, just like eating and drinking, is one of the inevitabilities of life; one of its positive necessities. And the Negro has had it for centuries; but it has never given him manhood. It does not *now*, in wide areas of population, lift him up to moral and social elevation. Hence the need of a new factor in his life. The Negro needs light: light thrown in upon all the circumstances of his life. The light of civilization.

Dr. Wayland fails to see two or three important things in this Negro problem:—

(a) That the Negro has no need to go to a manual labor school.[15] He has been for two hundred years and more, the greatest laborer in the land. He is a laborer *now;* and he must always be a laborer, or he must die. But:

(b) Unfortunately for the Negro, he has been so wretchedly ignorant that he has never known the value of his sweat and toil. He has been forced into being an unthinking labor-machine. And this he is, to a large degree, to-day under freedom.

(c) Now the great need of the Negro, in our day and time, is intelligent impatience at the exploitation of his labor, on the one hand; on the other hand courage to demand a larger share of the wealth which his toil creates for others.

It is not a mere negative proposition that settles this question. It is not that the Negro does not need the hoe, the plane, the plough, and the anvil. It is the positive affirmation that the Negro needs the light of cultivation; needs it to be thrown in upon all his toil, upon his whole life and its environments.

What he needs is CIVILIZATION. He needs the increase of his higher wants, of his mental and spiritual needs. *This,* mere animal labor has never given him, and never can give him. But it will come to him, as an individual, and as a class, just in proportion as the higher culture comes to his leaders and teachers, and so gets into his schools, academies and colleges; and then enters his pulpits; and so filters down into his families and his homes; and the Negro learns that he is no longer to be a serf, but that he is to bare his strong brawny arm as a laborer; *not* to make the white man a Croesus,[16] but to make himself a man. He is always to be a laborer; but now, in these days of freedom and the schools, he is to be a laborer with intelligence, enlightenment and manly ambitions.

But, when his culture fits him for something more than a field hand or a mechanic, he is to have an open door set wide before him! And that culture, according to his capacity, he must claim as his rightful heritage, as a man:— not stinted training, not a caste education, not a Negro curriculum.

The Negro Race in this land must repudiate this absurd notion which is stealing on the American mind. The Race must declare that it is not to be put into a single groove; and for the simple reason (1) that *man* was made by his Maker to traverse the whole circle of existence, above as well as below; and that universality is the kernel of all true civilization, of all race elevation. And (2) that the Negro mind, imprisoned for nigh three hundred years, needs breadth and freedom, largeness, altitude, and elasticity; not stint nor rigidity, not contractedness.

But the "Gradgrinds"[17] are in evidence on all sides, telling us that the colleges and scholarships given us since emancipation, are all a mistake; and that the whole system must be reversed. The conviction is widespread that the Negro has no business in the higher walks of scholarship; that, for instance, Prof. Scarborough has no right to labor in philology; Professor Kelly Miller in mathematics; Professor Du Bois, in history; Dr. Bowen, in theology; Professor Turner, in science; nor Mr. Tanner in art.[18] There is no repugnance to the Negro buffoon, and the Negro scullion; but so soon as the Negro stands forth as an intellectual being, this toad of American prejudice, as at the touch of Ithuriel's spear,[19] starts up a devil!

It is this attitude, this repellant, this forbidding attitude of the American mind, which forces the Negro in this land, to both recognize and to foster the talent and capacity of his own race, and to strive to put that capacity and talent to use for the race. I have detailed the dark and dreadful attempt to stamp that intellect out of existence. It is not only a past, it is also, modified indeed, a present fact; and out of it springs the need of just such an organization as the Negro Academy.

Now, gentlemen and friends, seeing that the American mind in the general, revolts from Negro genius, the Negro himself is duty bound to see to the cultivation and the fostering of his own race-capacity. This is the chief purpose of this Academy. *Our* special mission is the encouragement of the genius and talent in our own race. Wherever we see great Negro ability it is our office to light upon it not tardily, not hesitatingly; but warmly, ungrudgingly, enthusiastically, for the honor of our race, and for the stimulating self-sacrifice in upbuilding the race. Fortunately for us, as a people, this year has given us more than ordinary opportunity for such recognition. Never before, in American history, has there been such a large discovery of talent and genius among us.

Early in the year there was published by one of our members, a volume of papers and addresses, of more than usual excellence. You know gentlemen, that, not seldom, we have books and pamphlets from the press which, like most of our newspapers, are beneath the dignity of criticism. In language, in style, in grammar and in thought they are often crude and ignorant and vulgar. Not so with *"Talks for the Times"* by Prof. Crogman,[20] of Clark University. It is a book with largess of high and noble common sense; pure and classical in style; with a large fund of devoted racialism; and replete everywhere with elevated thoughts. Almost simultaneously with the publication of Professor Crogman's book, came the thoughtful and spicy narrative of Rev. Matthew Anderson of Philadelphia.[21] The title of this volume is *"Presbyterianism; its relation to the Negro;"* but the title cannot serve as a revelation of the racy and spirited story of events in the career of its author. The book abounds with stirring incidents, strong remonstrance, clear and lucid argument, powerful reasonings, the keenest satire; while, withal, it sets forth the wide needs of the Race, and gives one of the strongest vindications of its character and its capacity.[22]

Soon after this came the first publication of our Academy. And you all know the deep interest excited by the two papers, the first issue of this Society. They have attracted interest and inquiry where the mere declamatory effusions, or, the so-called eloquent harangues of aimless talkers and political wire-pullers would fall like snowflakes upon the waters. The papers of Prof. Kelly Miller and Prof. Du Bois have reached the circles of scholars and thinkers in this country. So consummate was the handling of Hoffman's "Race Traits and Tendencies"[23] by Prof. Miller, that we may say that it was the most scientific defense of the Negro ever made in this country by a man of our own blood: accurate, pointed, painstaking, and I claim conclusive.

The treatise of Prof. Du Bois upon the "Conservation of Race,"[24] separated itself, in tone and coloring, from the ordinary effusions of literary work in this land. It rose to the dignity of philosophical insight and deep historical inference. He gave us, in a most lucid and original method, and in a condensed form, the long settled conclusions of Ethnologists and Anthropologists upon the question of Race.

This treatise moreover, furnished but a limited measure of our indebtedness to his pen and brain. Only a brief time before our assembly last year, Prof. Du Bois had given a large contribution to the literature of the nation as well as to the genius of the race. At that time he had published a work which will, without doubt, stand permanently, as authority upon its special theme. *"The Suppression of the Slave Trade"*[25] is, without doubt, the one unique and special authority upon that subject, in print. It is difficult to conceive the possible creation of a similar work, so accurate and painstaking, so full of research, so orderly in historical statement, so rational in its conclusions. It is the simple truth, and at the same time the highest praise, the statement of one Review, that "Prof. Du Bois has exhausted his subject." This work is a step forward in the literature of the Race, and a stimulant to studious and aspiring minds among us.

One further reference, that is, to the realm of Art.

The year '97 will henceforth be worthy of note in our history. As a race, we have, this year, reached a high point in intellectual growth and expression.

In poetry and painting, as well as in letters and thought, the Negro has made, this year, a character.

On my return home in October, I met an eminent scientific gentleman; and one of the first remarks he made to me was—"Well, Dr. Crummell, we Americans have been well taken down in Paris, this year. Why," he said, "the prize in painting was taken by a colored young man, a Mr. Tanner from America. Do you know him?" The reference was to Mr. Tanner's "Raising of Lazarus," a painting purchased by the French Government, for the famous Luxembourg Gallery. This is an exceptional honor, rarely bestowed upon any American Artist. Well may we all be proud of this, and with this we may join the idea that Tanner, instead of having a hoe in his hand, or digging in a trench, as the faddists on industrialism would fain persuade us, has found his right place at the easel with artists.

Not less distinguished in the world of letters is the brilliant career of our poet-friend and co-laborer, Mr. Paul Dunbar.[26] It was my great privilege last summer to witness his triumph, on more than one occasion, in that grand metropolis of Letters and Literature, the city of London; as well as to hear of the high value set upon his work, by some of the first scholars and literati of England. Mr. Dunbar has had his poems republished in London by Chapman & Co.;[27] and now has as high a reputation abroad as he has here in America, where his luminous genius has broken down the bars, and with himself, raised the intellectual character of his race in the world's consideration.

These cheering occurrences, these demonstrations of capacity, give us the greatest encouragement in the large work which is before this Academy.

Let us enter upon that work, this year, with high hopes, with large purposes, and with calm and earnest persistence. I trust that we shall bear in remembrance that the work we have undertaken is our special function; that it is a work which calls for cool thought, for laborious and tireless painstaking, and for clear discrimination; that it promises nowhere wide popularity, or, exuberant eclat; that very much of its ardent work is to be carried on in the shade; that none of its desired results will spring from spontaneity; that its most prominent features are the demands of duty to a needy people; and that its noblest rewards will be the satisfaction which will spring from having answered a great responsibility, and having met the higher needs of a benighted and struggling Race.

## 18.

## *Tracts for the Negro Race*

Early in 1898 Crummell started work on a series of Tracts for the Negro Race. As originally conceived, there were to have been ten of these tracts on such themes as marriage, the family and the home, "leprous ministers," and "the duty of colored teachers." Crummell clearly was excited by this new venture. As he confided to a colleague, "*Our* people are poor, and the whites are but little interested in the matters which give me concern."[1] It is unlikely that Crummell ever completed his series of tracts, but at least these three were published before his death in September 1898. Each of the tracts ran to four printed pages and sold for ten cents.

### No. 1: The Losses of the Race
IN EVERY ATTEMPT to better the condition of wronged and degraded people the very first step should be to find the causes of their evils. As this step seems so largely ignored in the work for our Race, I venture to send forth this little paper.

I have the deep conviction, that many of our Ministers and Teachers are unaware, or else neglectful, of the great SPECIAL LOSSES OF THE RACE. And surely if they are blind to the prodigious calamities which, for centuries, have befallen us, how can they bring back to us the needed amends for those losses?

People *must* know the nature of their evils; or how can they find the remedy for them? No more than a physician can cleanse out the virus of a disease, unless he knows, first, the nature of that disease!

But—"Is it well to dwell upon calamities?" My answer is both No and Yes. (*a*) No! *i.e.* if you can see nothing save the dark things of life; if there is no "God of Hope" in your vision; if you can do naught but

—"Nurse despair,
And feed the dreadful appetite of death."[2]

But on the other hand, (*b*) Yes—if you are anxious to cure the evils of life: if you purpose, with Christ, to "destroy the works of the devil;"[3] if you are determined to turn calamity into light; to change disaster into saving providence! On this wise it *is* well to dwell upon calamities; for

1. Consider, just here, that no race of men can possibly live for centuries in bondage, without enduring the greatest calamities.

This is so universal, so well known a fact that no proof of it is needed.

The Negro Race in the United States has suffered the severest losses, mental, moral, spiritual, physical. Their suffering and losses are countless! "They *are*," I say; for their baleful influences follow us into these present days of freedom!

A few of them are so radical and so prodigious that, it seems to me impossible for us to make any real progress, to rise to any actual strength of excellence, until they are removed.

Look at these losses:

As I am speaking, mainly, of our *temporal* condition, I shall not dwell in this paper upon our *spiritual* disasters. I confine myself to a few *earthly* aspects of the case:—

1. For 250 years, we were, as a Race, deprived of the FAMILY and robbed of the HOME.

2. During this entire period we were barred from the ownership of property; and thus,

3. The ACQUISITIVE PRINCIPLE was extirpated.

4. The INTELLECT of the Race, for 250 years, was crushed and shrouded by penal laws; which closed the pages of books, forbade the opening of a School Room, shut out enlightenment from the mind, and barred the light of the Gospel from the soul!

This catalogue of losses could be indefinitely lengthened; but this is sufficient.

2. Now, the above items are the roots of society. They are the foundation-stones of all civil and social order, excellence, growth and manhood. Without them

—"All life dies, death lives and nature breeds
Perverse, all monstrous, all prodigious things."[4]

A generation of freedom has not, as yet, sufficed for our recovery of these grand organic elements of being. And yet it is manifest, that we cannot live without them! No people can live without them! And hence the most vigorous efforts are needed, to gain for ourselves the grand substitutes for these awful losses!

This is a life and death matter for our people. If we don't get back the FAMILY and the "family idea;" if we don't restore the HOME; if we don't cultivate widespread *family feeling* among our people; if we don't inspire, everywhere, family allegiance, family devotedness, family reverence and obedience; we shall be a lost people in this land!

Slavery, for 250 years, has robbed us of these qualities; but we must strive vigorously to regain them.

All the learning; all the riches; all the farms; all the industrial activities; all the political franchises; all the yearnings and clutching after office, cannot serve as substitutes for the ideas which cluster around the Family and the Home.

Next to the love of God these are the "first things" for our Race. But it is in this one point we have suffered our greatest loss. Just here we are a weak people. Just here, then, we must begin again to set up the standards of a true life.

3. Look into your Bibles, and see how the Almighty sets such great store upon the FAMILY. It is, first of all, *Marriage* at the creation of man; marriage which produces the family! See how He, everywhere, holds it up as the great and foremost of all human institutions! See how He guards it by His strongest laws, especially by the 7th Commandment! See how He fixes the inheritances of his chosen people by the limitations of the family! See how He arranges their sacrifices after the order of the family! See how He regulates Jewish life, in all generations, by the law of family life! See how He brought redemption, through Christ, out of the bosom of the family! See how family life, and family order are everywhere upheld, exalted, sanctified by the precepts, the teachings, the sacraments and the heavenly promises of the Lord Jesus, in the Covenant of Grace!

The Family; Parentage; Motherhood; the nurture of children; the ordering, the love, and the thrift of Households; reverence and obedience of the young; the fear of God; these are the foundation-stones of all human society. The other losses, I have referred to, will vanish with the gain of this. Given, everywhere, true, lofty, sacred ideas of Home; and then there will surely follow the ownership of property, intelligence, and the growth of the acquisitive principle.

4. "The Acquisitive Principle:"—a few words just here concerning the "acquisitive principle."

This loss has been one of our greatest misfortunes; for God made man to be a property-holder. He gave man a nature fitted for riches. To this end He put into the human constitution the principle of acquisitiveness; the capacity to get,—money, houses, property, etc.

The slave-system, for 250 years, declared that—"the Negro should not own anything,—not even his own body!" It made the man a chattel! And thus, for centuries, this grand principle of family and social growth has been driven out of the Negro nature. Hence it is, that we have lost, so widely, our grasp upon the things of earth. *We* know less than any other people the *value* of things! *We* are more improvident than any other class of citizens! *We* are the poorest people in the land! *We* hold a looser grip upon what we do get, than any others do! *We* lack the forecast which creates a fit and proper greed; and we have lost the lawful ambition which reaches out for wealth and riches!

These are the terrible losses of a poor people:—The loss of the Family and the Home! The loss of the capacity for gain and ownership! The loss of letters and learning! Worse than all, the loss of a true and uplifting religion!

How shall we recompense ourselves for these losses? Who shall give us restoral for these sore calamities?

It is all to come to us by teaching and instruction. Some philanthropists are to arise, and inculcate our people with the great ideas pertaining to the Family, the Home, and Acquisitiveness!

Who shall these Saviours of our people be? (*a*) Surely they will not come from afar. It is the rarest of things, that the men who raise and redeem a people are of foreign blood. The great regenerators of races and nations spring, generally, from their own ranks.

(*b*) So must it be with us. Our benefactors must be the Ministers of our own Churches; the Teachers of our own Schools; the Lecturers in our Public Halls. The revival, the strength, the regeneration of a people,—of any people, must come from *within;* they cannot come from without. Our Leaders must be men and women of our own Race, of our own blood!

The gift of grand opportunity and of higher culture, brings with it a deeper responsibility and an added duty, for the lowlier and neglected brethren of our Race. If our enlightened men and women do not devote themselves to the noble duty of race-progress and race-elevation, what is the use of their schooling and enlightenment? Why, in the course of providence have they had their large advantages, their superior opportunities?

The recognition of these losses is a matter of the vastest importance; for they must be replaced. *They must be!* Our race is the most needy race on American soil; and for our full restoration we need all the grand suggestions, which pertain especially to the domestic and social status of man.

Hence I would fain call upon all public men and women, upon our Ministers and Teachers and Public Speakers, to point out to the people these dire calamities; and to urge the need of their reparation.

Preach and teach, in the Pulpit and in the School, the idea of FAMILY; of family cohesion, yea, of family pride. Train the young to think much of their parentage. Call upon parents so to live, and so to act, that their children may be proud of their parents. Tell the people to make Homes. Inculcate the duty of the respectability and the honor of the Family! Proclaim, constantly, the dignity of Marriage, the sanctity of Motherhood, the glory of continuity of blood and lineage, and the abomination of lust, and illegitimacy.

Next to godliness, let this be the beginning of Race-reform and Race-progress.

### No. 2: Character: The Great Thing

NOTHING is more natural than the anxieties of wronged and degraded people concerning the steps they should take, to rise above their misfortunes and to elevate themselves. Thus it is that the colored people, in meetings and conventions, are constantly plied with the schemes their public speakers say will lift them up to higher levels.

1. (*a*) One prominent man will address an assemblage somewhat in this manner:—

"The only way to destroy the prejudice against our race is to become rich. If you have money the white man will respect you. He cares more for the almighty dollar than anything else. Wealth then is the only thing by which we can overcome the caste-spirit. Therefore, I say, get money; for riches are our only salvation."

(*b*) Another speaker harangues his audience in this manner:—

"Brethren, Education is the only way to overcome our difficulties. Send your children to school. Give them all the learning you can. To this end you must practice great self-restraint. Send them to College, and make them lawyers and doctors. Come out of the barber shops, the eating houses and the kitchens, and get into the professions; and thus you will command respect of the whites."

(*c*) But now up starts your practical orator. His absorbing fad is labor; and his address is as follows:—

"My friends, all this talk about learning, all this call for scholars, and lawyers, and doctors for our poor people is nonsense. Industrialism is the solution of the whole Negro problem. The black man must learn to work. We must have 'Manual Labor Schools' for the race. We must till and farm, ply the hoe and the rake, and thus, by productive labour, overcome inferior conditions, and secure strength and influence."

(*d*) We have another class of Teachers who must not be passed over. Our political leaders form not a small element in the life of our people, and exert no petty influence. In fact they are the most demonstrative of all classes; and they tell us most positively that "in a Democratic system, such as we are living under, no race can be respected unless it can get political influence, and hold office. Suffrage is the life of any people, and it is their right to share in the offices of the land. Our people can't be a people unless their leading men get positions, and take part in Government."

2. Now it would be folly to deny the importance of these expedients. For there *is* a real worth which the Almighty has put in money, in letters and learning, in political franchises, in labour and the fruits of labour. These are, without doubt, great agents and instruments in human civilization.

But I deny that either of them can gain for us *that* elevation which is our great and pressing want. For what we need, as a race, is an elevation which does something more than improve our temporal circumstances, or, alters our material condition. We want the uplifting of our humanity. We must have the enlargement of our manhood. WE NEED CHARACTER!

Many a man and many peoples, laden with riches, have gone down to swift destruction! In the midst of the grandest civilization many a nation has been eaten out with corruption, and gone headlong to ruin! The proudest monarchies and the most boastful democracies, have alike gone down suddenly to grim disaster!

3. There is no real elevation in any of these things. The history of the world shows that the true elevation of man comes from living forces.

But money is not a living force. Farms and property are not living forces; nor yet is culture of itself, nor political franchises. Those only are living forces which can uplift the souls of men to superiority:—living forces, not simply acting upon the material conditions of life, but permeating their innermost being; and moulding the invisible, but mighty powers of the reason and the will.

Now, when men say that money and property will elevate our people, they state only a half truth; for wealth only *helps* to elevate the man. There must be some manhood, precedent, for the wealth to act upon. So too when they declare that learning or politics will uplift the race, they give us but a half truth.

These all are simply aids and assistances to something higher and nobler; which both goes before and reaches far beyond them. They *are,* rightly used, agencies to that real elevation which is essentially an inward and moral process.

Don't be deceived by half truths; for half truths, lose, not seldom, the fine essence of real truth; and so become thorough deceits. Half truths are ofttimes prodigious errors. Half truths are frequently whole lies.

4. What then is the mighty power which uplifts the fallen?

It is Cowper who tells us,—

"The only amaranthine flower
Is Virtue; the only lasting treasure Truth."[5]

But what does the Poet mean by these simple but beautiful lines?

He means that for men, for societies, for races, for nations, the one living and abiding thing is character.

For character is an internal quality; and it works from within, outward, by force of nature and divine succours; and it uses anything and all things, visible and invisible, for the growth and the greatness of the souls of men, and for the upbuilding of society. It seizes upon money and property, upon learning and power as instruments for its own purposes; and even if these agencies should fail, character abides, a living and a lasting thing.

The other things are not internal and living things, useful as they are; and hence, of themselves, cannot produce the grand results which beget the elevation of humanity.

I say therefore that, unless a people has character, there is no elevation possible for them. In saying this, however, I would not by any means eschew the value of money and property, of education and political rights. These have their place in all the processes of personal or social growth; but they do not make men, nor regenerate society. Character alone does this.

It is character which is the great condition of life; character is the spring of all lawful ambitions and the stimulant to all rightful aspiration; character is the motive power of enterprise and the basis of credit; character is the root of discipline and self-restraint; character is the cement of the family; character is the consummate flower of true religion; and the crowning glory of civilization.

In fine, it is character which is the bed-rock of everything strong, masterful and lasting in all the organisms of life and society; and without it they are nothing but chaff and emptiness.

5. I am asked, perchance, for a more definite meaning of this word character. My answer is in the words of the Apostle St. Paul:—

"Whatsoever things are true, whatsoever things are honourable, whatsoever things are just, whatsoever things are pure, whatsoever things are lovely, whatsoever things are of good report, if there be any virtue, and if there be any praise, think on these things."[6]

These are the elements of character.

All this is equally applicable to a man, or, a community: for (*a*) If a *man* is not truthful and honorable, just and pure; he is not a man of character. (*b*) If a *family*, in a neighbourhood,—father, mother, girls and sons, are truthless and dishonorable, unjust and impure; no one can regard them as people of character. Just so too with a community, with a nation, with a race. If it is destitute of these grand qualities, whatever else it may be, whatever else it may have, if it is devoid of character; failure for it is a certainty.

6. Now if the Negro race in this nation wish to become a people; if they are anxious to prove themselves a stable, saving and productive element in this great Republic; if they are ambitious of advancement in all the lines of prosperity, of intelligence, of manly growth, and spiritual development; they must fall back upon this grand power of human being—character.

They must make this the main and master aim of all high endeavor. They must strive to free themselves from false notions, pernicious principles, and evil habits. They must exert themselves to the adoption of correct and saving ideas. They must lift themselves up to superior modes of living. They must introduce, as permanent and abiding factors of their life, the qualities of thrift, order, discipline, virtue and purity.

Now it is useless to deny the presence among us of drunken and profligate husbands, loose and slatternly wives, and licentious youths of both sexes. We see, not seldom, unprincipled hireling school teachers, greedy of self, hating their duties, and disliking children. We hear of leprous ministers in our pulpits, prostituting the holiest of offices; and we can, at once, put our finger upon the "damning spot,"[7] in all this varied iniquity:—it is the lack of character! It is not the want of money which is at the root of these disasters; not the need of education which is the great difficulty. No! It is the absence of that great inward quality—character!

Now the mightiest effort of the whole race, especially of Ministers and Teachers, should tend to this great acquisition. This should be put before and above everything else. If a choice *must* be made, it were better that our boys and girls should grow up poor and ignorant, than that they should be trained in the family, and in the school, devoid of character.

Is not this right? For think for a moment—What rot is there in the world which is as dreadful as a lad without honour, or a girl who is impure?

No such choice for our children is forced upon any of us. But character is the main thing; far superior to riches, estates, or learning, or voting.

## No. 3: The Care of Daughters

GIRLHOOD and the care of it is the topic of this tract:—And just here, it may be asked, What, next to infancy, is more beautiful than innocent girl-hood? We all know the attractiveness and charm of nature; everyone is delighted by

> "Splendor in the grass, and glory in the flower."[8]

All of us are made joyous at the rising beauty of the morn, in the magnificence of glowing sunsets. We know too the strength and majesty of noble manhood, the exquisite maturity of matronly womanhood. But, after all, as in nature we delight more in the dewy morn than in the full-orbed day, in the budding flower than in the full-bloomed rose,—nothing is so enchanting, nothing exercises so magic a spell as the sweetness, the simplicity, and the beauty of girlhood.

But as "the perversion of the best, is the worst;"[9] what greater calamity can befall a people than the loss of chastity in its girls! The moral defilement of youth is an awful disaster, irrespective of sex: but that disaster culminates in the case of girls. Man, no less than woman, is enjoined to virtue and purity. The consequences of guilt to the individual is the same in both cases. But so far as influences and results are concerned, moral defilement in girlhood is more calamitous. It is poison at the very fountain of life. One realizes the criminality of poisoning a stream miles away from its source: but what horror stirs the mind, when the dread infection is dropped at the very spot, whence the waters spring from the earth!

Notwithstanding, then, the agitation on sex-equality in our day, I dare to thrust into notice the conviction that woman's place in the world is unique. There is a specialty in her life and functions, which widely separates her sphere from that of man.

And hence, is it that womanhood, and therefore especially girlhood, carries with it a priceless treasure, which has never been given to man.

And so, it is difficult to exaggerate the importance of the care and solicitude, which parents should give their daughters. The fact, however, is that under the influence of our free and easy American life, where liberty ofttimes runs into license, anxiety upon this vital point has gradually slipped from the minds of parents. And owing to certain sad conditions, this evil works greater harm to the black race than to any other class in the whole population.

Two or three dreadful facts may be mentioned here. (*a*) Scores of colored girls are constantly allured, by advertisements for servants, into Northern cities: alas! soon to find themselves deceived. Ere long, unemployed and penniless, they are gradually dragged down to infamy and prostitution! (*b*) Again, at the National Capital, young and tender girls are enticed, from Southern homes, into its gilded houses of shame! (*c*) And then, all through the South, numbers of our girls become victims to the lust of unscrupulous white men,—a class who, crazy for the honor of white woman, regard the black woman as entitled to no chastity which white men are bound to respect.

And hence, the awful fact that numbers of blind and unsuspecting girls, many of them but little more than children, are lured into the dark avenues of ruin and death! All this is appalling!

For nigh three hundred years, the womanhood of our race has been violated by the wantonness of slavery: and now, albeit freedom is attained, still the despoiler is on the track of our children, and we are kept agonized by the slaughter of our innocents! For what deadlier evil can befall any people than the defilement of their girlhood? What more damning inheritance than the impurity, the dishonor, and the bastardy, which are the fruits of that defilement?

The causes of this dread calamity are twofold. (*a*) The indifference of the American mind toward the moral life of the Negro. From the very beginning, the white man has set a low value upon the chastity of the Negro woman. Some of the most distinguished men of the Nation have shown, by their illicit lives, that they regarded virtue in the Negress as a cheap and trifling thing. Secondly, (*b*) the Negro himself, although a rigorist in Africa as to the chastity of wife and daughter, soon fell into a state of license under the system of American slavery. And the evils of this license have survived a generation of freedom, and show themselves in the loss of the idea of FAMILY, in the lack of family training, in the neglect of moral oversight and guidance of children.

The time for the destruction of this gross enormity has fully come. How then is this inky tide of defilement to be stayed?

I. First of all comes the duty of Ministers and Teachers. Ministers are the instructors alike of teachers, and parents, and daughters: and then, schoolmarms, if they know the true intent of their calling, become the mothers of the little lasses and maidens entrusted to their care. Ministers, therefore, with downright scriptural plainness and pointedness, are to teach parents the duty of planting deep in the hearts of their girls the obligation to chastity of life. They should impress upon the heads of families, and especially upon mothers, the guilt and awfulness of fornication; they should proclaim the authority of the moral law; and urge particularly the binding force of the SEVENTH COMMANDMENT. Passing over, just here, the duties of teachers:

II. The duty of fathers and mothers comes next. In this connection, a number of important considerations arise:—(*a*) First comes the duty of training girls, from the first dawn of selfhood, into innocency. For this idea, next to that of God, stands foremost. (*b*) From the earliest childhood, little girls should be taught the modesty, simplicity, and purity both of thought and conduct, which especially becomes maidens; until these virtues become spontaneous. *At first* they are to be protected by that reserve and nonknowledge, which suits their tender age. (*c*) On the approach of early womanhood, when nature awakens to the mystery of life, they are to be given those direct truths and positive commands which impose responsibility and serve to set the will in the currents of excellence and purity. Mere ignorance at this period is no safeguard, but often proves a snare and a peril. Girls must be *taught:*—taught the sacredness as well as the mystery of their persons. They must be advised of the inviolability of the special trust which God has committed to maidenhood. They must be admonished of the obligation of the SEVENTH COMMANDMENT. They must be warned that there are sanctities of womanhood, which must be protected from all spot and stain, or they will commit the suicide of their own higher being! (*d*) Prudent and wholesale domestic arrangements have much to do in this training into innocency. And here a prodigious responsibility rests upon parents. Everything pertaining to home order, home comforts, home cleanliness, the properties of intercourse, the purity of manners, speech and habits, become matters of the vastest importance. If girls be deprived of privacy in households; if they are accustomed to the exposure of their persons in the family; if the sexes are not early separated in the rooming of children, how are they ever to grasp the ideas and practices of reserve and modesty? The one-roomed cabin has been the source and origin of countless immoralities!

III. All this, moreover, points out the duty of schoolmarms. They too are mothers to their girl scholars. If they do not realize this, they are mere hirelings, and have no right to take the place of teachers. Nay more, must they not ofttimes supersede the many ignorant, stupid, blind, yes, heartless, mothers, who, seemingly are dead to all ideas of motherhood?

A school is the place to make character, not merely to teach letters. And schoolmistresses, should strive, with warm motherly feelings, to build up character in their girls. They should hold up before them the highest ideals of excellence. They should enjoin the duty and glory of modesty, the priceless value of purity, the sanctity of their persons, the duties of cleanliness, tidiness, and especially chastity. For, in numerous places, so crude is the domestic condition of our people, that school teachers *must,* if true men and women, reduplicate themselves into other, divers services, to uplift their lowly people.

And there are things auxiliary to precepts, which serve as aids to virtue. These too must be brought to bear upon our girlhood. Our teachers should not listen to the "gradgrinds,"[10] who seem to think that the only thing Negro children should be trained for is to dig and delve, to cook and wash. No matter how poor, ragged and dirty these girls may be, no matter how miserable the cabins of their parents, throw in light upon their souls in the school room! Labor is a great thing; but character, virtue, and knowledge are greater. If they would save their girls, schoolmistresses must do *everything* to raise them above sense and animalism. However rude and dilapidated the school house, throw in light! Create a love of beauty by good pictures, even though they be cheap ones. Give the girls some of the harmonies and delights of music. Music and pictures are to put beauty, and ideas, and ideals into their minds, first *for the sake of their own lives;* and then to carry these ennobling ideas and ideals to their crude and miserable homes.

Destined, though they be, to lives of poverty and obscurity, yet, lift up these "heirs of ancestral woes" into a higher world than they have ever known. Schoolmistresses should remember that "man does not live by bread alone."[11] There is in the poor as well as the rich a hunger of the soul, which should be satisfied. Then throw in the light upon your girl children, and help them to see! There are "croakers" who will warn you of breeding discontent by these ideas of taste and beauty. But the true mother-teacher, striving to save her girls from infamy, will perceive that ideas and sentiments are the higher agencies for the elevation of human beings. Ideas and sentiments, moreover, are the rightful heritage of the lowest and most degraded. Fill their minds, therefore, with high, pure, noble, and uplifting thought, and so keep out the evil!

And as for "breeding discontent," that is your mission, from the infant class to the highest grade!—discontent with ignorance; discontent with low conditions of life; discontent with miserable homes and huts; discontent with rags and shoeless feet, and poor food; discontent with starving wages; discontent with crushed ambitions and a hopeless destiny! If teachers cannot stir up revolt against all these calamities, they are not fit to be the guides of youthful minds. One caution is needed here. See that the discontent that you breed is not morbid, but healthy and normal and aspiring.

And so, in conclusion, if we can only secure the womanhood of our race, we are safe. Men are the regulators of the trades, the farming, the business, the crafts, the labors of the world: *women* are the conservators of the manners of society, of morals, and the home. Girls are the apprentices of the future womanhood and maternity of a race. Everything possible, then, should be done, to secure the allegiance of their apprenticeship to virtue and purity.

# APPENDIX

# NOTES

# INDEX

# Appendix

## Provenance and
## Publishing History

Note: Location symbols are given in brackets. DLC = Library of Congress; DHU = Howard University; NN = New York Public Library.

1. The Social Principle among a People and Its Bearing on Their Progress and Development
   (i) Alexander Crummell, *The Social Principle among a People and Its Bearing on Their Progress and Development* (Washington, D.C., 1875). [DLC]
   (ii) Alexander Crummell, *The Greatness of Christ* (New York, 1882), 285–311.

2. The Destined Superiority of the Negro
   (i) Alexander Crummell, *The Greatness of Christ* (New York, 1882), 332–52.

3. The Assassination of President Garfield
   (i) Alexander Crummell, *The Greatness of Christ* (New York, 1882), 312–31.

4. The Dignity of Labour; and Its Value to a New People
   (i) Alexander Crummell, *Africa and America* (Springfield, Mass., 1891), 379–404.

5. A Defence of the Negro Race in America from the Assaults and Charges of Rev. J. L. Tucker, D.D., of Jackson, Mississippi
   (i) Alexander Crummell, *A Defence of the Negro Race in America from the Assaults*

and *Charges of Rev. J. L. Tucker, D.D., of Jackson, Mississippi* (Washington, D.C., 1883). A second edition was published that same year [DLC].

(ii) Alexander Crummell, *Africa and America* (Springfield, Mass., 1891), 83–125.

6. The Black Woman of the South: Her Neglects and Her Needs

(i) Alexander Crummell, *The Black Woman of the South: Her Neglects and Her Needs* (Cincinnati, 1883). [DLC]

(ii) Alexander Crummell, *The Black Woman of the South: Her Neglects and Her Needs* (Washington, D.C.: B. S. Anderson, n.d.). [DLC]

(iii) Alexander Crummell, *The Black Woman of the South: Her Neglects and Her Needs* (Washington, D.C.: Byron S. Adams, n.d.). [NN]

(iv) Alexander Crummell, *Africa and America* (Springfield, Mass., 1891), 59–82.

7. Excellence, an End of the Trained Intellect

(i) Alexander Crummell, *Africa and America* (Springfield, Mass., 1891), 343–54.

8. The Need of New Ideas and New Aims for a New Era

(i) Alexander Crummell, *Africa and America* (Springfield, Mass., 1891), 11–36.

9. Common Sense in Common Schooling

(i) Alexander Crummell, *Common Sense in Common Schooling* (Washington, D.C., 1886). [DLC, DHU]

(ii) Alexander Crummell, *Africa and America* (Springfield, Mass., 1891), 325–41.

10. Right-Mindedness: An Address before the Garnet Lyceum, of Lincoln University

(i) Alexander Crummell, *Africa and America* (Springfield, Mass., 1891), 355–78.

11. The Best Methods of Church Work among the Colored People

(i) Alexander Crummell, "The Best Methods of Church Work among the Colored People," *Church Magazine* 2 (June 1887): 554–62.

12. The Race-Problem in America

(i) Alexander Crummell, *The Race-Problem in America* (Washington, D.C., 1889). [DLC]

(ii) Alexander Crummell, *Africa and America* (Springfield, Mass., 1891), 37–57.

13. Incidents of Hope for the Negro Race in America

(i) Alexander Crummell, *Incidents of Hope for the Negro Race in America* (Washington, D.C., 1895). [DLC, DHU]

14. At Hampton Institute, 1896.
   I. (i) Alexander Crummell, "Founder's Day at Hampton Institute, January 30th, 1896, Address by Rev. Alex. Crummell, Rector Emeritus of St. Luke's Church, Washington, D.C.," *Southern Workman* 25 (March 1896): 46–49.
   II. (i) Alexander Crummell, "Address by Rev. Alexander Crummell, Pastor-emeritus of St. Luke's Church, Washington, D.C. AT EVENING PRAYERS, ON THE DAY OF PRAYER FOR COLLEGES, HAMPTON INSTITUTE. JANUARY 30TH, 1896," *Southern Workman* 25 (April 1896): 70–72.

15. Civilization the Primal Need of the Race
   (i) Alexander Crummell, *Civilization the Primal Need of the Race,* American Negro Academy, Occasional Papers, no. 3 (Washington, D.C., 1898). [DLC]

16. The Prime Need of the Negro Race
   (i) Alexander Crummell, "The Prime Need of the Negro Race," *Independent* 49 (Aug. 19, 1894): 1–2.
   (ii) Alexander Crummell, "The Prime Need of the Negro Race," in H. F. Kletzing and W. H. Crogman, eds., *Progress of a Race: or, the Remarkable Advancement of the American Negro* (Atlanta, Naperville, Ill., and Toronto, 1897), 361–67.

17. The Attitude of the American Mind toward the Negro Intellect
   (i) Alexander Crummell, *The Attitude of the American Mind toward the Negro Intellect,* American Negro Academy, Occasional Papers, no. 3 (Washington, D.C., 1898). [DLC]

18. Tracts for the Negro Race
   I. (i) Alexander Crummell, *The Losses of the Race,* Tracts for the Negro Race, no. 1 (Washington, D.C., 1898). [DHU]
   II. (i) Alexander Crummell, *Character: The Great Thing,* Tracts for the Negro Race, no. 2 (Washington, D.C., 1898). [DHU]
   III. (i) Alexander Crummell, *The Care of Daughters,* Tracts for the Negro Race, no. 3 (Washington, D.C., 1898). [DHU]

# *Notes*

## Introduction

1. W. E. B. Du Bois, *The Souls of Black Folk* (1903; rpt. New York, 1979), 161.

2. See Louis R. Harlan, *Booker T. Washington: The Making of a Black Leader, 1856–1901* (New York, 1972), and Louis R. Harlan, *Booker T. Washington: The Wizard of Tuskegee, 1901–1915* (New York, 1983).

3. Most of the biographical information in this introduction is taken from Gregory U. Rigsby, *Alexander Crummell: Pioneer in Nineteenth-Century Pan-African Thought* (Westport, Conn., 1987); Wilson Jeremiah Moses, *Alexander Crummell: A Study of Civilization and Discontent* (New York, 1989); and J. R. Oldfield, *Alexander Crummell (1819–1898) and the Creation of an African-American Church in Liberia* (Lewiston, N.Y., 1990).

4. Among white denominations the Protestant Episcopal church was conservative in tone and upper-class in character. It probably attracted less than 6 percent of churchgoers in Northern black communities. See Theodore Hershberg, "Free Blacks in Antebellum Philadelphia: A Study of Ex-Slaves, Freeborn, and Socio-Economic Decline," *Journal of Social History* 5 (1972): 186.

5. Crummell gives an account of this incident in his "Eulogium on Henry Highland Garnet, D.D." See Crummell, *Africa and America* (Springfield, Mass., 1891), 278–81.

6. Crummell Papers, MS C392, Schomburg Center for Research in Black Culture, New York; Crummell to Elizur Wright, 22 June, 1837, Elizur Wright Papers, Library of Congress, Washington, D.C.; Henry L. Phillips, *In Memoriam of the Late Rev. Alex. Crummell, D.D., of Washington, D.C.: An Address Delivered before the American Negro Historical Society of Philadelphia, November, 1898. With an Introductory Address by the Rev. Matthew Anderson, Pastor of the Berean Presbyterian Church* (Philadelphia, 1899), 5, 19; Daniel Murray, "A Sketch of the Life of Alexander Crummell," Daniel Murray Papers, reel 3, Library of Congress, Washington, D.C.

7. Crummell to John Jay, March 9, 1849, Jay Papers, Columbia University Library, New York.

8. Crummell went to Providence as lay reader of Christ Church. He became a deacon on May 29, 1842, and a minister in 1843.

9. Internal evidence suggests that the marriage was not a happy one. Crummell's domineering manner seems to have alienated Sarah, so much so that by the time of her death in 1878 she was living apart from her husband. Crummell's relationships with his children, especially his son Sidney, were equally strained.

10. See Howard Holman Bell, *Minutes of the Proceedings of the National Negro Conventions* (New York, 1970), 7–10.

11. Crummell Papers, microfilm edition, C38. In all, Crummell raised £1,934 for the Church of the Messiah.

12. Crummell was admitted to Queens' College on the recommendation of Thomas Babington Macaulay, J. A. Froude, Dean Arthur Stanley, and Bishop Samuel Wilberforce.

13. Crummell to Jay, Sept. 12, 1851, Jan. 27, 1852, Jay Papers. Crummell's symptoms, tremors or palpitations brought on by stress or excitement, were consistent with what we would now recognize as a valvular disorder of the right side of the heart, but, as Brodie's diagnosis suggests, it is quite likely that his illness was psychosomatic.

14. Crummell to Jay, Sept. 21, 1851, ibid.; Crummell, *Hope for Africa: A Sermon on Behalf of the Ladies Negro Education Society* (London, 1853), 47.

15. Crummell to Jay, Dec. 27, 1852, Jay Papers. Liberia was the brainchild of the American Colonization Society, founded in 1816, and, as such, was frequently associated with the principle of "involuntary emigration" back to Africa.

16. See Moses, *Alexander Crummell,* 71–72, 75–78; Oldfield, *Alexander Crummell,* 32, 34–36.

17. Crummell to Jay, April 15, 1853, Jay Papers.

18. Crummell to Jay, July 14 and August, 1848, ibid.

19. Sarah gave birth to three more children while the couple were in England: Frances Auriol, born in Bath on June 17, 1849; Sophia Elizabeth, born in Cambridge on March 13, 1851; and Dillwinna (?), born in Ipswich on May 2, 1852. Crummell's eldest son, Alexander, choked to death on a button in June 1851.

20. Winwood Reade, *The African Sketch Book* (London, 1873), 257; For Liberia, see Tom W. Shick, *Behold the Promised Land: A History of Afro-American Settler Society in Nineteenth-Century Liberia* (Baltimore, 1980).

21. "A copy of part of the proceedings of the Christmas Convocation for 1854 of the Episcopal Church in Liberia held at New York, Montserrado County," Papers of the Domestic and Foreign Missionary Society, box 27, Archives and Historical Collections, Episcopal Church, Austin, Tex.

22. See J. R. Oldfield, "The Protestant Episcopal Church, Black Nationalists, and Expansion of the West African Missionary Field, 1851–1871," *Church History* 57 (1988): 31–45.

23. Oldfield, *Alexander Crummell,* 104–7; Hollis B. Lynch, *Edward Wilmot Blyden: Pan-African Patriot, 1832–1912* (New York, 1970), 50–52.

24. Crummell to Samuel Denison (Secretary of the Foreign Committee of the Board of Missions), Jan. 16, 1872, Papers of the Domestic and Foreign Missionary Society.

25. Of Crummell's three surviving children, only Sidney and Frances returned to the United States with their mother. Sophia, by this time married to a Liberian citizen, chose to remain in West Africa. Dillwinna seems to have died soon after Crummell and his family arrived in Liberia in 1853.

26. *Washington Post,* Sept. 11, 1898.

27. Crummell to Frazier Miller, March 13, 1895, to John Edward Bruce, Nov. 4, 1895, Feb. 28, 1896, Crummell Papers.

28. Alfred A. Moss, *The American Negro Academy: Voice of the Talented Tenth* (New Orleans, 1981), 23–25.

29. Ibid., 27–45.

30. After Crummell's first wife, Sarah, died in 1878, he married Jennie M. Simpson, a New Yorker, in 1880. See Crummell Papers, microfilm edition, C4.

31. Crummell to Bruce, June 1, 1897, Crummell Papers. Besides his long sojourn of 1848–53, Crummell was in England in 1862, 1865, and 1872.

32. Crummell to Bruce, Sept. 27, Nov. 5, 1897, Jan. 21, 1898, ibid.

33. Crummell to Bruce, March 22, 1898, to Miller, June 20, Aug. 10, 1898, Jennie M. Crummell to John Wesley Cromwell, Sept. 3, 1898, ibid.; Churchman, Sept. 24, 1898, p. 428.

34. Du Bois, The Souls of Black Folk, 59–60.

35. See C. Vann Woodward, The Strange Career of Jim Crow (New York, 1955); Howard N. Rabinowitz, Race Relations in the Urban South, 1865–1890 (New York, 1978); Joel Williamson, The Crucible of Race: Black-White Relations in the American South since Emancipation (New York, 1984).

36. Paul A. Groves, "The Development of a Black Residential Community in Southwest Washington, 1860–1897," Records of the Columbia Historical Society 71 (1973): 260–61; Constance Green, The Secret City: A History of Race Relations in the Nation's Capital (Princeton, N.J., 1967), 36, 38.

37. See, for instance, Alexander Crummell, The Future of Africa (New York, 1862), 126–27, and Africa and America, 415, 418.

38. Particularly striking in this context is Crummell's statement in 1882 that blacks would have been "more blessed and far superior, as pagans, in Africa than slaves on the plantations of the South." See chap. 5.

39. See chap. 4.

40. See chap. 9.

41. See chap. 8.

42. See chap. 1.

43. Ibid.

44. Winthrop Hudson, Religion in America (New York, 1965), 224–25; David Reimers, White Protestantism and the Negro (New York, 1965), 34.

45. Joseph Louis Tucker, The Relations of the Church to the Colored Race. Speech of the Rev. J. L. Tucker, D.D., of Jackson, Mississippi, before the Church Congress, Held in Richmond, Va., on the 24–27 Oct., 1882 (Jackson, Miss., 1882); Herbert G. Gutman, The Black Family in Slavery and Freedom, 1750–1925 (New York, 1976), 531–41.

46. Gutman, The Black Family in Slavery and Freedom, 534; Journal of the General Convention of the Protestant Episcopal Church, 1883, appendix 11, 597–98; George F. Bragg, The History of the Afro-American Group of the Episcopal Church (Baltimore, 1922), 151.

47. Bragg, The History of the Afro-American Group of the Protestant Episcopal Church, 151–52; Reimers, White Protestantism and the Negro, 67; Churchman, Sept. 24, 1898, p. 428; Crummell to Miller, Sept. 18, 1894, Crummell Papers.

48. See chap. 12.

49. None of this is to deny the importance of Washington's secret civil rights activities, but "his power as a race leader grew from his accommodationist public image and his strong following among whites, not from his secret activities." See Louis R. Harlan, ed., The Booker T. Washington Papers (Urbana, Ill., 1975–84), 5:xxii.

50. See chap. 16.

51. Crummell to Miller, June 20, 1898, Crummell Papers.

52. See chap. 15.

53. Crummell to Cromwell, Oct. 5, 1897, Crummell Papers.

54. See chap. 16.

55. Harlan, Booker T. Washington Papers 4:369–71; Crummell to Miller, July 28, 1898, Crummell Papers.

56. Moss, *American Negro Academy*, 50.

57. Sketch of Alexander Crummell in the George Forbes Papers, Rare Books Department, Boston Public Library.

58. In the eighteen pieces in this selection, there are over fifty quotations from the Bible, only two of which appear more than once, Joshua 9:21 and Matthew 4:4.

59. Crummell Papers, MS C44.

60. See chap. 2.

61. Crummell also quotes from "A Sonnet Composed upon Westminster Bridge," "Laodamia," "Ode to Duty," "Ode: Intimations of Immortality," "Rob Roy's Grave," and "September 1802. Near Dover."

62. See chap. 12.

63. Sketch of Alexander Crummell in the George Forbes Papers.

64. Crummell's often-repeated story concerning John C. Calhoun, blacks, and the classics is particularly illuminating in this regard. See chaps. 12 and 17.

65. The list of these African and West Indian travelers is impressive and includes Michael Adanson, John Bigelow, Richard Burton, Henry Coleridge, Alexander Laing, John Ledyard, Mungo Park, Anthony Trollope, and May French-Sheldon. Crummell quoted at length from Bigelow and Park, while the same passage from Adanson's *Voyage to Senegal* (1759) appears in both "The Destined Superiority of the Negro Race" and "Incidents of Hope for the Negro Race in America." Another key text is William Ellery Channing's "Emancipation" (1840), a review of Joseph John Gurney's *Familiar Letters to Henry Clay, of Kentucky, Describing a Winter in the West Indies*, from which Crummell quoted on no less than three separate occasions.

66. See chap. 8.

67. See chaps 15 and 16.

68. *Washington Post*, Sept. 11, 1898.

69. See, for instance, chap. 12.

70. Alexander Crummell, *Destiny and Race: Selected Writings, 1840–1898*, ed. Wilson Jeremiah Moses (Amherst, Mass. 1992).

## 1. *The Social Principle among a People and Its Bearing on Their Progress*

1. Luke 16:8.

2. "And the Lord God said, It is not good that the man should be alone; I will make him an help meet for him." Genesis 2:18.

3. The Greek army that accompanied Cyrus from Sardis to Babylon (401 B.C.) was later forced to retreat after the battle of Cunaxa.

4. James Cook (1728–79), English navigator, made voyages of discovery to New Zealand and Australia.

5. George Anson (1697–1762), English admiral, sailed round the world in 1740–44.

6. John Howard (1726?–90), philanthropist, led the fight for prison reform in England. William Wilberforce (1759–1833), English reformer, was the chief parliamentary spokesman for the movement to abolish slavery and the slave trade. Thomas Clarkson (1760–1846), abolitionist and reformer, was a leading member of the (London) Committee for the Abolition of the Slave Trade; significantly, one of Crummell's earliest ventures into print was his *The Man: the Hero: the Christian! A Eulogy on the Life and Character of Thomas Clarkson* (New York, 1847). Robert Raikes (1735–1811) was a wealthy businessman who promoted the Sunday school movement in England.

7. The Second Opium War (1856–60).

8. I am advised by an intelligent friend, that the above allegations need modification; that some few such organizations have been made in two or three of the Southern States and in the City of Baltimore. The "COLORED EDUCATIONAL CONVENTION" of Virginia deserves distinguished consideration and great commendation. [AC]

9. Alexandre Dumas fils (1824–95) was a French dramatist, novelist, social reformer, and member of the French Academy. Dumas's great-grandmother on his father's side was Maria Cessette Dumas, a Santo Domingo black.

10. There was, in fact, no reference to mixed marriages in the North Carolina constitution of 1868. Crummell probably had in mind Section 2 of Chapter 193 of the public laws of North Carolina which banned "all marriages between a white person and a negro or Indian, or between a white person and a person of negro or Indian descent, to the third generation inclusive" (Feb. 12, 1872).

11. Mount Blanc is the highest mountain in the French Alps.

12. Shakespeare, Henry V 3.1.6–7.

13. Bishop Butler. [AC] The Works of Joseph Butler (Edinburgh, 1810), 1:20–21. The quotation is from Butler's Analogy of Religion to the Constitution and Course of Nature, first published in 1736.

14. "Be strong, and quit yourselves like men, O ye Philistines, that ye be not servants unto the Hebrews, as they have been to you: quit yourselves like men, and fight." 1 Samuel 4:9.

15. "For thou art a holy people unto the Lord thy God, and the Lord hath chosen thee to be a peculiar people unto himself, above all the nations that are upon the earth." Deuteronomy 14:2.

16. "And the Lord said unto Cain, Where is Abel they brother? And he said, I know not: Am I my brother's keeper?" Genesis 4:9.

17. Felicia Dorothea Hemans, "Evening Song of the Tyrolese Peasants," ll. 1–4.

18. "Be thou familiar, but by no means vulgar; / The friends thou hast, and their adoption tried / Grapple them to thy soul with hoops of steel." Shakespeare, Hamlet 1.3.57–59.

19. "For I could wish that myself were accursed from Christ for my brethren, my kinsmen according to the flesh." Romans 9:3.

## 2. The Destined Superiority of the Negro

1. "Therefore as the fire devoureth the stubble, and the flame consumeth the chaff, so their root shall be as rottenness, and their blossom shall go up as dust; because they have cast away the law of the Lord of hosts, and despised the word of the Holy One of Israel." Isaiah 5:24.

2. Exodus 12–14.

3. Ezekiel 33–34, 36, 40, 43.

4. Psalms 18:25–26.

5. "And it repented the Lord that he had made man on the earth, and it grieved him at his heart." Genesis 6:6.

6. "These are the generations of Noah: Noah was a just man and perfect in his generations, and Noah walked with God." Genesis 6:9. "But with thee will I establish my covenant; and thou shalt come into the ark, thou, and thy sons, and thy wife, and thy sons wives with thee." Genesis 6:18.

7. Cornelius Tacitus, *Germania* (A.D. 98).

8. Luke 8:15.

9. Richard Chenevix Trench, *Notes on the Parables of Our Lord* (London, 1841), 81. Trench (1807–66) was an English cleric, poet, and scholar who became archbishop of Dublin in 1863.

10. Walter Scott, *Ivanhoe* (1819). In the climax to the story, Ivanhoe's rival, the dishonorable Sir Brian de Bois-Guilbert, falls dead, untouched by his opponent's lance, the victim of his own contending passions.

11. "But God giveth it a body, as it hath pleased him, and to every seed his own body." 1 Corinthians 15:38.

12. Henry Wadsworth Longfellow, *A Psalm of Life* 4.4.

13. Of course, this was written before the European partition of Africa, which gathered pace during the 1880s.

14. Edmund Burke, *A Philosophical Enquiry into the Origins of Our Ideas of the Sublime and Beautiful*, ed. J. T. Boulton (London, 1958), 49.

15. Presumably a chameleon.

16. "But knowledge to their eyes her ample page / Rich with the spoils of time did ne'er unroll." Thomas Gray, "Elegy Written in a Country Churchyard," ll. 49–50.

17. "Yet cheerfully thou glinted forth / Amid the storm." Robert Burns, "To a Mountain Daisy," l. 15.

18. "The history of West Indian emancipation teaches us that we are holding in bondage one of the best races of the human family. The negro is among the mildest, gentlest of men. He is singularly susceptible of improvement from abroad." *The Works of William E. Channing, D.D.* (Boston, 1880), 838. Crummell obviously added this quotation later for inclusion in *The Greatness of Christ* (1882). Channing's "Emancipation," a review of Joseph John Gurney's *Familiar Letters to Henry Clay, of Kentucky, Describing a Winter in the West Indies* (1840), originally appeared in 1840.

19. Alexander Kinmont, *Twelve Lectures on the Natural History of Man, and the Rise and Progress of Philosophy* (Cincinnati, 1839), 218.

20. Michael Adanson, *A Voyage to Senegal, the Isle of Goree, and the River Gambia* (London, 1759), 40, 214. Crummell nearly always refers to Adanson as "Adamson."

21. Alexander Raleigh (1817–80) was minister of Hare Court Chapel, Canonbury, London, and closely involved with missionary work in Africa, but I have been unable to trace this quotation.

22. "I have made a covenant with my chosen, I have sworn unto David my servant." Psalms 89:3.

23. Liberia and Haiti.

24. Toussaint L'Ouverture (1748–1803), an ex-slave, led the revolt against French colonial rule in Santo Domingo in 1791 and later became the island's dictator. Henry Christophe (1767–1820) was president of the northern state of Haiti (1806–11) and then king (1811–20). Benjamin Banneker (1731–1806), mathematician and astronomer, served on the commission to survey the District of Columbia in 1799. Stephen Allen Benson (?–1865) was president of Liberia between 1856 and 1864. Samuel Crowther (c. 1809–90), an ex-slave, was consecrated bishop of the Niger territory by the Church of England in 1861.

## 3. The Assassination of President Garfield

1. Preached Sunday, July 10, 1881. [AC]

2. "And he bowed the heart of all the men of Judah, even as the heart of one man; so that they sent this word unto the king, Return thou, and all thy servants." 2 Samuel 19:14.

3. Thomas Hood, "The Death Bed," stanzas 1–3.

4. "I cannot go / Where UNIVERSAL LOVE not smiles around, / Sustaining all yon Orbs and all their Sons, / From *seeming Evil* still educing *Good*, / And Better thence again, and *Better* still, / In infinite Progression." James Thomson, "A Hymn on the Seasons," ll. 111–16.

5. "But as for you, ye thought evil against me; but God meant it unto good, to bring to pass, as it is this day, to save much people alive." Genesis 50:20.

6. "Although affliction cometh not forth of the dust, neither doth trouble spring out of the ground." Job 5:6.

7. "Let every soul by subject unto the higher powers. For there is no power but of God: the powers that be are ordained of God." Romans 13:1.

8. "Honor all men. Love the brotherhood. Fear God. Honor the king." 1 Peter 2:17.

9. "Ich dien" is the motto of the Prince of Wales.

10. See n. 7 above.

11. "For for this cause pay ye tribute also: for they are God's ministers, attending continually upon this very thing." Romans 13:6.

12. "Governments are instituted among Men, deriving their just powers from the consent of the governed." Declaration of Independence.

13. "God, who at sundry times and in divers manners spake in time past unto the fathers by the prophets." Hebrews 1:1.

14. See, for example, "The Federalist Number 1," *The Federalist Papers* (1788).

15. Reform of the civil service had been an issue since 1865. Garfield's assassination brought the movement to a head; in August 1881 the National Civil Service Reform League was founded, and the new president, Chester A. Arthur (1881–84), was instrumental in abandoning the old spoils system.

16. "Zealous, yet modest; innocent, though free; / Patient of toil; serene amidst alarms; / Inflexible in faith; invincible in arms." James Beattie, *The Minstrel* 1.97–99.

17. "Yet tears to human suffering are due; / And mortal hopes defeated and o'erthrown / Are mourned by men, and not by man alone." William Wordsworth, "Laodamia," ll. 164–67.

## 4. The Dignity of Labour; and Its Value to a New People

1. William Wordsworth, "Rob Roy's Grave," stanza 9.

2. Sartor Resartus. [AC] See *The Works of Thomas Carlyle* (London, 1896), 1:181–82.

3. "Thou therefore endure hardness, as a good soldier of Jesus Christ." 2 Timothy 2:3.

4. "But Jesus answered them, my Father worketh hitherto, and I work." John 5:17.

5. Wordsworth, *The Excursion* 4.343.

## 5. *A Defence of the Negro Race in America from the Assaults and Charges of Rev. J. L. Tucker, D.D., of Jackson, Mississippi*

1. See chap. 1, n. 13.

2. Paper read at the "CHURCH CONGRESS" [Prot. Epis. Church], Richmond, Va., Oct., 1882. [AC]

3. See the testimony of the celebrated African travellers—Mungo Park, Ledyard, Adanson, Laing, &c, &c. [AC]

4. Being filled with all unrighteousness, fornication, wickedness, covetousness, maliciousness; full of envy, murder, debate, deceit, malignity, whisperers. Rom. 1:29.

Knowing this, that the law is not made for a righteous man, but for the lawless and disobedient, for the ungodly and for sinners, for unholy and profane, for whoremongers, for liars, for perjured persons, and if there be any other thing that is contrary to sound doctrine, I Tim. 1:9 and 10. [AC]

5. Genesis 45–47.

6. Tucker, *Relations*, 13.

7. William Bell White Howe (1827–94).

8. Tucker, *Relations*, 36. This and similar remarks came in the form of a series of "endorsements" included in a lengthy appendix to Tucker's published address.

9. Ibid., 45. Alexander Gregg (1819–93) was Episcopal bishop of Texas.

10. All of these men were ex-slaves. Henry Highland Garnet (1815–82) settled in New York and was a classmate and near neighbor of Crummell; following spells in England and Jamaica (1848-c.1856), Garnet returned to the United States where he became a leading proponent of African emigration. Frederick Douglass (1817–95) escaped to the North in 1838 and was later to become the preeminent black leader of his generation. Samuel Ringgold Ward (1817-c.1866) toured England in the early 1850s in behalf of the Canadian Anti-Slavery Society; considered one of the great black orators of his day, Ward left England in 1855 for Jamaica where he spent the rest of his life. J. W. C. Pennington (1807–70) was one of the first black abolitionists to visit England; after the Civil War, Pennington ministered to an African Methodist Episcopal church in Natchez, Mississippi, and from 1867 until his death served the Fourth (Colored) Congregational Church in Portland, Maine.

11. That is, the General Assembly of the Presbyterian church.

12. Simon Legree is the cruel slave master in Harriet Beecher Stowe's *Uncle Tom's Cabin* (1853).

13. See "A Journey to the Back Country" and "Sea Side and Slave States," by Frederick Law Olmstead. [AC] Frederick Law Olmsted, *A Journey in the Back Country* (New York and London, 1860), 63–64, 118, 123–24, 268–70, 302–3, 445–46; Olmsted, *A Journey in the Seaboard Slave States* (New York and London, 1856), 94–95, 115, 148, 211, 296–97, 403.

14. Samuel Taylor Coleridge, "Fears in Solitude," ll. 42–53. Coleridge (1772–1834), English poet, essayist, and critic, was a close friend of William Wordsworth.

15. See chap. 2, n. 12.

16. It must be remembered, too, that this increase of the colored people is entirely by native birth. More colored people left these States during every one of these decades than came to them.

It will be noticed also that the rate of growth by birth in a state of freedom has been much more rapid than in a state of slavery; thirty-four per cent, being the rate since they were emancipated, while twenty-two per cent was the average of increase during the last two decades in a state of slavery. These facts clearly indicate that the physical condition of the colored people has been greatly improved since they became free men, and no longer merchantable chattels to be bought and sold.—From "THE FIELD," in *paper of Presbyterian Board of Missions for Freedmen.* [AC]

17. Paul Langford, ed., *The Writings and Speeches of Edmund Burke* (Oxford, 1989), 8:177. The quotation comes from Burke's *Reflections on the Revolution in France*, first published in 1790.

18. This is the number reported by Hon. Augustus Orr, State School Commissioner of Georgia, in 1878. This statement included *all* Southern States except Arkansas, Florida, and Lousiana. The number at this time must well nigh reach 1,000,000. See "Our Brother in Black," p. 166, By Rev. A.S. Haygood, D.D. [AC] The numbers reported by Orr were, in fact, for the "entire South," including Arkansas, Florida, and Louisiana, the difference being that in these states "careful estimates" had been made. See Atticus G. Haygood, *Our Brother in Black: His Freedom and His Future* (New York, Cincinnati, and Nashville, 1881), 166.

19. Tucker, *Relations*, 90.

20. Ibid., 3, 5.

21. John Locke, *An Essay concerning Human Understanding*, ed. Peter H. Nidditch (Oxford, 1975), 655, ll. 19–21 ("Of Probability").

22. For this and what follows, see Tucker, *Relations*, 3–4, 7, 13, 21.

23. The reader will bear in mind that these and similar statements of Dr. Tucker are absolutely contradictory of the statements of Southern men made at the period of Southern "Secession." *Then* the Southern clergy published to the world, as one ground of justification of their course, "THEIR RESPONSIBILITY FOR HUNDREDS OF THOUSANDS OF NEGRO CHRISTIANS, WHOM THEY HAD CONVERTED." Then as *slaves*, they were CHRISTIANS. *Now*, as *freemen*, they are "HYPOCRITES," going down to perdition! The reconcilement of these inconsistencies I leave to others. [AC]

24. Alexander Pope, *An Essay on Man* 1.121–22.

25. The editor and proprietor of the *People's Advocate*, a local black newspaper published in Washington, D.C., was John Wesley Cromwell (1845–1927). Cromwell also was the author of *The Negro in American History* (1914).

26. Tucker, *Relations*, 17.

27. In the spring of 1879 thousands of black tenant farmers from Tennessee, Texas, Mississippi, and Louisiana fled to Kansas, the quintessential free state, in search of land, education, and civil rights. See Nell Irvin Painter, *Exodusters: Black Migration to Kansas after Reconstruction* (New York, 1976).

28. Tucker, *Relations*, 27.

29. See speech of Rev. Dr. Allen, before Presbyterian General Assembly, 1883. [AC]

30. Butler's Analogy, Ch. V. [AC] See *The Works of Joseph Butler* 1:121.

31. Tucker, *Relations*, 27.

32. Tucker did not use this precise form of words, but the sentiment was implicit in the foregoing remarks.

33. Tucker, *Relations*, 27.

34. "Send no more Northern Missionaries down here who barely know a negro when they see him." Ibid.

35. Presumably the slave insurrection of 1712.

36. The New York Draft Riots.

37. John Jay (1745–1829), his son William (1789–1858), and grandson John (1817–94) were all supporters of abolition and active in efforts to aid free blacks in New York City. Crummell was personally acquainted with John Jay (1817–94), who befriended him after he was refused admission to the General Theological Seminary in 1839. Matthew Clarkson (1758–1825), a Revolutionary soldier, introduced a bill into the New York Assembly in 1789–90 for the gradual abolition of slavery. Rufus King (1755–1827), Federalist statesman, opposed the three-fifths clause in the Constitution and, later, the Missouri Compromise of 1820. James Kent (1763–1847) was a jurist and the author of Kent's *Commentaries* (1826–30); in 1821 Kent added his voice to those political reformers who urged the New York State constitutional convention not to disfranchise any portion of the black community.

38. Elias Boudinot (1740–1821), a Revolutionary statesman, succeeded David Rittenhouse as director of the United States Mint in 1795; Boudinot later retired from public life to concentrate on his biblical studies. Various Shotwells were active in the abolitionist cause, among them Joseph Shotwell, a merchant of Rahway, New Jersey, and Anna H. Shotwell, who founded a Colored Orphan Asylum in New York City in 1836. Anthony Benezet (1713–84), a teacher and philanthropist, wrote *A Caution and Warning to Great Britain and Her Colonies on the Calamitous State of the Enslaved Negroes* (1766), one of the earliest abolitionist tracts.

39. Benjamin Rush (1745–1813) was a physician and author of *An Address to the Inhabitants of the British Settlements in America, upon Slave-keeping* (1773); in 1774 he helped to organize the Pennsylvania Society for Promoting the Abolition of Slavery. Benjamin Franklin (1706–90), printer, author, philanthropist, inventor, statesman, and diplomat, was an early convert to abolition and lent his support to the movement for an independent black church in Philadelphia.

40. The sisters Sarah Moore Grimké (1792–1873) and Angelina Emily Grimké (1805–79) were antislavery crusaders and advocates of women's rights. James Gillespie Birney (1792–1857) ran as a presidential candidate for the Liberty party in 1840 and 1844. Albert Brisbane (1809–90) was a leading social reformer and proponent of the ideas of Charles Fourier.

41. Tucker, *Relations*, 26.

42. "With righteous Æthiops (uncorrupted Train!)." Maynard Mack, ed., *The Poems of Alexander Pope* (London, 1967), 8:499, l. 256. The quotation is from Pope's translation of Homer's *Iliad*, originally published in 1715–20.

## 6. *The Black Woman of the South: Her Neglects and Her Needs*

1. See John Wesley Cromwell, *The Negro in American History* (Washington, D.C., 1914), 133.

2. Phillis Wheatley (c.1753–84), first major African-American poet, published her *Poems on Various Subjects, Religious and Moral* in 1773.

3. "And the princes said unto them, Let them live; but let them be hewers of wood and drawers of water unto all the congregation; as the princes had promised them." Joshua 9:21.

4. "The evil that men do lives after them, / The good is oft interred with their bones." Shakespeare, *Julius Caesar* 3.2.81–82.

5. "Slaves cannot breathe in England, if their lungs / Receive our air, that moment they are free; / They touch our country, and their shackles fall." William Cowper, *The Task* 2.40–42.

6. "The fair humanities of old religion." Samuel Taylor Coleridge, *Piccolomini* 2.4.124.

7. "Emancipation." By Rev. W. E. Channing, D.D. Works of W. E. Channing, D.D. A.U.A. ed. Pp. 820. [AC] See chap. 2, n. 18. In the original the last sentence reads: "The African carries within him much more than we the germs of a meek, long-suffering, loving virtue." The quotation can be found on p. 838.

8. Henry Nelson Coleridge (1798–1843), an English barrister and writer, published *Six Months in the West Indies in 1825* in 1826. Anthony Trollope (1815–82) was a well-known English novelist; Crummell probably had in mind Trollope's *The West Indies and the Spanish Main* (1859). Sir Richard Burton (1821–90) was an English explorer; his many publications included *The Lake Regions of Central Equatorial Africa* (1859) and *Wanderings in West Africa from Liverpool to Fernando Po* (1863).

9. James Hunt (1833–69), English ethnologist, was the author of *The Negro's Place in Nature: A Paper Read before the London Anthropological Society* (1864). George Robbins Gliddon (1809–57), English-born Egyptologist, was the coauthor, with Josiah Nott, of *Types of Mankind: or Ethnological Researches* (1854).

10. "Woman." From the French of M. J. Michelet, page 132. Rudd & Carleton, New York. [AC] Jules Michelet, *Woman (La Femme)*, from the French of M. J. Michelet (New York, 1860), 132.

11. Mungo Park, *Travels in the Interior Districts of Africa: Performed in the Years 1795, 1796 and 1799 etc.*, rev. ed. (London, 1817), 299–300.

12. See "Jamaica in 1850." By John Bigelow. [AC] John Bigelow, *Jamaica in 1850: or, The Effects of Sixteen Years of Freedom on a Slave Colony* (London, 1851), 199.

13. Wordsworth. Sonnets dedicated to Liberty. [AC] The sonnet in question is "September 1, 1802."

14. "Aunt Chloe" is Uncle Tom's wife and a central character in Harriet Beecher Stowe's *Uncle Tom's Cabin* (1853).

15. Fanny Kemble Butler, *Journal of a Residence on a Georgian Plantation in 1838–39* (London, 1863), 33–34, 78–79, 148, 188.

16. "Ritualism" was a movement within the Church of England which advocated the strict observance of symbolic religious rites.

17. "Sister Dora" was Dorothy Wyndlow Pattison (1832–78), a surgical nurse who devoted herself to the care of the poor in and around Walsall, Birmingham. Charles Fuge Lowder (1820–80), an Anglican minister, was responsible for setting up a mission to the London dockyards.

## 7. Excellence, an End of the Trained Intellect

1. See the comments in James McPherson, *The Abolitionist Legacy: From Reconstruction to the NAACP* (Princeton, N.J., 1975), 215.

2. Muhammed Ahmed (1849–85), usually the Mahdi or al-Mahdi, was a religious reformer and political leader who in 1881 established a theocratic state in the Sudan; William Ewart Gladstone (1809–98), English liberal statesman, was prime minister

1868–74, 1880–85, 1886, and 1892–94. In 1884 Gladstone's cabinet sent General Charles George Gordon to the Sudan to supervise the withdrawal of the khedive of Egypt's garrisons, which could no longer hold out against the Mahdi. Gordon's subsequent death at the hands of the Mahdi's forces at Khartoum (1885) cost Gladstone much popularity.

3. George William Curtis (1824–92), author and orator, was an early advocate of civil service reform.

4. "Quandoque bonus dormitat Homerus," literally "Sometimes even the good Homer nods." The quotation is taken from Horace's *Ars Poetica*, l. 359.

5. John Milton (1608–74), English poet, is best known for his epic poem *Paradise Lost* (1667).

6. Thomas Babington Macaulay (1800–1859) was an English politician, essayist, poet, and historian. He also was one of four men who helped to arrange for Crummell's admission to Queens' College, Cambridge, in 1849.

7. Daniel Adams (1773–1864), physician and educator, was the author of *The Scholar's Arithmetic* (1801), *Adams' New Arithmetic* (1827), and *Primary Arithmetic* (1848). Urbain Jean Joseph Le Verrier (1811–77) was a French astronomer.

8. William Cowper, "Verses Supposed to Be Written by Alexander Selkirk, during His Solitary Abode in the Island of Juan Fernandez," stanza 6.

9. Shakespeare, *A Midsummer Night's Dream* 5.1.12–13.

10. "May not taste be compared to that exquisite sense of the bee, which instantly discovers and extracts the quintessence of every flower, and disregards all the rest of it." Fulke Greville, *Maxims, Characters, and Reflections, Critical, Satyrical, and Moral* (London, 1756), no. 232.

11. Possibly Robert Blakey (1795–1878), professor of logic and metaphysics at Queen's College, Belfast, but I have been unable to trace this quotation.

12. "They perfect nature and are perfected by experience." Francis Bacon, *Essays* (London, 1597), no. 50 ('Of Studies').

13. "—Beauty—a living Presence of the earth, / Surpassing the most fair ideal Forms / Which craft of delicate Spirits hath composed / From earth's materials—waits upon my steps; / Pitches her tents before me as I move, / An hourly neighbour." William Wordsworth, *The Excursion*, Preface, ll. 42–47.

## 8. The Need of New Ideas and New Aims for a New Era

1. Crummell, *Africa and America*, iii–iv.

2. Numbers 11–14.

3. "We look before and after; / We pine for what is not." Percy Bysshe Shelley, "To a Skylark," ll. 86–87.

4. "And thus the native hue of resolution / Is sicklied o'er with the pale caste of thought." Shakespeare, *Hamlet* 3.1.84–85.

5. "Why need such men go desperately astray, / And nurse 'the dreadful appetite of death?'" William Wordsworth, *The Excursion* 4.601–2.

6. "Let wealth and commerce, laws and learning die, / But leave us still our old nobility." John Manners, duke of Rutland, *England's Trust* 3.227–8.

7. "A love of freedom rarely felt, / Of freedom in her regal seat / Of England;

not the schoolboy heat, / The blind hysterics of the Celt." Alfred, Lord Tennyson, *In Memoriam* 109.13–16.

8. See Charles Darwin, *The Descent of Man* (London, 1871), 1:iv.

9. "TRENCH ON WORDS."—Introductory Lecture. [AC] Richard Chenevix Trench, *On the Study of Words: Lectures Addressed (Originally) to the Pupils at the Diocesan Training School, Winchester* (London, 1851), 18–19.

10. "And custom lies upon thee with a weight, / Heavy as frost, and deep almost as life!" Wordsworth, "Ode: Intimations of Immortality from Recollections of Early Childhood" 8.131–32.

11. "I called the New World into existence, to redress the balance of the Old." George Canning, speech, Dec. 12, 1826. George Canning (1770–1827), English statesman, was foreign secretary (1807–9, 1822–27) and later prime minister (1827). The quotation refers to Canning's acknowledgment of the independence of the Spanish-American colonies in 1823 in retaliation against the French invasion of Spain, the logic being that if French influence was henceforth to predominate in Spain, it should not be "Spain with the Indies."

12. John Donne, "To Sir Henry Goodyere," ll. 13–17.

13. Presumably a gloss on Proverbs 9:12. See chap. 9, n. 1.

14. I Cor., 16;13. [AC]

15. Luke I;17. [AC]

16. "Forbade to wade through slaughter to a throne, / And shut the gates of mercy on mankind." Thomas Gray, "Elegy Written in a Country Churchyard," ll. 67–68.

17. Cornelius Tacitus, *The Annals* (A.D. 115–17), 3.44–45 and 16.16.

18. "Keep therefore and do them; for this is your wisdom and your understanding in the sight of the nations, which shall hear all these statutes, and say, Surely this great nation is a wise and understanding people." Dueteronomy 4:6.

19. "One decree / Spake laws to *them*, and said that by the soul / Only, the Nations shall be great and free." William Wordsworth, "September, 1802. Near Dover," ll. 12–14.

20. "I may not hope from outward forms to win / The passion and the life, whose fountains are within." Samuel Taylor Coleridge, "Dejection: an Ode," 3.45–46.

## 9. Common Sense in Common Schooling

1. Presumably a gloss on Proverbs 9:12.

2. "To give light to them that sit in darkness and in the shadow of death, to guide our feet into the way of peace," Luke 1:79.

3. *The Poems of Alexander Pope*, ed. Mack, 8:315, ll. 729–30. The quotation is from Pope's translation of Homer's *Iliad*.

4. "From labour health, from health contentment springs." James Beattie, *The Minstrel* 1.109.

5. "As a jewel of gold in a swine's snout, so is a fair woman which is without discretion." Proverbs 11:22.

6. "What could have been done more to my vineyard, that I have not done it? wherefore, when I looked that it should bring forth grapes, brought it forth wild grapes?" Isaiah 5:4.

7. "That our sons may be as plants grown up in their youth; that our daughters may be as corner stones, polished after the similitude of a palace." Psalms 144:12.

8. "Behold, all souls are mine; as the soul of the father, so also the soul of the son is mine: the soul that sinneth, it shall die." Ezekiel 18:4.

## 10. Right-Mindedness

1. "Twas thus, by the glare of false science betrayed, / That leads, to bewilder, and dazzles, to blind." James Beattie, "The Hermit," ll. 33–34.

2. "Into our Minds, into the Mind of Man / My haunt, and the main region of my song." William Wordsworth, *The Excursion*, Preface, ll. 40–41.

3. Richard Brinsley Sheridan (1751–1816), English playwright, was a member of Parliament between 1780 and 1811. The quotation can be found in Lewis Gibbs, *Sheridan* (London, 1947), 93.

4. The *Historiae* by Cornelius Tacitus (A.D. 56–120) concerned the Roman Empire from A.D. 69 to 96.

5. Dante Alighieri (1265–1321) was an Italian poet. His works included *The Divine Comedy* (c.1310–14).

6. Robert Southey (1774–1843), English poet and essayist, is perhaps best known for his *Life of Horatio Lord Nelson* (1813).

7. John Ruskin (1819–1900), writer, critic, and artist, had a profound impact on public taste in England during the nineteenth century.

8. Edmund Burke (1729–97), Irish-born statesman, was the author of *Reflections on the Revolution in France* (1790).

9. "But I keep under my body, and bring it into subjection: lest that by any means, when I have preached to others, I myself should be a castaway." 1 Corinthians 9:27.

10. Sir Edward Dyer, "My Mind to Me a Kingdom Is," l. 1.

11. "One of the most certain of all lessons of military history . . . is the superiority of discipline to enthusiasm." Thomas Arnold, *Introductory Lectures on Modern History* (Oxford and London, 1842), 198. The illustration Crummell referred to was of the Jacobite victory over Cope's regulars at Prestonpans in 1745.

12. Dominie Sampson, a character in Walter Scott's *Guy Mannering* (1815), is described as "a poor, modest, humble scholar, who had won his way through the classics, but fallen to the leeward in the voyage of life."

13. "For the body is not one member, but many." 1 Corinthians 12:14.

14. Ibid., 23–24.

15. "Sursum corda," literally "Lift up your hearts." Said as part of the eucharistic liturgy.

16. Wordsworth, "Ode to Duty," l. 1.

17. "All is, if I have grace to use it so, / As ever in my great Task-Master's eye." John Milton, "On His Having Arrived at the Age of Twenty-Three," ll. 13–14.

18. "These rules regard; / These helps solicit; and a steadfast seat / Shall then be yours among the happy few / Who dwell on earth, yet breathe empyreal air, / Sons of the morning." Wordsworth, *The Excursion* 4.228–32.

19. "The river glideth at his own sweet will." Wordsworth, "Sonnet Composed upon Westminster Bridge, September 3, 1802," l. 12.

20. See chap. 2, n. 10.

## 11. The Best Methods of Church Work
### among the Colored People

1. That is, the Protestant Episcopal church.

2. I am unable to give the statistics of the great Methodist denominations of colored people.

The following statement of the Rev. Richard de Baptiste will show the magnitude of the Baptist (colored) body in the United States:

1,071,902 colored Baptist church-members.

311 associations.

| 255 associations reported | | | 9,079 | churches. |
|---|---|---|---|---|
| 218 | " | " | 4,590 | ministers. |
| 90 | " | " | 2,603 | Sunday-schools. |
| 94 | " | " | 143,832 | Sunday-school pupils. |
| 58 | " | " | $1,334,092 | valuation of church property. |
| 153 | " | " | $ 181,663.41 | contributions for religious and educational work.   [AC] |

3. The word "compulsory" should doubtless be taken, very largely, in its literal sense, and as allowing no exercise of personal choice; but there is no doubt that, in numerous cases, compulsion was simply the influence and example of superiors. [AC]

4. "Young Ireland" was an Irish nationalist movement of the 1840s.

5. Joseph Crane Hartzell (1842–1928) was a Methodist minister who worked in the South during the 1870s and 1880s and later was consecrated missionary bishop for Africa.

6. "Root, hog, or die. This is the refrain of each of the nine verses of the Bull-Whacker's Epic." J. H. Beadle, *Life in Utah* (Philadelphia and Chicago, 1870), 227.

7. Under date of Jan. 29, 1887, an English clergyman writes to me, "My brother, a colonial bishop, has a good many colored congregations, but only one colored missionary. There are a large number of catechists who receive no pay, but conduct service in the out-islands." [AC]

8. Nashotah House in Nashotah, Wisconsin, was founded in 1841 as a semimonastic center for study, worship, and evangelism. Berkeley Divinity School was established in 1854 by Bishop John Williams; originally located in Middletown, Connecticut, Berkeley was moved to New Haven in 1928. Kenyon College in Gambier, Ohio, was chartered in 1824 as the Theological Seminary of the Protestant Episcopal Church in the Diocese of Ohio.

### 12. The Race-Problem in America

1. The kingdoms of Aragon and Castile were united under the Spanish crown in 1808.

2. "I watch the wheels of Nature's mazy plan, / And learn the future by the past of man." Thomas Campbell, *The Pleasures of Hope* 1.319–20.

3. "Duties of Higher toward Lower Races." Canon Rawlinson, Princeton Review, Nov., 1878. [AC] George Rawlinson, "The Duties of Higher toward Lower Races," *Princeton Review* 1 (Nov. 1878): 804–47.

4. See "Physics and Politics," by Bagehot, pp. 84, 85. [AC] Bagehot was in this instance refuting the supposed influence of climate ("land, sea, and air") in eradicating racial differences. See Walter Bagehot, *Physics and Politics; or, Thoughts on the Application of the Principles of 'Natural Selection' and 'Inheritance' to Political Society* (London, 1872), 84–85.

5. See Herbert Spencer, *The Principles of Biology* (London, 1864), 1:141, 150.

6. For similar comments, see Emma Elizabeth Brown, *The Life of James Russell Lowell* (New York, 1895), 221, 242.

7. "That fatal and perfidious bark." John Milton, "Lycidas," l. 100.

8. "We have no slaves at home.——Then why abroad? / And they themselves, once ferried o'er the wave / That parts us, are emancipate and loos'd." William Cowper, *The Task* 2.36–39.

9. For similar comments, see Atticus G. Haygood, *Pleas for Progress* (Nashville, 1889), 26–27, 54.

10. Jurgen Herbst, ed., *Josiah Strong: Our Country* (Cambridge, Mass., 1963), 56–57. The settlement of New Glarus, Wisconsin, was founded in 1808 by immigrants from one of the Swiss cantons.

11. "Coelum, non animum mutant, qui trans mare currant," literally "They who cross the seas, change their sky but not their disposition." Horace, *Epistolae* 1.11.27.

12. George Rawlinson (1812–1902) was Camden Professor of Ancient History at Oxford University (1861–89) and canon of Canterbury Cathedral (1872–1902). A firm advocate of mixed marriages, Rawlinson believed that benevolence and self-interest dictated that whites should "absorb and assimilate" black Americans. "Before a century was over," he predicted, "only the skilled physiologist might be able to perceive the existence of a Nigritic element in the composite nation." See Rawlinson, "The Duties of Higher toward Lower Races," 846–47.

13. Strong was not advocating "universal assimilation" but the creation of a "new Anglo-Saxon race of the New World." He made this quite clear in chap. 14 of *Our Country* when he reiterated Herbert Spencer's conviction that "the eventual mixture of the allied varieties of the Aryan race, forming the population, will produce a more powerful type of man than has hitherto existed, and a type of man more plastic, more adaptable, more capable of undergoing the modifications needed for complete social life." See Herbst, *Josiah Strong: Our Country*, 211.

14. *The Bradenham Edition of the Novels and Tales of Benjamin Disraeli* (London, 1927), 12:245. The quotation is from Disraeli's *Endymion* (1880).

15. "And God said, Let the earth bring forth grass, the herb yielding seed, and the fruit tree yielding fruit after his kind, whose seed is in itself, upon the earth: and it was so." Genesis 1:11.

16. Alfred, Lord Tennyson, *In Memoriam* 55.5–8.

17. "From Nature's chain, whatever link you strike, / Tenth or ten-thousandth, breaks the chain alike." Alexander Pope, *An Essay on Man* 1.245–46.

18. George Bancroft (1800–1891) was a historian and diplomat.

19. See also chap. 17.

20. William S. Scarborough, *First Lessons in Greek* (New York and Chicago, 1881). Scarborough was a professor at Wilberforce University.

21. Crummell refers here to John Manners, duke of Rutland (1818–1906), who was postmaster general in Disraeli's second cabinet (1874–80) and later chancellor of the duchy of Lancaster (1886–92).

22. See chap. 8, n. 6.

23. Prince William George of Denmark (1846–1913) became King George I of Greece in 1863. Jean Baptiste Bernadotte (c.1763–1844), one of Napoleon's generals, was named heir to the Swedish throne in 1810. Benjamin Disraeli (1804–82), novelist and statesman, was prime minister in 1868 and 1874–80. Albert Gallatin (1761–1849), born in Geneva, was secretary of the treasury under Jefferson and Madison (1801–14) and minister to England (1826–27). Carl Schurz (1829–1906), from Liblar, near Cologne, arrived in the United States in 1852 and became United States senator from Missouri (1869–75) and secretary of the interior under President Hayes.

24. John Hampden (1594–1643) was an English parliamentarian who refused to pay Charles I's illegal ship money in 1636.

25. Algernon Sydney (1622–1682), English republican, was executed for treason in 1682. His influential *Discourses concerning Government* was published posthumously in 1698.

26. "DEMOCRACY IN AMERICA," B.2, Ch.2. [AC] "Aristocracy links everybody, from peasant to king, in one long chain. Democracy breaks the chain and frees each link." Alexis de Tocqueville, *Democracy in America*, ed. J. P. Mayer and Max Lerner (New York, 1966), 2:653 ("Of Individualism in Democracies").

27. "But God hath chosen the foolish things of the world to confound the wise; and God hath chosen the weak things of the world to confound the things which are mighty." 1 Corinthians 1:27.

28. "He hath put down the mighty from their seats, and exalted them of low degree." Luke 1:52.

29. "Now unto the King eternal, immortal, invisible, the wise God, be honor and glory for ever and ever. Amen." 1 Timothy 1:17.

## 13. Incidents of Hope for
## the Negro Race in America

1. This sermon was preached, by special request, before the three congregations,— 15th St. Presbyterian Church, and the two Congregational Churches in Washington; and is published by the request of the "Ministers' Union," in whose presence it was afterwards read. [AC]

2. Crummell was presumably referring here to Henry McNeal Turner (1834–1915), a leading proponent of emigration to Africa who not only managed to alienate intellectuals like Crummell but also clashed with Booker T. Washington.

3. Two facts may be noticed under this head—(a) That the Negro has supplanted the aboriginal populations, in several quarters, on the American Continent and its Isles; (b) That there is not a spot on which he has been placed but what there he lives and thrives. [AC]

4. I must leave it to each reader to judge for himself the census reports of 1880 and 1890:—

PERCENTAGE OF INCREASE

| *White* | *Negro* |
|---|---|
| 1870 to 1880 – 29.22 | 34.85 |
| 1880 to 1890 – 26.68 | 13.51 [AC] |

5. See "Stroud's Slave Laws." [AC] George M. Stroud, *A Sketch of the Laws Relating to Slavery in the Several States of the United States of America* (Philadelphia, 1827), 85–96.

6. Shakespeare, *Othello* 5.2.7.

7. The following may be regarded as a fair estimate of the American Continent, and Islands:

| | |
|---|---|
| United States | 8,000,000 |
| Brazil | 6,500,000 |
| Cuba | 1,500,000 |
| South and Central American Republics | 2,500,000 |
| Hayti | 3,000,000 |
| British possessions | 1,500,000 |
| Dutch, Danish and Mexican | 400,000 |
| French | 350,000 |

[AC]

8. Hayti and St. Domingo. [AC]

9. Henry Diaz (d. 1662) was a black officer who helped to drive the Dutch out of Brazil. Abraham Hannibal, an ex-slave, was bought as a present for Peter the Great (1672–1725) and later was promoted to general of the artillery. Juan Lateno (c. 1516–c. 1597), another ex-slave, studied at the University of Granada and later (c. 1556) became professor of Latin in the city's cathedral school; he was the author of the *Austriad* (1573) and the *Translatione* (1576), as well as several minor poems. Anthony William Arno (b. 1703) graduated in law from the University of Halle in 1729 and the following year received his doctorate from Wittenberg University.

10. John Eliot (1604–90) was a scholar and missionary to the Indians. His translation of the Bible appeared in two parts in 1661 and 1663. A copy was presented to Andover Theological Seminary in 1818 by James Chater, a Baptist missionary.

11. The religious growth of the race is closely shown by the following statistics:—

Dr. H. K. Carroll, in "The Independent," says that the aggregate of colored church members in the United States is, in round numbers, 2,674,000, distributed as follows: Baptists, 1,403,559; Methodists, 1,190,638; Presbyterians, 30,000; Disciples of Christ, 18,578, and Protestant Episcopal and Reformed Episcopal together, somewhat less than 5,000. According to the census there has been an increase of 1,150,000 colored church members during the last thirty years, which Dr. Carroll thinks is *unparalleled in the history of the Christian Church.* The value of Negro church property is $26,626,000, and the number of edifices is 22,770. [AC] H. K. Carroll, "The Negro in His Relations to the Church," *Independent* 47 (Dec. 19, 1895): 1712–13. Carroll, in fact, gave the number of black churches as 23,770.

12. See chap. 5, n. 42.

13. See chap. 2, n. 20.

14. Mungo Park (1771–1806), Scottish explorer, is perhaps best known for his *Travels in the Interior of Africa* (1799). David Livingstone (1813–73) was a Scottish missionary and explorer; Henry Morton Stanley (1841–1904), English-born explorer, rescued Livingstone in 1872. May French-Sheldon (1848–1936), American explorer, was the author of *Sultan to Sultan* (1892), an account of her expedition to Zanzibar and East Africa in 1891.

15. See chap. 2, n. 19.

16. See chap. 2, n. 18, and chap. 6, n. 7.

17. Edward Wilmot Blyden (1832–1912), educator, politician and black nationalist, spent most of his life in Liberia and Sierra Leone. On a visit to the United States in 1895, Blyden delivered an address before the Bethel Historical and Literary Society, referred to here. Crummell's sometimes stormy friendship with Blyden dated back to the early 1850s.

18. William H. Powell, *The Battle of Lake Erie* (1873).

19. Commodore Perry was the great Hero in the great naval battles on Lake Erie and Lake Champlain. A goodly number of Negroes were sent to the Commodore, to reinforce his marines. He took umbrage, and complained at the sending of so many Negroes to his ships! But such was their bravery and efficiency in the engagements, that, in his reports, he afterwards speaks of these black naval heroes in the warmest and most enthusiastic manner. [AC] See George Washington Williams, *A History of the Negro Race in America, from 1619 to 1880* (New York, 1885), 2:28–30.

20. The figure in question, Perry's black servant, Hannibal, is depicted shielding his face from the impact of a cannonball. His white companions, meanwhile, remain impassive and seemingly oblivious to the danger. See Albert Boime, *The Art of Exclusion: Representing Blacks in the Nineteenth Century* (London and Washington, D.C., 1990), 185–86.

21. The Honorable C. C. Pinckney of South Carolina, in his day, celebrated as an Orator and Statesman, in the memorable debate on the Missouri question, made the following statement:—"In the Northern States, numerous bodies of them [the Negroes] were enrolled, and fought, side by side with the whites, the battles of the Revolution." "*Numerous* bodies!" The statement is literally true. In many cases they fought, in the ranks with whites: but, aside from this, regiments were enlisted, in Massachusetts, New Hampshire, Rhode Island, Connecticut, New York, who fought and died for the independence of the Colonies. History assures of the conspicuous valor of these men, at Bunker Hill, Fort Griswold, Red Bank, Valley Forge, Saratoga, &c, &c.

So much for the Revolutionary War.

In the War of 1812, they showed the greatest gallantry. At the conclusion of the war General Jackson issued a proclamation in which he spoke in glowing terms of their bravery, declaring—"I *expected much of you* . . . You have done *more than I expected.*" [AC] See Williams, *A History of the Negro Race in America* 1:362, 2:26–27.

22. Garnet Joseph Wolseley (1833–1913), English field marshal, wrote extensively on the American Civil War, but I have been unable to trace this quotation.

23. The simple contrast of a homeless, houseless unlettered race, thirty years ago; with the growth of this people into some 30,000 Teachers, nigh 2,000,000 pupils; many Academies and Colleges, and Seminaries, *since* the day of Emancipation; should satisfy any one of the onward march of the race. [AC]

24. "No pent-up *Utica* may contract your Pow'rs / But the whole boundless Continent is Yours." Jonathan Mitchell Sewall, Prologue to Joseph Addison's *Cato*, ll. 82–83. Park Benjamin (1809–64) adopted this couplet as the motto of his journal, the *New World* (1839–45), published in New York.

25. See chap. 3, n. 16.

26. "Fame is the spur that the clear spirit doth raise / (That last infirmity of noble mind) / To scorn delights, and live laborious days." John Milton, "Lycidas," ll. 70–72.

## 14. At Hampton Institute, 1896

1. "And all they that heard *them* laid *them* up in their hearts, saying, What manner of child shall this be! And the hand of the Lord was with him." Luke 1:66.

2. Albert Howe (1836–1925), manager of the Hampton farm, also supervised construction of the school's first brick building, Academic Hall.

3. Oliver Otis Howard (1830–1909), Union general, became commissioner of the Bureau of Refugees, Freedmen, and Abandoned Lands in May 1865.

4. Mary Tiletson Hemenway (1820–94), a wealthy philanthropist and Bostonite, gave about $35,000 to Hampton.

5. That is, the Armstrong League of Hampton Workers.

6. Probably Elbert B. Monroe, who was a Hampton trustee.

7. Crummell had previously visited Hampton in December 1886. See *Southern Workman* 16 (Jan. 1887): 2.

8. "Trust no Future, howe'er pleasant! / Let the dead Past bury its dead! / Act,— act in the living Present! / Heart within, and God o'erhead!" Henry Wadsworth Longfellow, *A Psalm of Life*, stanza 6.

9. "There is a tide in the affairs of men, / Which, taken at the flood, leads on to fortune." Shakespeare, *Julius Caesar* 4.3.218–19.

10. Mr. Wilkins Micawber, a character in Charles Dickens's *David Copperfield* (1850), is always confident that something will "turn up."

11. "No man is an *Island*, entire of itself." John Donne, *Devotions upon Emergent Occasions*, no. 17.

12. Damon and Pythias were two inseparable friends of Greek legend.

13. The close friendship of Jonathan and David is described in 1 Samuel 18–20.

14. "All are but parts of one stupendous whole; / Whose body Nature is, and God the soul." Alexander Pope, *An Essay on Man* 1.267–68.

15. "Man's heart th' Almighty to the future sets, / By secret and inviolable springs." Edward Young, *Night Thoughts* 7.119–20.

16. This quotation is possibly a gloss on 2 Kings 19:16 ("Lord, bow down thine ear, and hear; open, LORD, thine eyes, and see: and hear the words of Sennacherib, which hath sent him to reproach the living God").

## 15. Civilization the Primal Need of the Race

1. "But he answered and said, It is written, Man shall not live by bread alone, but by every word that proceedeth out of the mouth of God." Matthew 4:4. See also Deuteronomy 8:3 and Luke 4:4.

2. Philip Melancthon (1497–1560), humanist and theologian, was a friend of Martin Luther.

3. For similar comments, see Francis Augustus Cox, *The Life of Philip Melancthon, Comprising an Account of the Most Important Transactions of the Reformation* (London and Edinburgh, 1815), 272–73.

4. Desiderius Erasmus (1469–1536), humanist, was probably the greatest scholar of the northern Renaissance.

5. See chap. 2, n. 16.

6. See chap. 8, n. 20.

7. See chap. 8, n. 19.

8. Horatio Nelson (1758–1805), English admiral, defeated the French fleet at the battle of Trafalgar (1805).

## 16. The Prime Need of the Negro Race

1. "Ay, but to die, and go we know not where; / To lie in cold obstruction and to rot." Shakespeare, *Measure for Measure* 3.1.117–18.

2. "Every good gift and every perfect gift is from above, and cometh down from the Father of lights, with whom is no variableness, neither shadow of turning." James 1:17.

3. "Mislike me not for my complexion, / The shadowed livery of the burnish'd sun, / To whom I am a neighbour, and near bred." Shakespeare, *The Merchant of Venice* 2.1.1–3.

4. Fisk, a black college in Nashville, Tennessee, was chartered by the American Missionary Association in 1866; Clark, a black college in Atlanta, Georgia, was founded in 1869 by the Freedmen's Aid Society of the Methodist Episcopal Church; Lincoln, a black college near Philadelphia, formerly Ashmun Institute, was founded in 1854.

5. Howard, a black college in Washington, D.C., was established in 1867 by the Freedmen's Bureau. For Oberlin College, see chap. 17, n. 8.

## 17. The Attitude of the American Mind toward the Negro Intellect

1. "For ever, and for ever, farewell, Cassius!" Shakespeare, *Julius Caesar* 5.1.117.

2. See chap. 2, n. 16, and chap. 15, n. 5.

3. See chap. 13, n. 6.

4. *Baptism*, for well nigh a century, was denied Negro slaves in the colonies, for fear it carried emancipation with it. Legislation on Education began at a subsequent date. In 1740 it was enacted in SOUTH CAROLINA: "Whereas, the having slaves taught to write or suffering them to be employed in writing, may be attended with great inconvenience. Be it enacted, That all and every person or persons whatsoever who shall hereafter teach or cause any slave or slaves to be taught to write, or shall use or employ any slave as a Scribe in any manner of writing, hereafter taught to write; every such person or persons shall forever, for every such offense, forfeit the sum of £100 current money."

The next step, in South Carolina, was aimed against mental instruction of *every kind*, in reading and writing.

A similar law was passed in Savannah, Georgia. In 1711, in the Colony of Maryland, a *special enactment* was passed to bar freedom by baptism and in 1715, in South Carolina! See *"Stroud's Slave Laws."* [AC] Stroud, *A Sketch of the Laws Relating to Slavery in the Several States of the United States of America*, 88–89, 94–95.

5. At the time when France was on the eve of plunging deeply into the slave trade and of ruining her colonies by the curse of Slavery, the ABBE GREGOIRE stept forth in vindication of the Negro, and published his celebrated work—"The Literature of Negroes." In this work he gives the names and narrates the achievements of the distin-

guished Negroes, writers, scholars, painters, philosophers, priests and Roman prelates, in Spain, Portugal, France, England, Holland, Italy and Turkey who had risen to eminence in the 15th century.

Not long after BLUMENBACH declared that "entire and large provinces of Europe might be named, in which it would be difficult to meet with such good writers, poets, philosophers, and correspondents of the French Academy; and that moreover there is no savage people, who have distinguished themselves by such examples of perfectibility and capacity for scientific cultivation: and consequently that none can approach more nearly to the polished nations of the globe than the Negro." [AC] See Henri Grégoire, *An Essay concerning the Intellectual and Moral Faculties and Literature of Negroes: Followed with an Account of the Life and Works of Fifteen Negroes and Mulattoes Distinguished in Science, Literature, and the Arts* (Paris, 1808); Johann Friedrich Blumenbach, *On the Natural Varieties of Mankind* (1885; rpt. New York, 1969), 312. The quotation is from Blumenbach's *Contributions to Natural History*, first published in 1790.

6. John Chavis (c. 1763–1838), black educator and Presbyterian minister, attended Washington Academy, later Washington and Lee University, and Princeton University.

7. Jesse Peters (n.d.), Baptist minister, was cofounder of the Silver Bluff Baptist Church, South Carolina (1793).

8. "Oberlin College" in Ohio was the first opening its doors to the Negro in 1836. [AC] Oberlin College in Oberlin, Ohio, was founded by New England Congregationalists in 1833.

9. Theodore S. Wright (1797–1847), Presbyterian minister and black abolitionist, led the struggle for black voting rights in New York State during the 1840s.

10. Crandall's school in Canterbury, Connecticut, was opened in 1833. See Leon F. Litwack, *North of Slavery: The Negro in the Free States, 1790–1860* (Chicago, 1961), 127.

11. See Crummell, "Eulogium on Henry Highland Garnet, D.D." in *Africa and America*, 279–280.

12. William Dean Howells (1837–1920), novelist and critic, edited and wrote the introduction to Paul Laurence Dunbar's *Lyrics of Lowly Life* (1896).

13. George Thomas Barnes (1833–1901), native of Augusta, Georgia, and leading Democrat, represented Georgia in the United States Congress (1885–91).

14. See Heman Lincoln Wayland, "The Higher Education of the Colored People of the South," *Journal of Social Science* 34 (Nov. 1896): 68–72. Wayland (1830–98), formerly professor of rhetoric and logic at Kalamazoo College, Michigan, was from 1872 editor of the *National Baptist*.

15. "I am not so old as some of my young friends may suspect, but I am too old to go into the business of 'carrying coals to Newcastle.'. . . The colored citizen of the U.S. has already graduated with respectable standing from a course of 250 years in the University of the old-time type of Manual labor. The South of to-day is what we see it largely because the colored men and women at least during the past 250 years, have not been lazy 'cumberers of the ground,' but the grand army of laborers that has wrestled with nature and led these 16 States out of the woods thus far on the high road to material prosperity. It is not especially necessary that the 2,000,000 of our colored children and youth in the southern common schools should be warned against laziness, and what has always and everywhere come of that since the foundation of the world." The Rev. A. D. Mayo, M.A., LL.D. Address before State Teachers' Association (Colored), Birmingham, Ala. [AC]

16. Croesus (d. c. 546 B.C.), last king of Lydia, was renowned for his great wealth.

17. Thomas Gradgrind, a character in Charles Dickens's *Hard Times* (1854), makes no allowance for human weakness and treats all people merely as ciphers.

18. William S. Scarborough (b. 1852), noted linguist, taught at Wilberforce University; his textbook, *First Lessons in Greek*, was published in 1881. Kelly Miller (1863–1939) served on the faculty at Howard University (1890–1934), first as a mathematics professor, then as dean of arts and sciences, and finally as professor of sociology. William Edward Burghardt Du Bois (1868–1963), historian, sociologist, and black activist, was a professor of classics at Wilberforce University (1894–96) and later professor of history and economics at Atlanta University (1897–1910). John Wesley Edward Bowen (1855–1933) taught at Gammon Theological Seminary, Atlanta, and later became its president (1906–33). Charles H. Turner (n.d.) was a biology instructor at Clark University, Atlanta. Henry Ossawa Tanner (1860–1937), a black artist, spent most of his life in France.

19. Ithuriel is an angel in John Milton's *Paradise Lost* who is commissioned by Gabriel to search for Satan in Paradise. Ithuriel is armed with a spear which "no falsehood can endure."

20. William Henry Crogman (1841–1931) taught classics at Clark University and later became its president (1903–21). *Talks for the Times* was published in 1896.

21. Matthew Anderson (1845–1928), graduate of Oberlin (1874) and Princeton Theological Seminary (1877), was pastor of the Berean Presbyterian Church in Philadelphia from 1880 until his death in 1928. *Presbyterianism: Its Relation to the Negro* was published in 1897.

22. I owe Mr. Anderson an apology for omitting this reference to his book on the delivery of this address. It was prepared while its author was in a foreign land, but had passed entirely from his memory in the preparation of this address. [AC]

23. Kelly Miller, *A Review of Hoffman's Race Traits and Tendencies of the American Negro*, American Negro Academy, Occasional Papers, no. 1 (Washington, D.C., 1898).

24. W. E. B. Du Bois, *The Conservation of Races*, American Negro Academy, Occasional Papers, no. 2 (Washington, D.C., 1898).

25. W. E. B. Du Bois, *The Suppression of the African Slave-Trade to the United States of America, 1630–1870* (New York, 1896).

26. Paul Laurence Dunbar (1872–1906), black poet, was the author of *Majors and Minors* (1895) and *Lyrics of Lowly Life* (1896).

27. The English edition of *Lyrics of Lowly Life* was published by Chapman and Hall in 1897.

## 18. Tracts for the Negro Race

1. Alexander Crummell to Frazier Miller, June 20, 1898, Crummell Papers.

2. See chap. 8, n. 5.

3. "He that committeth sin is of the devil; for the devil sinneth from the beginning. For this purpose the Son of God was manifested, that he might destroy the works of the devil." 1 John 3:8.

4. John Milton, *Paradise Lost* 2.624–25.

5. "The only amaranthine flow'r on earth / Is virtue; th'only lasting treasure truth." William Cowper, *The Task* 3.268–69.

6. Philippians 4:8.

7. This quotation is possibly a gloss on Shakespeare's *Macbeth* 5.1.34 ("Out damned spot! out, I say").

8. "Be now for ever taken from my sight / Though nothing can bring back the hour / Of splendour in the grass, of glory in the flower." William Wordsworth, "Ode: Intimations of Immortality from Recollections of Early Childhood," ll. 177–79.

9. "Corruptio optimi pessima," literally "the worst is the corruption of the best." This Latin proverb is echoed in Shakespeare's *Sonnet 94*, l. 13 ("For sweetest things turn sour by their deeds").

10. See chap. 17, n. 18.

11. See chap. 15, n. 1.

# Index